The Europeanization of the World

The Europeanization of the World

On the Origins of Human Rights and Democracy

JOHN M. HEADLEY

PRINCETON UNIVERSITY PRESS
PRINCETON AND OXFORD

Published by Princeton University Press, 41 William Street,
Princeton, New Jersey 08540
In the United Kingdom: Princeton University Press, 3 Market Place,
Woodstock, Oxfordshire OX20 1SY

Library of Congress Cataloging-in-Publication Data

Headley, John M.
The Europeanization of the world : on the origins of
human rights and democracy / John M. Headley
p. cm.
Includes bibliographical references and index.
ISBN: 978-0-691-13312-6 (hardcover : alk. paper)
1. Democracy. 2. Human rights. 3. Globalization—
Political aspects. I. Title.
JC423.H425 2007
321.8—dc22 2007010470

British Library Cataloging-in-Publication Data is available

This book has been composed in Palatino

Printed on acid-free paper. ∞

press.princeton.edu

Printed in the United States of America
1 3 5 7 9 10 8 6 4 2

Remota itaque iustitia, quid sunt regna nisi
magna latrocinia?
–Aug. *De civ. Dei, IV.4*

For my many grandnieces
and grandnephews
and for their generation,
lest they ignore, forget,
or never even encounter

Contents

Illustrations

Preface

For the reader, the preface, coming first in a book, can convey the impression that the work developed logically from a reasonable beginning. For the author, however, the preface comes last and compels its writer to perceive and admit the stumblings and false starts, his doubts and debts along the way. In the present instance the experience of writing this book, its composition, stems from a remote corner of the historical profession, on the part of one who early felt dissatisfaction with the all too easy orientation of our history toward the nation-state and its almost preordained beginnings; on the part of one who looked to other forms of polity and human political organization in the historical record for transcending such parochialism or at least making it more historically bound: first the church in its potential universality, then empire—perhaps more Spanish and Spanish colonial than Holy Roman, but still never too far removed from the wondrously archaic features of the Germanic experience. My first discernible, specific debt I owe to long acquaintance with Tommaso Campanella, that notorious seventeenth-century Dominican prisoner, with his marvelously Italianate drive toward the global, the universal, and the transformation of the world. Following an extended study of this radical prophet, I awakened from my own thoughts to discover that the world around me had meanwhile become transformed by a new sort of universality, by global processes, producing that seemingly unaccountable reality—globalization—which now commands our attention. I could not help but recognize that this entity, good or bad, was very much the result of that civilization of which I am a product, and which I have respected and have made such long effort to study, explore, understand.

In the preparation of this book I have incurred a legion of debts toward friends and associates from whom I have received advice, suggestions, comfort, reassurance, and the reading of individual parts: Jerry Bentley, Melissa Bullard, Ian Crowe, Susan Danforth, Anne D. Hall, Peter Headley, Don Higginbotham, Hans J. Hillerbrand, Peter I. Kaufman, Timothy Kircher, Lloyd Kramer, D.W.Y. Kwok, Hsi Huey Liang, Michael Lienesch, Bruce Mazlish, Terence McIntosh, Michael McVaugh, Kenneth Nebenzahl, Gerda Nischan, Barbara Norton, Anthony Papalas, Robert Policelli, Gerald Postema, Celia Pratt, Paul Rahe, Jonathan Reid, Jay Smith, Maria Smith, John Sweet, John B. Tomaro, Keith Windschuttle, Ronald Witt, Jessica Wolfe, and T. C. Price Zimmermann.

Some persons deserve special mention: Price Zimmermann for his unsurpassed weighing of words in two crucial sections; Paul Rahe for his careful, appreciative reading of the entirety, his valuable suggestions, and his decisive support; Robert Policelli for his reliable and prompt expedition; Barbara Norton for sustained advice and aid in the preparation and assemblage of the manuscript; Celia Pratt of the University of North Carolina at Chapel Hill map division, and Susan Danforth, curator of Maps and Prints, John Carter Brown Library, for their ready assistance with the illustrations. As the present work concerns the beginnings of globalization, the maturing of civilizations and the larger, long-range principles of human history, I was fortunate, even at the late stage of submission to the Press, that by serendipity, following a thirty-year lapse, I renewed an association with one of the principal pioneers in the study of globalization, Bruce Mazlish. Professor Mazlish generously apprised me of his own most recent work—*Civilization and Its Contents* (2004) and *The New Global History* (2006), published the week before I made my own submission. Both Mazlish's books have relevance for the larger implications of my present work, although such implications are not made evident in the body of the work. From the first I found most fruitful Mazlish's willingness to consider the need to divest ourselves henceforth of thinking in terms of civilizations, especially given the pressures and the concept and reality of globalization. Second, in consulting earlier drafts of parts of the forthcoming *New Global History,* I considered valuable his addressing the need for "a higher morality" created by the increasing evidence of globalization. The idea allowed me to see in a new light the role of my second principle examined at length here—that of political dissent—insofar as it may relate to my first principle, the equalizing dynamic in the idea of a common humanity: not necessarily a higher morality but one distinguished by tolerance, compromise, moderation, even playfulness and humor. With the West still the principal agent in pushing an assemblage of diverse cultures toward a new, globalized way of life, Indian civilization might prove the most receptive, given its British phase and preparation; China less readily compliant, given its long understanding of itself as the Middle Kingdom to which all other polities and peoples must be subservient; and Islam, unique in its totally circumscribed religious wrappings, recently reinforced by conflict, inherently the least susceptible and the most resistant.

Among other forms of indebtedness and obligation, I wish to acknowledge the many services extended to me by both the personnel of Davis Library and the History Department of the University of North Carolina at Chapel Hill. Finally, by no means least, I am glad to recognize the support and understanding, evident at crucial stages of the manuscript's odyssey, of Brigitta van Rheinberg, now the editor-in-chief at Princeton University Press.

Most of chapter 1 and the beginning sections of chapters 2 and 3 have been based upon previous articles and publications that in this instance have been reshaped and to which evidence has been added for the larger context of this book. In this respect I want to thank the *Journal of World History* for allowing me to draw heavily upon "The Sixteenth-Century Venetian Celebration of the Earth's Total Habitability: The Issue of the Fully Habitable World for Renaissance Europe," vol. 8, no. 1 (1997): 1–27, and "The Universalizing Principle and Process: On the West's Intrinsic Commitment to a Global Context," vol. 13, no. 2 (2002): 291–321; likewise *Renaissance Quarterly* for the first part of "Geography and Empire in the Late Renaissance: Botero's Assignment, Western Universalism and the Civilizing Process," vol. 53, no. 4 (2000): 1119–55, and Ashgate, publisher of *Confessionalization in Europe, 1555–1700* (2004), for its last article, "Thomas More's Horrific Vision: The Advent of Constituted Dissent," 347–58.

Regarding translations, those readers interested in the sixteenth-century original can refer to the earlier articles cited for the extended passages of Latin, German, and especially Italian that I have translated. In later cases where I have used the work of a more recent author in English translation, I checked the use of critical terms but depended otherwise upon the translation in an authoritative edition. All biblical references are to the Vulgate (Stuttgart, 1975 edition).

Last, at the outset, let it be emphasized that while the present work is a formal, professional historical study of two major themes claimed to be unique and constitutive of Western civilization as it passes the threshold of its own creation into the withering process of globalization, the nature and broad implications of those themes or principles are such as to intrude very much upon present-day issues. Thus, the academic and apparently arcane by their very implications invade the current world.

The Europeanization of the World

Introduction

As dusk begins to settle on the abruptly curtailed "American century," the time seems long overdue for an assessment of that hitherto distinct civilization, the West, which is in the process of merging now with other civilizations and cultures. It may seem inappropriate for a study aspiring to relevance and to revision, and thus apparently requiring a specialist in modern history, to be attempted instead by a scholar of early modern European history. Yet an awareness of the earlier period affords a readier access to first principles, their development, and an appreciation of their uniqueness, as well as their capacity for transference to a global context. For however remote, tangential, and irrelevant sixteenth-century Europe may appear to some, it is one of the main tenets of this analysis that the Renaissance decisively and effectively prepared the global context for the European engagement of the world's peoples. As the early seventeenth-century French geographer Pierre d'Avity put it, "[The geographers] have wanted to make the world as a single community known to all men who are its citizens."[1] If globalization has become the major focus of social studies and the new frontier for historians, the European Renaissance then provides the proper moment to begin examining a process that increasingly enfolds us all.

As Western civilization becomes the primary agent in the present process of globalization, wherein the multitude of cultures, societies, and peoples of our planet are being reduced to a common, modern civilization, we seek to distinguish and assess some of the West's unique characteristics that are operating in this vast planetary transformation. Three are exceptional developments of our civilization: modern science and technology, the idea of a common humanity, and the capacity for self-criticism and dissent. Regarding the first, the distinguished social philosopher Ernest Gellner has claimed for Western science a "culture-transcending knowledge" that works to effect a sort of cognitive replumbing of the people of the globe.[2] This distinctive development is certainly the least debatable and, because of the obvious case that has been made for it, will not be treated here.

The second distinctive characteristic, with its program of natural, human rights, warrants attention as a formative and enduring characteristic of the West. To some extent a culture-transcending quality can also be claimed for it. The transcendence of this contribution is indeed explicitly announced in the idea of a common humanity as a single moral, biological totality, despite the apparent difficulty which many of the more collective societies might at first have with Western notions of rationality and individuality. The initial, if imperfect, manifestation of this idea first expresses itself in a religious form derived from Christian roots. In the course of the Renaissance, the more fragile and inevitably more particularistic notion of civilization will largely displace and frequently disfigure but never entirely lose the ongoing momentum of commitment to a universal jurisdiction of a common, all-inclusive humanity. This idea persists throughout the period studied here, 1500 to 1800, which provides the principal context for analyzing its continuity during the shift from the specifically religious to the more secular register.

The third of these distinctive characteristics, and the second of the two political principles to be examined, is the faculty for self-criticism. This feature really amounts to a state of mind, one ultimately attributable to Socrates' "examined life" and broadly described as a capacity for criticism, review, and dissent, which through a long historical process ultimately culminated in constitutional democracy. Certainly constitutional democracy, representative and elective, involves a number of practices, attitudes, and institutions not limited to two-party government but also including the presence of a free press, independent judicial review, and respect for the rule of law and the rights of minorities. The discussion in this book limits itself to the heart of this vast subject, namely, the immediacy of political dissent with its inherent idea of freedom; it seeks to disclose the beginnings of political parties in the European world, specifically in Britain and its first empire, culminating in the Federalist period, which followed immediately upon the acceptance of the U.S. Constitution. To a significantly lesser extent because of its complexity and unique history, as well as the need for moderation, this second political principle, the permitting, even expectation, of dissent, has culture-transcending aspirations and is thus potentially exportable to the peoples of other civilizations.

Two clarifications are in order. First, it is indeed true that other developments in current Western civilization may seem to be more influential and immediately exportable, such as capitalism and the world market—or, even more prominent and pervasive, American popular culture and consumerism. But these apply specifically to recent modern developments, especially in the twentieth century, and occur outside our period of consideration. Second, the use of the term "European" rather than "Western" in the title may appear problematic. But Europe and Europeans have come to identify and define a distinct civilization that matured in the extreme westernmost end of the Eurasian landmass in the period under analysis. Despite their long, august pedigree, "West" and "Western" are terms avoided in the body of this work or as much as possible curtailed; it was not until the late nineteenth century that the term "West" came to displace "European"—undoubtedly a process reinforced by America's increasing prominence—and to represent the entire collectivity of our civilization.[3] It will thus be used here either to indicate the period of our civilization following that designated as Europe and European, after approximately 1900, or as a convenient term referring to the total course of this civilization from the Stoic-Christian origins to the present. Consequently, according to such a periodization—Christian, European, Western—the title of this book refers to a still initial, brittle engagement of European civilization with the globe and its peoples; it deliberately stops short of the great period of colonialism and imperialism in the nineteenth century.

The strange anomaly of this European civilization that grades later into the West is nicely captured in a recent observation provoked by Denis Diderot's criticism of European imperial practices, which poses "the paradox that the most arrogant of civilizations is at the same time the most radically given to criticism of itself."[4] But this paradox is trumped by another, even more astonishing—that the civilization that in its colonialism and imperialism gave us the most savage, inhuman treatments of indigenous populations, not to mention the ultimate inhumanity of Auschwitz, was the same that promoted the idea of a common humanity and programs of human rights accompanied subsequently by a myriad of private organizations that continue to address poverty, hunger, disease, and multifarious needs throughout the globe. Yet perhaps this is not a paradox at all but can best be understood as integral to the complexity and varieties of the human animal.

An emphasis upon exceptionality, uniqueness, and the universalizing aspirations of the West more than implicitly challenges those currents that have come to prevail in American academe since the 1960s. The present study, however, refuses to become entangled in this ongoing debate or mired in confronting counterclaims of other civilizations to a comprehensive understanding of humankind or to the value and role of political dissent by means of diversity. In order to free this work from such distractions and maintain the unity of its argument, let it be clearly stated at the outset that there can be found in such claims only disparate, scattered cases, random lights—the Confucian Mencius, for example, or the Arab social philosopher Ibn Khaldūn—over the past twenty centuries that lack a sustained, continuous tradition, coherent in its formulation, comprehensive in its potential application and ever capable of achieving institutional expression. The stock recourse of those making counterclaims is most frequently evinced by appeals to truly attractive, unusual figures such as the emperors Akbar or Asoka in Indian civilization. But where the continuity? the sustained influence? the religiously neutral legal framework? the institutionalization of such high-minded practices?[5] Nonetheless, these scattered moments point to a larger universality upon which the Western impetus can attempt to graft itself.[6]

Developments within American academe since the 1960s have worked to marginalize or reject, while vilifying, what formerly seemed to be most solid and meritorious in the Western tradition. Admittedly, much in that tradition did need criticism and reformulation. Yet such an effort does not warrant a total denial of its enduring value. Extreme relativism and subjectivism have recently been rampant, their proponents urging that the center cannot, should not, never did, and will not hold. The West may be responsible for much of the present state of the world, including some horrendous features. Nevertheless, there is much in the Western tradition that we need to recognize, nurture, and enhance, rather than vehemently denigrating the entirety and indiscriminately pursuing the celebration of variety and difference for their own sakes. Absent the two distinctively Western political principles studied here, enthusiasm for diversity alone can descend into a nasty tribalism; absent the frameworks these principles provide, the opportunities for justice can only suffer. More important perhaps than anything else is the intellectual need to establish a common ground that also respects difference. And insofar as the West's intellectual inheritance addresses this issue, it creates at its best a framework for discussion, for reasoned argument, and the quest for a more inclusive justice, thereby extending a common basis of negotiation to all others. In brief, this book concerns itself with the unique creation, the historical beginnings, of that arena, that framework.

It would appear imprudent to extend such a study outside one's own competence as a historian of the Renaissance and Reformation into the present and even beyond. Here, without the same presumed authority, I must consider these enduring issues—more as an ordinary citizen. Furthermore, against the judgment and advice of several of my readers, I nevertheless remain determined to intrude this inquiry into the present day and not suppress the considerations that appear in the Epilogue—considerations dictated by the nature of the subject. The attempt to define the ultimate long-range political characteristics of our civilization and to recognize their universal purpose and seemingly inexorable development commits the investigator to entering at least to some extent the tricky currents of present controversy. To blandly refuse the challenge would be irresponsible. Nevertheless, one can only accept this responsibility by recognizing that one is acting in a different register and that whatever apparent "polemic" ensues, it must not intrude upon the principal historical exposition of this study; it must be insulated from the body of the work, the historical analysis and exposition of two unique political principles, and confined to an Epilogue that whoever wishes to do so can ignore.

The present study seeks to pursue a historical analysis and deliberately eschews any polemical, much less triumphalist, exposition of its two themes. Whatever its implications for the present, the object here is to deepen our historical appreciation of two distinctive features of our civilization—the idea of a common humanity that reveals itself in programs of human rights, and the tenability of political dissent that expresses itself in constitutional democracy; they bear within themselves the ideas of equality and of political freedom, respectively. Nor can this study linger in weighing the claims of other civilizations to a notion of universal humanity, where fleeting, fitful expressions contrast with the sustained, continuous concern of the West. Nor again, other than by brief allusion or in endnotes, can the issue of the potential grounds for an effective future coalescence or concord between a Western program of human rights and a Chinese-Confucian style program of human rites gain consideration. Likewise, any reference to the current political climate has been limited to an Epilogue, which justifies its inclusion here only by addressing the intrinsic question regarding the exportability of the two potentially universal features defined by this study: human rights and constitutional democracy.

An opening geographic chapter sets the stage in the Renaissance engagement of the peoples of the globe. In its cartographic contribution, linked with improved navigational skills, the Renaissance establishes the global context. Chapter 2 addresses the first of our two political principles—the idea of a common humanity. In chapter 3, that aspect of constitutional democracy mentioned earlier will be treated in two stages: the unlikely but necessary opening of formal, constructed dissent in Reformation Germany, followed by the more obvious development of party government in Britain and Anglo-America. An Aftermath seeks to bring the subject more into the present. Finally, an assessment of the future exportability of the two political principles will be the subject of a concluding Epilogue.

In the exposition of such a theme, with its potential universality over space and time, one embarks upon a representation of European civilization that is frankly more positive and attractive than has prevailed in the academic discourse of the past several decades. While admitting some validity to the criticism that has been leveled against the West, this book seeks to educe an achievement that has been allowed recently to suffer obscurity: namely, that uniquely positive voice in the long development of our civilization as it crosses the threshold into a more amorphous modern civilization for the planet.

Before the knowledge of Western civilization's distinctiveness disappears—and it *is* disappearing in the immense wash of globalization—this analysis aspires to define the two paramount political aspects of that civilization, the greatest of all in its resourcefulness and aspirations, the most awful and unnatural in its exploitation of power.

Chapter 1

The Renaissance Defining and Engagement of the Global Arena of Humanity

> The Renaissance remains—despite every criticism and revision—the crux of European history as a whole: the double moment of an equally unexampled expansion of space, and recovery of time. It is at this point, with the rediscovery of the Ancient World, and the discovery of the New World, that the European state-system acquired its full singularity. A ubiquitous global power was eventually to be the outcome of this singularity, and the end of it.
>
> —Perry Anderson, *Lineages of the Absolutist State* (1974)

The fifteenth century's recovery of Ptolemy's *Geographia* mobilized a complex of forces constituting within the Western tradition a comprehensive, unifying, universalizing process released upon the globe by Renaissance Europe, and now significantly reinforced by an incipient geographical culture. The inherent imperialism of Europe's geographical knowledge, best known in the work of the Royal Geographical Society during the nineteenth century,[1] had its earliest manifestations in the new trajectory upon which England somewhat belatedly embarked after 1575.[2] But it emerged earlier and quite expectably in the practices and attitudes of the Catholic world of Spain and of Rome in America, Asia, and Africa—in short, wherever new lands and non-European peoples appeared, and even where they did not. In contrast to the better-known English example, with its distinctively emergent national character, the Iberian, reflecting a Mediterranean culture with pronounced classical roots and antecedents, evinced a more universalizing character in its commitment to a civilizing process.

Epitomizing early modern Europe's direct application of geography to empire, there looms the formidable presence of the Count-Duke of Olivares, the great minister of Philip IV of Spain. Withdrawn into his study amidst the maps and globes that provided him with a picture of the world as a single theater of operation and opportunity, he determined the policy of the far-flung Spanish *monarquía* for over two decades (1621–43) and worked from the beginning to present his young, hesitant master as the Planet King (*rey planeta*).[3] This world statesman conveyed that inevitable delight in the sense of control and of possession imparted by a map or, better yet, by the satisfying physicality of a globe. Truly, as Sir Thomas Elyot had opined a century earlier, "What more delightful than following voyages on maps through the imagination in a warm study"—statesmen's imaginations being larger than most.[4]

In any account of the earliest beginnings of geography as a potential discipline, the terms *geography* and *cosmography* and their connotations become intertwined. This apparent interchangeability reflects their common source in Claudius Ptolemy's own *Geographia*, which, in its first Latin translation by Jacopo Angeli de Scarperia (1406), was titled *Cosmographia*. At the outset of his *Geographia*, Ptolemy defines geography "as the pictorial representation of the entire known earth and with what it is generally associated"; chorography, from which it is distinguished, treats the individual local parts.[5] The geography inherited from classical antiquity included three branches: the mathematical, the chorographic, and the descriptive, the first best evinced by Ptolemy, the last by Strabo.[6] Ptolemy mathematized geography by treating the celestial and terrestrial globes as equivalent, applying the same grid system to each, and reaffirming the parallel belts or climates.[7] The charting of the heavens and the earth remained so enmeshed that Ptolemy's crucial third projection for the earth's surface, presented in book 7, may actually have been constructed using an armillary, the traditional sphere for the construction of the heavens.[8] The gradual detachment of these terms, *geography* and *cosmography*, from one another and from their substantive connotations led in the course of the sixteenth century to the displacement of *cosmographia* in favor of *geographia*, the former name still lingering, suggestive of the slow, erratic genesis of a new discipline.

Among the new types of knowledge that germinated during the Renaissance, geography is of particular historical interest. Although most modern geographers understand their field to have become established as a distinct formal discipline only in the course of the later nineteenth century, effectively dismissing its dramatic developments in the sixteenth century, the claim that geography constituted a discipline was made in their own time by the early practitioners of this study. Indeed, they made important and fundamental advances in the mathematical and chorographic branches of this emerging subject as well as its better-known descriptive branch, which distinguished these early efforts in the eyes of twentieth-century geographers.

Any emphasis on the dignity and scientific character of geography as an emerging discipline must also admit the practical and subjective distortions its advocates made for economic and political ends. As evinced in the production of a map, geographical knowledge quickly assumed the form of a commodity subject to the interests of princely patronage and to the political and commercial claims of empire. The map became a politically and commercially charged product. During the later 1520s, in the Castilian-Portuguese controversy over the longitude of the Moluccas (the Spice Islands in the East Indies) for the very division of the world, the geographers, the new scientific experts of the day, were brought to the negotiating table of high diplomacy, where each side sought to advance its own rival, partisan claims. In its basic acquisitiveness—or, better, its essentially rhetorical nature—this new discipline could not afford to be neutral and detached.[9]

The imperializing, universalizing element appears to have been integral to sixteenth-century Europeans' exploitation of this new form of knowledge. Maps represented a language of power anticipating empire: to name, to locate mathematically, to define cartographically in relation to others became the essential preparatory step for possession, control, mastery.[10] The development of perspective in the Renaissance afforded Europeans the conceptual key to global dominance. Something of the seed of this recognition occurred in the thought of Leon Battista Alberti, that great pioneer of perspective's study and uses, when he confidently sought to apply to the visible world the universal, mathematical vision of proportionality first revealed to the age in Ptolemy's *Geographia*.[11]

The late Renaissance in Europe needs to be more fully understood in terms of this burgeoning of map making and geographical knowledge as those oceanic barriers, according to the second-century BCE cosmographer Crates of Mallos, presumably separating continents, collapsed in the sixteenth century's intellectual mastery of the globe before the intrusive advances of those impious ships earlier proclaimed by Horace. At the century's end England, the last of the major European powers to enter the competition for overseas colonies, turned with notable focus and attention to the field of education in geography; the universities of Oxford and Cambridge pressed upon their incoming students a rapidly expanding program of geographic knowledge that would lay the foundations to a new sort of empire—what Diderot would protest two centuries later as "the pretensions of one single people to the universal monarchy of the seas."[12] More generally, geography, maps, and charts with their steady improvement afforded the European sea captain a new sort of assurance and effective power for the conquest of the globe.[13]

Once the European engagement of the globe had been effected—however tenuously—through cartography, improved navigation, and discovery, in the course of the sixteenth century it continued to be sustained and secured by a unique exercise of oceanic sea power unknown to all other civilizations, excepting a brief flourish of naval might by the Ming dynasty in the Indian Ocean during the first third of the fifteenth century. Indeed, there followed what has been called the politicization of oceanic space, pursued by the emerging territorial states of Europe.[14] Moreover, with the beginning in 1565 of 250 years of regular trade between Spanish America and China, known as the Manila Galleon, Spain wrought a silver chain of global girth that served as the first deposit in the establishment of a world economy.[15] It was to be sea power, first exercised by Portugal and Spain, then by the Dutch, and finally by the British, that made the development of the New World a European monopoly and allowed Europe to establish significant toeholds in and beyond the Indian Ocean. Cast into the balance after 1800, the European predominance came to displace for two centuries the economic and cultural preeminence Asia had long enjoyed.

Imperial and Global Motifs in the Advent of the New Geography

Universalizing and imperializing forces inherent in this new theater of intellectual enterprise, the study of geography, afforded Europe the supreme advantage of defining the global arena. The energies released by the new discipline of geography in the form of mathematical perspective and the graticule or net of mathematical coordinates equipped Europeans, especially Iberians, with improved cartography and navigation and opened up the world to their aggressiveness, allowing them to begin to establish a global arena of opportunity, exploitation, and conquest.

Deep within the recesses of the medieval university's curriculum, in the quadrivium of the seven liberal arts, those four recognized studies communicated by number rather than by word—arithmetic, geometry, music, and astronomy—lay a practical mathematics involving geometry and optics. The latter held important implications for perspective. Sacrobosco's *On the Sphere* (*De sphaera*, 1220), a standard textbook, had played a part in this area since the mid-thirteenth century. Shortly thereafter John Pecham's (1230?) *Common Perspective* (*Perspectiva communis*) became the standard textbook on optics at the universities and remained so to the end of the sixteenth century. Although the work did not address the distancing factor and the rationalization of space, it nevertheless sought to describe how objects appear to an observer.[16] During the mid-fourteenth century at the University of Paris, perspective, hence optics, came to be treated as a mathematical science, to be taught along with the quadrivium's original subjects.[17] By the time Antonio Pollaiuolo executed the tomb for Pope Sixtus IV in 1484, he included perspective as the eighth liberal art.[18] And by the turn of the century, when Albrecht Dürer came to explain the word *perspectiva* as meaning a "seeing through" (*ein Durchsehung*) rather than a "seeing clearly," the earlier optical sense, a perspectival view of space had emerged. No longer satisfied with the foreshortening of individual objects, perspective now went on to the creation of a systematic space, a managed distancing: the entire composition was turned into a window, allowing one to look into this rationalized, artificial space.[19] The great art historian Erwin Panofsky identified this linear, perspectival construction as expressive of "a quite specific, indeed specifically modern sense of space, or if you will, sense of the world." What was the meaning of this slide from *Raumgefühl* to *Weltgefühl* by means of a mere *wenn man so will*?[20] *Welt* not only entails most immediately the physical universe, drawing with it profound implications for its measurement and description in a nascent geography, but more broadly suggests a total perspectival consciousness and a distinctively Western perception of reality.[21]

Yet one of the distinctive features of geography as a new, incipient type of knowledge was its necessary and essential links with practicality and application; whatever its mathematical roots in the university, geography from the start represented an applied science with connections to learned humanistic circles outside the university, such as that of the mathematician and polymath Paolo Toscanelli (1397–1482) in Florence or the Jewish astronomers patronized by Portuguese monarchs. In this latter case Abraham Zacuto (1450–1522) significantly promoted the reception of Islamic astronomy and cartography by the Portuguese as they moved out into the Atlantic to claim new islands and as they inched their way so fatefully down the western coast of Africa during the fifteenth century.[22] Building upon and generating an improved knowledge of geography through successive cartographic refinements, European navigation provided the tangible evidence and announcement of the diverse roots and practicalities of the new science. Moreover, through navigation Christianity would at last be able to implement globally its claims to universality.[23] The compass came to serve as metaphor for a type of knowledge that augured Europe's encompassment and potential conquest of the globe.

No single event so mobilized and reoriented this new learning as the recovery and translation into Latin of Ptolemy's

Geographia. This event profoundly reflected what we have come to expect of humanism and the Renaissance: it occurred within the circle of young aficionados for the study of classical Greek, created by the presence of the distinguished diplomat and teacher Manuel Chrysoloras in Florence at the end of the fourteenth century. In the *Geographia*, Ptolemy defines his subject "as a survey of the earth in its just proportions," and he calls upon its practitioners "to concentrate upon the position rather than the quality [i.e., nature] of a place." It can well be judged the most significant single work among the classical texts recovered by the Italian Renaissance, for it would beckon artists and astronomers, cartographers and navigators to apply a mathematical proportionality to the visible world (fig. 1).[24]

Through Jacopo Angeli's translation from the Greek, Ptolemy now described to the Latin world of scholarship three projections. In its first cartographic publication (Bologna, 1477), the last projection, on a modified conic surface, pictorially revealed to the learned public the then known inhabited world, the *oikoumene*. It is difficult to imagine the awe that intellectual achievement inspired; perhaps the only comparable modern effect is that of the *Apollo 8* photograph, taken from lunar orbit, of Earthrise. Ptolemy's depiction of the *oikoumene*, or more probably a fourteenth-century Byzantine reconstruction based upon his third projection, treated the purchasers of the volume at a glance to a perspective on all that mattered, far superior to what the gods had been enjoying from Mount Olympus. This capacity to stand outside and beyond this planet and plot its surface through perspective and mathematics culminated at the end of the century in the tangible aesthetic as well as the intellectual experience of the first terrestrial globe, produced by Martin Behaim, a Nuremberg geographer in Lisbon, in the same year Columbus sailed west.

Pressing further the implications of this tangible reduction of the macrocosm to the microcosm through the mapping of

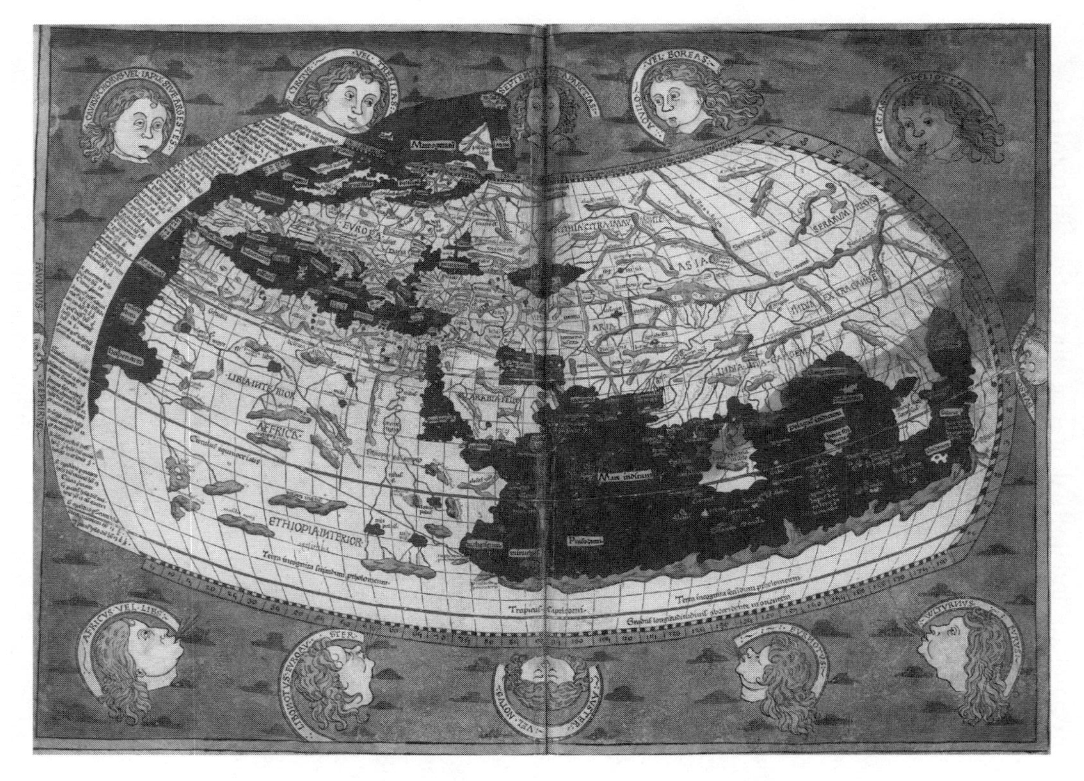

Figure 1. Ptolemy's *Oikoumene* from the Ulm 1482 edition of the *Geographia*. Courtesy of the John Carter Brown Library.

the earth effected in the subsequent decades, we can begin to appreciate the intellectual and aesthetic delight readers derived from the mathematical achievement of the Duisburg cartographer Gerard Mercator (1512–94). In his own choice of the word *atlas* after 1569 to designate his structured collection of maps, he raises the aesthetic experience of intellectual possession to the level of godlike mastery and comprehension. Combining both divine and human qualities in an almost supernatural inclusiveness, this microcosmic rendering of the macrocosm, this intellectual yet graphic compression, borders upon the archetypal Hermetic experience of mastery, possession, empire through *gnosis*.[25]

We think of the Renaissance as humanism's recovery of classical rhetoric. Yet we take for granted, even ignore, that transposition of the mind, that intellectual effort to attempt to bring the vestiges of an age and its culture into focus from an established vantage point. This aspect of perspective, of seeing, when applied to time, created an incipient mental distancing—a perspective less mathematical than emotional and cognitive—which both evinced and promoted in the self a new and deepening complexity. Similarly, the application of perspective to space, best known to us in Renaissance painting, was concurrent with and complementary to Europe's geographical accomplishments, which moved it toward conquest of the globe. Moreover, at the very least in the mathematical uses of perspective, what has long been recognized as the hallmark of Renaissance painting applied as well to contemporary cartography: in their recourse to perspective, painters and cartographers moved together, and its early uses were often conjoined in the same person as manifested in the careers of the Limbourg and the van Eyck brothers, Alberti, Leonardo, Dürer, the Dieppe School, and finally El Greco.[26] Serving to nurture Brunelleschi's two perspectival experiments, undertaken about 1418—which would establish linear perspective in painting—the Ptolemaic seeing from one fixed point, with its mathematical construction of space, invaded Florentine high lay society; artists, the scientifically gifted, and wealthy patrons could be found convening at a new scriptorium engaged in the reproduction of Ptolemaic atlases, whose hand-colored maps, not accidentally, were referred to as paintings or pictures (*pitture*).[27] Indeed, it appears that, more than rhetoric or even philology, perspective—the mind's capacity intellectually to project and to survey both in time and in space—best assembles the enterprise as well as the import of that cultural movement identified as the Renaissance. Only if we appreciate the decisive nature of this distinct common ground shared by cartographers and artists in the construction of a rationalized space, can the so-called Age of Discovery, with all its implications, be conceptually integrated into the main course of the European Renaissance.

Yet perspective alone by no means exhausts the immediate significance of the Latin publication of Ptolemy's *Geographia*. Despite its grave limitations, which through the course of successive editions led to its final displacement by Ortelius's atlas of 1570, Ptolemy's work possessed another feature instructive to our purpose: Ptolemy cast over the face of the *oikoumene* a net of mathematical coordinates, or graticule—the latitude and longitude of the Alexandrian school—whereby he could presumably establish with mathematical exactitude the location of individual places. The assumption that permitted such mathematization arose from his confidence that the earth's surface was essentially homogeneous. The grid would shortly be extended from the ecumenical patch to the entire globe and constitute a vital feature of the new geography. Following his first voyage, Columbus himself called for a new map for navigation wherein the collocations afforded by latitude and longitude (no matter how inaccurate the latter) might replace the wind rose of earlier cartography as a locative device.[28] The grid not only came to be extended globally to an expanded ecumene but was increasingly refined and tightened to become another metaphor for human existence in the dawning modern age.

During the fifteenth century, churchmen and the church itself fed the mounting interest in a larger world and the new geographical culture. In Venice the Camaldolese monk Fra Mauro benefited from Ptolemy but in some instances went beyond him in accuracy, especially in opening up an enclosed Indian pond into what became the vast Indian Ocean. Pope Alexander VI's Treaty of Tordesillas (1494) between Portugal and Castile, which sought to divide the colonial world according to a hypothetical meridian, would have been impossible without Ptolemy's coordinates. To balance the mathematical emphasis provided by Ptolemy's recovery, the contemporary recovery of the classical Greek Strabo's *Geography* through papal patronage and the Florentine circle of scholars associated with Cardinal Nicholas of Cusa (Nicholas Cusanus) now introduced the chorographic and descriptive aspects, the sense of place, as a counterweight to the more theoretical aspects of geography. Strabo spoke to the contemporary interest in travel and distant lands. With Pius II, in the mid-fifteenth century the geographical current would enter Christendom's highest office.[29]

From the beginning of the sixteenth century an awakening sense of a new type of knowledge appeared and continues to resound to this day. From the Swiss canton of St. Gall the eminent polymath Joachim Vadian, in his edition of the classical geographer Pomponius Mela (1518), gave a significant twist to Plato's admonition that no man is human without a knowledge of arithmetic: now those are designated *inhumani* who lack a knowledge of geography. He went on to celebrate the fact that Vespucci's discovery of America (!) showed this land to be populated in all its zones, as the Portuguese also made clear in their penetration of the Southern Hemisphere.[30] In his dedicatory letter to the Archbishop of Salzburg, which figured as the preface to his *Cosmographicus liber* of 1524, Peter Apian (1495–1552), a pioneer of astronomical and geographical instrumentation, wrote not only of the *geographica disciplina* but also of the *geografica* [!] *et cosmographica professio*. To a learned public still feeling its way amid the explosive knowledge of the globe, Apian defined geography in terms of cartography, although the term had yet to be minted and his *continens* was not yet identical to the modern continent.[31] Geography was groping its way toward definition. Likewise with Philip II's chief cartographer, his *cosmógrafo mayor*, Alonso de Santa Cruz, who served the House of Trade at Seville from 1536 to 1564: the prologue to his *Geography of All the Islands of the World* (*Islario general de todas las islas del mundo*) defined geography as the description or picture of the earth (*terra*), while cosmography was a science or discipline that treated the universe (*mundo*); the author then proceeded to define the vocabulary of his subject.[32] Toward the end of his life Santa Cruz found a young collaborator and intellectual heir in Juan López de Velasco, who composed the greatest single geographical synthesis of *ambas Indias* ("both Indies," East and West) in the sixteenth century, although it was not published until three hundred years later. His *Geografía y descripción universal de las Indias* provided the most coherent synthesis of regional geography for a New World that included the Pacific area and the extreme Far East as well as the Americas. Appointed to the Council of the Indies as its first royal cosmographer, *cosmógrafo real*, this autodidact, this self-made man composed a searching questionnaire of thirty questions—the true harbinger of the new bureaucratic age—directed to five hundred communities in the New World.[33] The resulting *Relaciones geográficas*, in its topographic and ethnographic aspects, its inquiry into the resources of the new lands and their populations, introduces us to the chorographic level of sixteenth-century geography. In its effort to provide detailed information suitable to government, administration, and policy, the work exemplifies the natural link between geography and empire.

Geographers' efforts to define their field and confer intellectual respectability upon it led to the resumption of geography's mathematical roots in the university and the more public advancement of its practical and descriptive aspects. Giuseppe Moletti, who preceded Galileo in the chair of mathematics at Padua, consciously addressed all the terms and rules pertaining to geography when he participated in Girolamo Ruscelli's translation and edition of Ptolemy's *Geographia* (1561). In treating maps, tables, and the collocation of coordinates, he sought to drive his subject *alla perfettione della scienza*. Emulating Ptolemy, he aspired to produce an entirely new geography of the whole earth, but "as it is found today" (*come hoggidì si trouva*), with its coordinates.[34] And soon afterward publications from Pisa turned emphatically in the direction of that descriptive type of geography that was now emerging with greater frequency from the press.[35] By 1616, a distinct chair for geography had been established at Leyden, which was rapidly becoming Europe's foremost university.[36]

This rudimentary survey of the tentative beginnings of geography as a distinct form of knowledge appears here not simply because the subject seems to have escaped the direct attention of historians in suggesting a different and expanded understanding of the Renaissance. Rather, the specifically universalizing theme associated with the advancement of geography also claims our attention. No other intellectual discipline serves the total comprehensive aspirations, whether exploitative or missionary, of a civilization as does geography. In its immediate address to the lands and peoples of the earth, when associated with the improved technology of sixteenth-century navigation, geographic knowledge brought the entire globe within its survey and eventual compass. In keeping with its Ptolemaic roots, geography was closely linked with cosmography, which pertained to the astronomical system; yet the former, as the study of the earth, in the course of the century came increasingly to be detached and defined separately from the latter. Such a rich heritage served to establish the specifically universalizing character of geography as a new knowledge that could be exploited for religious, political, economic, and military purposes upon a global stage.

In the sudden experience of January 1640 forced upon Peter Heylyn, cleric and royal partisan of Charles I as well as geographer, there is much that is illustrative of an age undergoing rapid transformation. While being transferred to Westminster in the detainment of hostile custody, Heylyn reports being abruptly accosted by a man with a statement applicable most immediately to the royalist cleric but also to the new age: "Geographie is better than Divinitie."[37] Besides the startled theologian himself, scholars have puzzled over its meaning; with the cooling advantage of almost four centuries' removal it might here be hazarded as announcing that geography is safer and more useful than the political entanglements of religion.

Yet decades before Heylyn's curious experience the geography of the late Renaissance had attained both its culmination and its consolidation in the *Theatrum orbis terrarum* of Abraham Ortelius. There had been previous collections of maps. But in his sustained effort to normalize and coordinate a personal assemblage of the best maps of the century, this Antwerp scholar provided Europe not only with the first actual atlas, but with what his friend Mercator praised as a single, effective *enchiridion* or manual. For if Ptolemy's *Geographia* represented an icon, invoking the human ability to know and to master the globe, the *Theatrum* of the later sixteenth century, dedicated to Philip II of Spain, presented itself as a manual for the European mastery of the globe.[38] With the posthumous publication of the first atlas so named in 1595, Mercator himself would further confirm that fact for seafaring Europe.

It was a very different Europe from that of classical mythology that sat for her portrait at the hands of the distinguished engraver Franz Hogenberg and now confronts us on the title page of this extraordinary work (fig. 2). While the other continental figures of Asia and Africa look downward or aside and America is depicted as suitably enthralled in cannibalism, while Magellanica has achieved a fractured representation of truncated plasticity, from her eminence Europe confronts us directly—crowned, sceptered, with a rudderlike cross thrust into the globe—an attestation of knowledge and of global expansion. Amidst the accompanying prefatory material a poem announces that "Spain has dared to extend Europe's empire across the unknown seas."[39]

The improved navigation and new confidence that suddenly made the whole world accessible to Europe revealed more profound and subtler aspects to the opportunities and challenges afforded by geography as a new form of knowledge. The thoughts of two humanists command our attention: Simon Grynaeus, the Hellenic scholar and Protestant theological leader at Basel, at the beginning of the century, and Michel de Montaigne at its end.

Grynaeus's career exemplifies the passage of humanism's critical techniques from literary to mathematical, cosmographical, physical, botanical, medical, and metallurgical texts: to be sure, humanism and science here coalesce. To Grynaeus, the discovery of a new continent was no accident but the product of man's rational powers; the systematic inquiry into nature as part of the divine revelation became a religious and specifically Christian duty. Anticipating the later and more extensive collections of the humanist scholar Giovanni Battista Ramusio and of Ramusio's better-known English counterpart, Richard Hakluyt, the chief promoter of English discoveries,

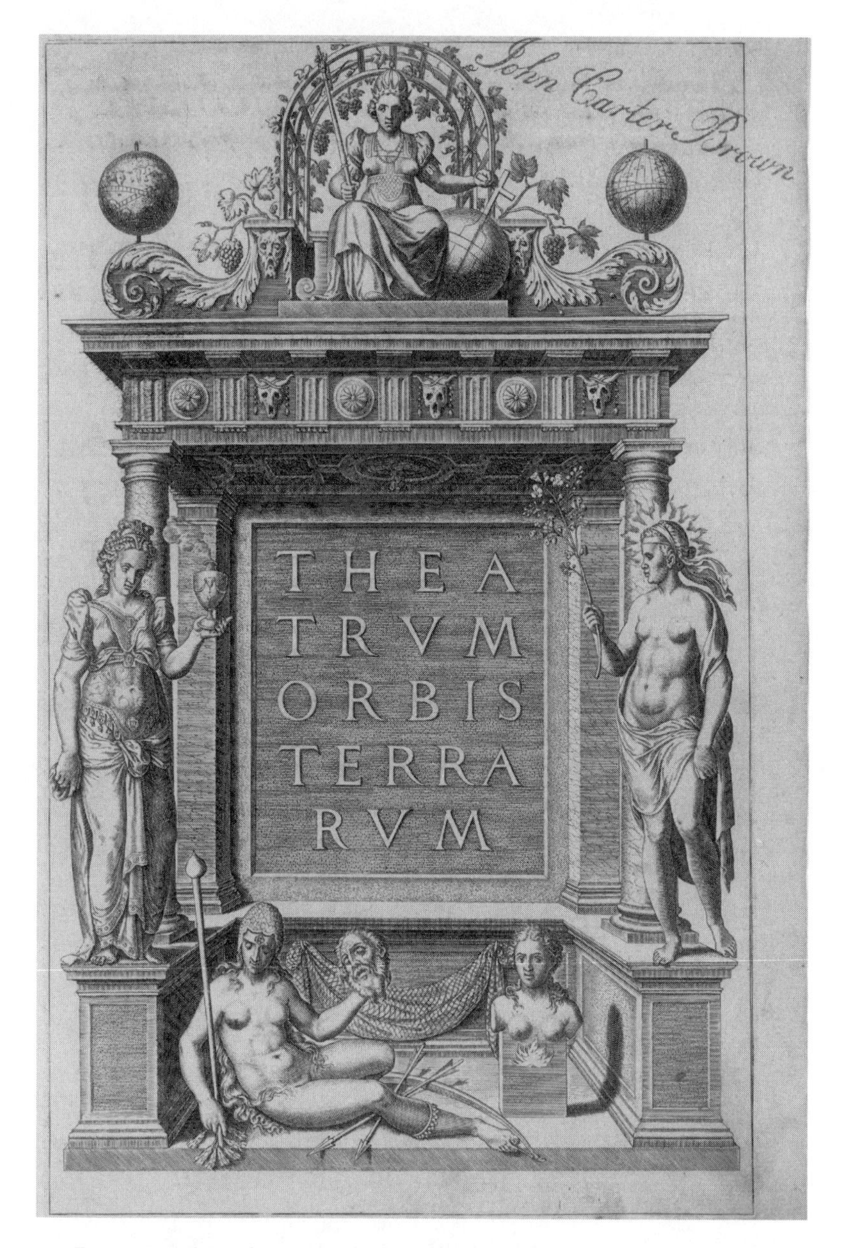

Figure 2. The title page of Abraham Ortelius's *Theatrum orbis terrarum*, 1570. Courtesy of the John Carter Brown Library.

Grynaeus's *Novus orbis* (1532) brought together a number of accounts of exploration, some predating Columbus. In a prefatory letter Grynaeus proclaimed mathematics and physics as the highest auxiliary disciplines of theology, for natural philosophy provided another type of knowledge of the supreme Architect—an intellectual development that would culminate with Robert Boyle and the scientific accomplishments of the Royal Society over a century later. In a resonant passage Grynaeus acclaimed rational man's overcoming, mastering, and harnessing of every apparent obstacle that Nature might present "once the reliability and constancy of Nature had been established at home":

> Indeed, the acuity of [the human] mind surpasses all of the forces of Nature, and as it finds its own way through all obstacles, fulfilling the desire which secretly and silently devours every well-formed intelligence . . . and as it perceives You more closely, Father, in Your works, it will become all the more deeply perturbed and its visceral appetite will burn all the more intensely. Thus it follows You through all seas, to all ends of the Earth as if crazed.[40]

Thus had the intellectual *contemplatio mundi*, the contemplation of the world, now raised by a broadly conceived geographical knowledge to a pitch of religious fervor, become a ravenous thirst, recognizing no barriers, to master the globe. Was it really this that the Christian God had intended—this encompassing universalization? *Plus oultre*, the emperor Charles V's device, "Still further"—indeed! No wonder that, after the Spanish juggernaut of conquest and exploration turned to Asia and China in the 1560s, it left in its wake in the governor's palace at Santo Domingo the motto, written over the escutcheon, "The World Sufficeth Not."[41]

In the essays of Montaigne we encounter a less appalling, more attractive aspect to the universalizing ingredient in European civilization. From the tower-study on his estate outside Bordeaux, he reflected upon the ransacking of America: "So many cities razed, so many nations exterminated, so many millions of people put to the sword . . . and [all] for the traffic in pearls and pepper!" And earlier: "Our world has just discovered another world, and who will guarantee that it is the last of its brothers?"[42] Montaigne concluded all his life musings in the culminating master idea of the *commun humain*, the definition and affirmation of the common, human pattern, universally applicable amidst the immense diversity—the intrinsic solidarity and mutuality of all humankind—rising to that wonderful statement in "On Repentance" that we each bear within ourselves the entire form of the human condition.[43] It has been said that the discoveries—American, African, and Asian—of this period thus invented humanity. Here presumably is intended not the traditional, classical idea of *humanitas* as an individual, subjective endowment, but rather, in another dimension of this key term, an incipient notion of the human race as a single collectivity.[44]

This sudden exposure to a fully inhabited (or so it seemed) yet extra-Christian world, this abruptly expanded ecumene with its variety of peoples, in time created an increasingly secular, religiously neutral lens that gradually revealed humankind's common biological and moral unity. In the terrible shock that Europeans inflicted upon hitherto unknown peoples, the contacts between the peoples posited the fact of humanity as an ideal to be realized in some distant future. Beyond the brutal impact and the immense problem of Adam's newfound children, the intellectual instruments afforded by the decisive reemergence of Stoicism and natural law, the traditional means for promoting such community, faltered in achieving the universal commitment implicit in the ideal of a single humanity. But in the context of so much explication, the hope presented by this universal ideal briefly attained articulation. As Alphonse Dupront, an intellectual historian of early modernity, argued in 1946: "The true fruit of the 'Discovery of the World' is the certitude of a *commun humain*."[45]

For sixteenth-century Europe, redolent with new geographical knowledge and reawakened imperial instincts, the obvious political architect was none other than the Catholic king, Philip II of Spain. By 1580, through the personal union thrust upon Portugal and the consequent alignment of the two Iberian colonial empires—the expanding worlds of Castile and Portugal—no monarch on earth, other than the Mongol khans, had ever commanded so much real estate. Philip's immediate extra-European holdings revealed a colonialism unique in its effort to incorporate the indigenous populations into a total, comprehensive Catholic system. The broadly held belief of most cartographers in the existence of a great southern continent, known since the 1540s as Terra Australis or Magellanica and presumably pulsating with other peoples and abounding in resources, held out the seeming opportunity for further exploitation and proselytizing in a world whose boundaries still awaited definition (fig. 3).

At the end of the century, in Rome, Europe sat for one of its earliest portraits—by the hand of Giovanni Botero, ex-Jesuit, acting as descriptive geographer. The nature of Botero's assignment, which served to generate the composition of his *Global Reports* (*Relationi universali*), compelled him to look beyond the Spanish monarchy to the presence of Christianity in general throughout the globe. Indeed his patron and lord, Federico Borromeo, Cardinal-Archbishop of Milan, had inquired what the newly constituted globe signified for the Christian religion in general.[46] The assignment required an extensive exercise in the third branch of geography, the descriptive, together with an assessment of political conditions throughout the globe and opportunities for the papacy. Writing in 1591,

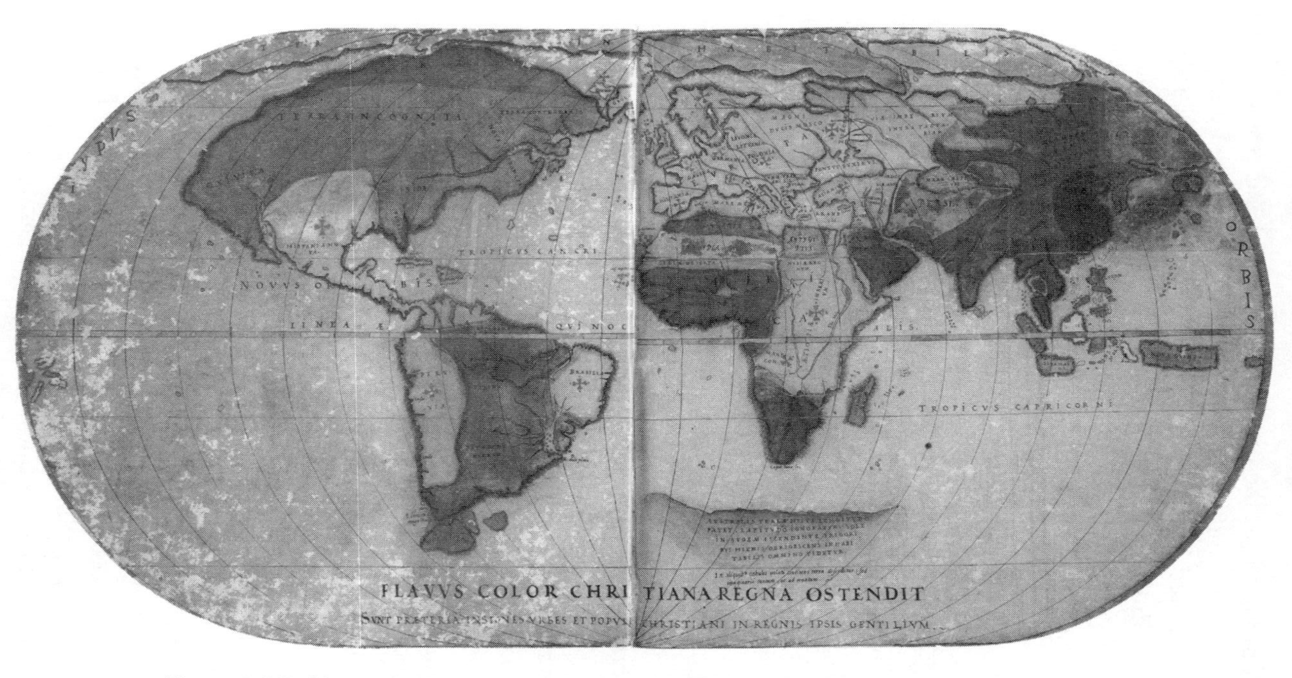

Figure 3. World map by Inacio Moreira, late 1590s. Alert to the new opportunities offered to Christendom at the end of the sixteenth century, the Portuguese cartographer Inacio Moreira, serving in the retinue of the Jesuit inspector general, Alessandro Valignano, when the latter visited the emperor of Japan in 1585, sought to show by the lighter areas the ostensible progress of Christendom in a world on the eve of what was soon to witness the European rise to dominance. Courtesy of Kenneth Nebenzahl.

Botero announced at the outset of his project the new claims of geography to intellectual recognition: just as the Egyptian priest, as quoted by Plato in *Timaeus*, could scold the Greeks for being children in their ignorance of the past, now Botero berated his contemporaries for their ignorance of geography.[47] Less technical and mathematical than political and narrative, his addressing of geography would engage the imperializing features of the new subject.

In fact, Botero presents two portraits of Europe, each situated at the very beginning of parts 1 and 2 respectively of his report. The first is broadly historical, cultural, and geographical. Despite the specifically ecclesiastical assignment of the book, it is significant that his point of reference is not *Christianitas* (Christendom), but *Europa*. The second, Botero's political portrayal of Europe, was that of a continent multicellular in its internal features, physically defined and demarcated by rivers and mountain ranges and distinguished by a variety of political governments all pulsating with explosive power; a tense balance of forces (*con tal contrapeso di forze*) kept its parts in relative and momentary respectful order. But this moment of portrayal Botero compared to the political expectancy noted by the great Roman poet Vergil in the cities of Italy before Rome and its legions burst upon the Mediterranean world. Similarly, Europe harbored almost uncontrollably expansive energies.[48]

The present brief consideration of perspective, this new way of seeing, now expressed in a new geography and coupled with political power, can best be concluded by referring to the emperor, Charles V, the first and preeminent Lord of all the World. For one not particularly gifted with respect to intellectual matters and even rather incurious, Charles acquired during his long reign a most respectable knowledge of the new, burgeoning cartography, as well he might, for his expanding global real estate. He made use of maps not simply for his own edification but also for administrative purposes.

Nor was he immune to the aesthetic, subjective experience; indeed, the distinguished French humanist and soldier Martin Du Bellay spoke of the emperor as giving such attention and study to a map of lower Provence and the Alps "that he began to think that he had the country in his grasp, instead of just the maps." In keeping with such cartographic enthusiasm it is reported that at Charles's death, among the few objects of bedside proximity was to be found a copy of "Tolomeo"—presumably Ptolemy's *Geographia*.[49]

The Fully Habitable World for Renaissance Europe

> I see that you are still directing your gaze upon the habitation and abode of men. If it seems small to you, as it actually is, keep your gaze fixed upon these heavenly things, and scorn the earthly. For what fame can you gain from the speech of men, or what glory that is worth the seeking? You see that the earth is inhabited in only a few portions, and those very small, while vast deserts lie between [*vastas solitudines interiectas*] those inhabited patches [*maculis*], as we may call them; you see that the inhabitants are so widely separated that there can be no communication whatever among the different areas; and that some of the inhabitants live in parts of the earth that are oblique, transverse, and sometimes directly opposite your own [*partim obliquos, partim transversos, partim etiam adversos stare vobis*], from such you can expect nothing surely that is glory.
>
> —Cicero, *De re publica*, VI.19–20

By the beginning of the sixteenth century, Venice had become the main center of map production in Europe. Although the house of Antonio Lafreri at Rome could claim to be the largest cartographic establishment in Italy, it specialized in maps of cities and those that celebrated historical events. Venice projected a far more cosmopolitan, even global, awareness and commitment.[50] The cosmographer to the republic of Venice, Giacomo Gastaldi, surpassed all other cartographers of the age in producing the most accurate maps of areas of the earth's surface—some hitherto unknown.[51] He clearly benefited from his friendship with the humanist scholar Giovanni Battista Ramusio, whose intellectual enterprise in the course of the late 1530s drew upon a network of aristocratic and talented luminaries who made available to him the best of Renaissance learning and science and the latest news from the New World. The result of this wide access together with Ramusio's own talents bore fruit in the formidable venture revealed by the *Navigations and Voyages* (*Navigazioni e viaggi*). This work offered both a source and a vehicle for some of Gastaldi's own production.[52]

Ramusio's great collection of travel materials sought to include all past and present literature on voyages of discovery. An earlier and more extensive presentation than the *Principal Navigations* later offered by Richard Hakluyt to the English, Ramusio's *Navigations and Voyages* constituted the first such collection of historical documents; it represented the culmination of the energies, enterprise, and learning of its accomplished editor. With his pronounced gifts in the study of the classics and especially geography, Ramusio advised the highest circles of Venetian society, government, the university, and the press. From 1515 he served as secretary to the Venetian Senate, and after July 7, 1553, as secretary to the all-important Council of Ten. In 1534–38, Ramusio began compiling the *Navigations and Voyages*. His work presented for the first time a general synthesis of the experiences that had recently transformed the contours and dimensions of the earth.[53] Composed in the vernacular and organized spatially rather than chronologically, it had a somewhat disjointed production: the first of its three volumes, which covered the Portuguese enterprise in Africa and in the Indian Ocean, appeared in 1550; the third volume, about the Spanish conquests in South and Central America, appeared in 1556; and the second volume, largely devoted to the French voyages in North America, appeared in 1559, two years after Ramusio's death.[54]

In 1563, when Ramusio's collaborator and printer Tommaso Giunti published the second edition of volume 1, he included a prefatory letter detailing the vicissitudes that explained the delays in publication, among them the death of his great friend Ramusio. In the course of his reflections he made a striking pronouncement: acclaiming the geographical knowledge of his day, which was unknown to the ancients, he stated that "it is clearly able to be understood that this entire earthly globe is marvelously inhabited, nor is there any part of it empty, neither by heat nor by cold deprived of inhabitants."[55]

Our immediate task is that of trying to pick up the implications of this confident statement. Most immediately in the larger context of sixteenth-century thought, several resonances of possible meaning present themselves from this celebratory exclamation: (1) that all the world is sufficiently temperate for sustaining human life; (2) that people know that all the world can sustain human life and may act upon that notion; (3) that all the world has become accessible to human beings by means of navigation and cartography; (4) that God's creation is glorified as something that has been made on our account—according to Copernicus, for us (*propter nos*—for us Europeans?); and (5) that the volume celebrates a totally humanized (Europeanized?) world.[56]

In actual fact the statement proved somewhat premature and anticipatory so far as the experience of exploration up to that time had established. In Ramusio and Giunti's day, exploration had only provided sufficient evidence to allow one safely to assume that the Arctic was habitable; the Antarctic remained those unknown southern lands—*terra australis incognita*—far into the twentieth century. Yet if America presented an epistemological and cognitive problem of the first magnitude, it was not to be resolved solely by the corrosive of experience upon the solid block of authority and the accumulation of navigational penetrations and cartographic precisions. Supplementing experience and emerging in the prefatory letters of Ramusio himself obtrudes a pervasive conviction based upon the deductive reasoning of Platonism: that God in his infinite potentiality had created a *plenum*, a fullness, that disallows any exceptional developments, making impossible any voids—metaphysical, biological, or anthropological. Suggestive of an intellectual climate soon to be reinforced by the presence of the Church's arch-heretic, Giordano Bruno, this philosophical-religious assumption of a pervasive rationality and an essential uniformity pointed toward the completion of a still experientially, empirically incomplete realization regarding the earth's total habitability in 1563.

The subject of the earth's habitability has apparently never received any sustained consideration and review in studies of the Age of Discovery.[57] Regarding whatever actual lands were discovered, the discovery that they were populated proved to be of decisive importance. Our analysis focuses upon the construction of the idea of the earth's total habitability and its significance for Renaissance Europe from the late fifteenth century in geography's new beginnings.

The origins of Columbus's "Enterprise of the Indies" can be seen emerging in the margins of the admiral's copy of Pierre d'Ailly's *Imago mundi* (1410). In chapter 8 of that work the learned cardinal turned to the question of the extent (*quantitate*) of the habitable earth. The world he had inherited had been perceived ever since Pythagoras as spherical, and its habitable part had been confined to little more than the *orbis terrarum*, the lands around the Mediterranean. Herodotus had introduced the significant term *oikoumene*—"ecumene," or "inhabited earth"—which, through the intercommunication of its inhabitants, imparted the sense of "known world" or "familiar world." Herodotus's criticism opened up the ecumene from its oceanic confinement and surrounded it with "distant lands," for the present only dimly perceived but presumably capable of becoming to some degree "known."[58] The resulting T-O map—so called because it has the appearance of a T, with Asia above the cross-stroke and Europe and Africa to the left and right of the downstroke that represented the Mediterranean, all inside an entirely ocean-bounded O—constituted one of the two fundamental cartographic types of the medieval inheritance (fig. 4).

The second type of medieval map was the zonal, based on climatic differentiation.[59] Beginning with Aristotle and advanced by Eratosthenes in the third century BCE, Greek speculation hazarded a spherical earth divided into climatic bands that now posited not only an ecumene in the north, constituted by Europe, Africa, and Asia and situated in the Tropic of Cancer, but also its possible mirror image in a matching ecumene stretching from the Tropic of Capricorn to the Antarctic, the two forever separated either by an impassable torrid zone or by a vast scheme of oceanic barriers. Crates of Mallos and the Stoics reconstituted this picture into four island continents, each inhabited, yet lacking any intercommunication (fig. 5).[60] Cicero, as presented in the epigraph to this section, sent the eminent Roman general Scipio Africanus Minor skyward, allowing him to see now four inhabited portions of the earth widely separated by ocean and without communication among the constituent parts. In the first century BCE, Horace endowed navigation with moral import: "For no purpose did a wise god divide the lands with estranging

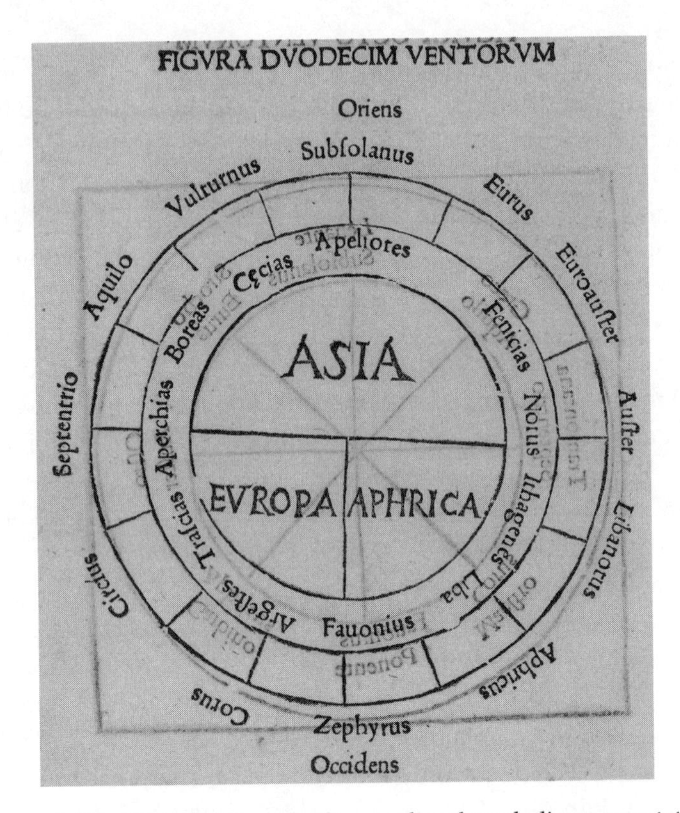

Figure 4. The T-O map, the prevailing medieval symbolic representation of the world according to the Lilio rendering. Courtesy of the John Carter Brown Library.

Ocean, if our impious ships nevertheless race across waters that should be left untouched." And Ocean, as Seneca the Younger gazed upon it, presented to him both a moral threat and an intellectual challenge (fig. 6).[61]

In the twilight of the Roman Empire in the West, the Neoplatonic commentator and early popularizer of science Macrobius returned to Scipio's global vision revealed in Cicero's *De re publica* (VI.19–20) and significantly reworked its import. Macrobius, impressed with the same continental disconnections and isolation, reframed the argument. In an interesting

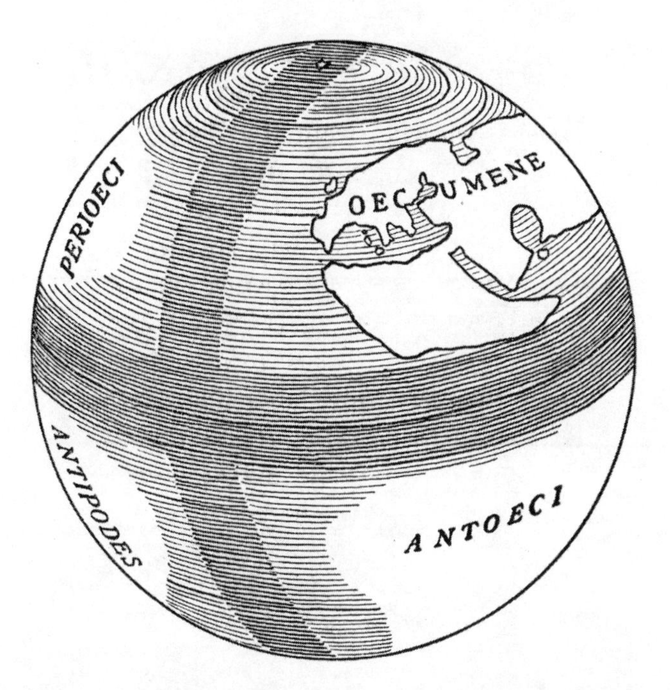

Figure 5. The globe according to Crates of Mallos (second century BCE) showing the four noncommunicating continental patches. An equatorial and meridional ocean divides the earth into four quarters, each believed inhabited but not communicating with the others. E. L. Stevenson, *Terrestrial and Celestial Globes*, I.7, fig. 5 (New Haven, 1921).

appeal to reason that allowed the other three continental patches (*maculas*) to be understood as inhabited similarly to our own patch, Macrobius lamented not the comparatively trivial issue of one man's fame being muted, but rather the veritable separation among the types of humans, the four world peoples, lacking as they did the capacity for continuous, reciprocal communication and exchange.[62] Such partitioned confinement appeared to be the doom of the human condition.

As a late-medieval Christian, Cardinal d'Ailly inherited another dimension to this geographic-ethnographic puzzle, raising the issues to a new level of complexity: namely, the

Liber. II. Fo. XXII.

longe recedunt: veram tenent salutaremq; temperiem. Locus nos admonet: vt quoniam diximus rē quæ a nullo possit refelli: vtrunq; tropicum circum zodiaco terminos facere: nec vnq̄ solem alter utrum tropicum excedere posse: vel sursum vel deorsum meando: trans zodiacum vero circum: id est trans vstam: q̄ tropicis claudit̃: ex vtraq; parte incipere temperatas: Quæramus quid sit qđ ait Virgilius: quem nullius vnq̄ disciplinæ error inuoluit. Duæ mortalibus ægris
Munere concessæ diuum: & via secta per ambas:
Obliquus qua se signorum vertitur ordo.
Videt̃ em̄ dicere his versibus: zodiacū p̄ tēperatas ductū: & solis cursum p̄ ipsas ferri: qđ nec opinari fas est: quia neutrū tropicū solis cursus excedit. Nunc igit̃ illud attendit: qđ dixim⁹: & intra tropicū in ea perusta parte: q̄ vicina est tēperatę: habitatores esse. Nā Siene sub ipo tropico est: Meroe aūt tribus milibus octingētis stadiis in perustā a Siene ītrorsum recedit: & ab illa vsq; ad terrā cynamomi feracē: sunt stadia octingēta. Et p̄ hęc oīa spatia pustę: licet rari: tñ vita fruunt̃ habitātes. Vltra vero iā inaccessum est ꝓpter nimiū solis ardorē. Cū ergo tātū spatii ex pusta vitā ministret: & sine dubio circa vicinā alteri⁹ tēperatę. i. ἀγρέκωρον, tātundē spatii habere p̄ pustę fines: & parē māsuetudinē: nō neget̃. Paria em̄ in vtraq; parte sunt oīa. Ideo credēdū est: p̄ poeticā tubā q̄ oīa semp in maius extollit: dixisse: viā solis sectā p̄ tēperatas: qm̄ ex vtraq; parte fines perustę in eo sunt similes tēperatis: q; se patiunt̃ habitari. An forte poetica licētia particulā ꝓ simili pene particula posuit: & p̄ sub ambas: p̄ ambas dicere maluit? Nā reuera duct⁹ zodiaci sub ambas tēperatas vltro citroq; p̄uenit: non tñ per ambas. Scimus aūt & Homerū ipm: & in oībus imitatorē ei⁹ Maronē sępe tales mutasse particulas. An: qđ mihi vero ꝓpius videt̃: p̄ ambas ꝓ inter ambas voluit ītelligi? Zodiacus em̄ īter ambas tēperatas voluit̃: nō p̄ ambas. Familiariter aūt p̄ ꝓ inter ponere solet: sicut alibi quoq;. Circum perq; duas in morem fluminis arctos. Neq; enim anguis sydereus arctos secat: sed dum & amplectitur & interuenit: circum eas & inter eas voluit̃ nō per eas.

Per pro inter.

D iii

Figure 6. Macrobius's view of the world, early fifth century CE. Courtesy of the John Carter Brown Library.

Adamic or monogenetic origin of the entire human race. This issue of monogenesis had been secured by an array of Latin church fathers—Lactantius, Augustine, Isidore of Seville, and Bede—who rejected the possibility of the antipodes' being inhabited. Augustine went on to admit that the human race did have monsters or physical types; he maintained, however, that such births were not to be considered subhuman but rather as so many occasions for us to extend to them human sympathy and tolerance. Thus, for Augustine and Isidore, monstrous or divergent types came to represent so many ornaments of God's creation and so many opportunities for relaxed, respectful, charitable treatment by others. For Augustine, this rejection of the antipodes stemmed not from any biblical literalism or distrust of science, but rather from moral reasons: a common, single descent affirmed the compass of a common humanity.

Nevertheless, the medieval church here walked the tightrope of a paradox: the affirmation of a single, common human descent required the denial of an inaccessible yet habitable antipodes but the inclusion of its imagined monstrous types within the long-known ecumene. To put it another way, charity and human tolerance required the answer to the question about the monsters to be the opposite of that regarding an inhabited antipodes. Once both questions could be answered affirmatively—the fact of monsters and the accessibility of inhabited antipodes—the floodgates of potential intolerance and racism would be opened, sweeping away the comfortable, generous myth of a common human origin and dissolving the explicitly Christian arguments of human brotherhood insofar as they rested upon humanity's monogenetic origin. Fortunately for the church, however, only one direct challenge occurred before Columbus's landfall in the New World. In Augustinian panoply, Pope Zachary easily squelched the idea of a populated antipodes in 748. A victory for the church and for authority to the detriment of scientific accuracy? Certainly—but also a victory for charity and for the party of humanity. Next time, in an age of greater communication by both sail and print, the outcome would be different.[63]

Having considered the geographic-ethnographic tradition and its implications as received by the learned of d'Ailly's generation, we may return to the text and margins of the *Imago mundi*. Virtually copying Roger Bacon's earlier and influential *Opus maius* (*Greater Work*), Cardinal d'Ailly saw the issue of habitability as a function of sun and ocean, heat and water. He referred to Ptolemy, who with respect to water in one instance gave one-sixth of the earth's surface to be habitable, in another one-fourth, extending the ecumene lengthwise from east to west above the equator. Deploying classical authorities, d'Ailly argued for a modest distance between the coast of Spain and the eastern coast of India. He advanced the scriptural passage in Esdras 4 that six-sevenths of the earth was inhabited and the rest water. He concluded that the confined world of Ptolemy fell short of what could be inhabited.[64]

Excitedly, Columbus proceeded to deploy, weigh, and review the authorities mentioned in an anxious effort to expand, where possible, the land surface of the earth, stretch Asia toward Europe, and concur with the cardinal that water did not cover three-quarters of the earth's surface. He eventually was able to reassure himself that the sea was quite navigable everywhere (*tot navigabilem*) and that extreme heat did not prevent passage.[65] The problem of habitability involved at all times the problem of accessibility. Yet relatively easy accessibility of communicating continents did not in itself suffice for Columbus's enterprise; he also had to have confidence in the uniform continuous surface of a terraqueous globe.

D'Ailly composed his *Imago mundi* in 1410, four years after Ptolemy's *Geographia* had been rendered in Latin. Although the first publication of *Geographia* had to wait until 1475 and even then lacked any maps, a new conception of the globe began to move in step with the empirical achievements of Portuguese navigation. That Ptolemy could cast a grid of mathematical coordinates over a partly spherical projection of an expanded *oikoumene* both presumed and posited a continuous and essentially uniform surface to the globe. Ptolemy effectively broke with the Scholastic, Aristotelian tradition of the separate spheres of water and earth, which reinforced the view of a habitable landmass surrounded by the great river, Ocean; instead, water and earth made up a single terraqueous globe. This conceptual breakthrough proved of decisive importance for Copernicus in book 1, chapter 3, of his *De revolutionibus*, titled "How Earth Together with Water Forms One Globe." In that chapter Copernicus made of the earthly globe a planet—integral, compact, perfectly spherical, capable of hurtling through space on its own.[66]

But before Copernicus's application of the idea to astronomy, an intellectual momentum developed among some mathematically and geographically inclined scholars, headed by Paolo Toscanelli in Florence, that put them hardly one step behind ongoing Portuguese discovery. Toscanelli presupposed an ocean as an integral part of the earth, inviting navigation, which made all the earth's land formations accessible to man. The recovery at this time of the descriptive geographer Strabo for the Ptolemaic discussions occurring in Florence—discussions hitherto heavily weighted in favor of mathematics and theory—helped to undermine Ptolemy's idea of the Indian Ocean as a landlocked sea. Toward the end of his life, in a letter dated June 25, 1474, to the canon of Lisbon—a copy of which served soon to embolden Columbus—Toscanelli, operating within the mathematized space of Ptolemy's grid, plotted on his own map twenty-six uniform spaces of 250 miles each directly west from Lisbon to Hangzhou. China's accessibility became a simple westward sail; mathematics seems to have thus taken all the romance, drama, and heroics out of what still appeared to most a bold, brash adventure. Indeed, Ocean, previously seen as an impassable barrier, had become by the last third of the fifteenth century, at least in Florence, an intercontinental highway for those impious ships. More than one mind at this time saw a fourth continent as an obvious discovery waiting to be made.[67] The veritable opening up of the world to general accessibility would raise for a still-Christian civilization the issue of rapid evangelization and universal redemption of all antipodeans, antoecians, and whomever else, as the oceanic barriers of the Cratesian-Macrobian world collapsed before superior European theory and navigation.

Even before the news of Columbus's landfall resounded in Europe, Latin Christendom seemed to have lost its diffidence regarding the antipodes and the problems created by their existence. Impelled by a new confidence born of curiosity, greed, and the evidence of a superior technology, Europe embarked on a sudden binge regarding the habitability of still-to-be-discovered *terra firma*. In the first construction of a globe in 1492, Martin Behaim depicted a world that had exploded beyond its Ptolemaic confines; in the inscription on this globe he describes the polar region, understood as Iceland, Norway, and Russia, as now being known to us, annually visited, and attainable by ship like all the rest of the world.[68] The following year, but before learning of Columbus's achievement, the cartographer Hieronymus Münzer wrote to the king of Portugal. Maintaining that "the habitable East is very near the habitable West" and that the king should make them known to each other, he mocks the authority of the Islamic cosmographer Alfraganus, who claimed that only one-fourth of the earth was above the sea, "for in matters referring to the habitable earth, we should believe experience and trustworthy accounts rather than fantastical opinion."[69]

At every stage the issue of habitability involved that of accessibility, dragging with it the task of rapidly expanding and redefining a Christian ecumene that affirmed the universal redemption of the human race and effectively extended it under forced conditions to the globe. The growing recognition of the earth's universal habitability could only make more acute the problem of squaring the Adamic origin of all mankind with the swelling contours and complexity of its membership. Scraps of evidence about the actual inhabitants of the antipodes had been accumulating since the early fourteenth century, especially from missionaries who had sailed to Madagascar and beyond. In a long letter to Philip VI of France, dated July 26, 1330, the Dominican William Adam, traveling toward the South Pole, affirmed at one point the reality of the antipodes and stated that "we Christians are not the tenth part, not even the twentieth part [of the population of our world]." He hastened to add that although Christians were crammed into a small corner of that world, they were more than compensated in terms of "divine grace, the operation of miracles, natural prudence, civility, military talent, good government, and the just exercise of ruling."[70]

Yet only with the discovery of the western Indies did the issue of the earth's wide habitation become explicit. Francesco Guicciardini, the most sophisticated historian of Renaissance Europe, reflected upon the meaning of newfound populated continents in the course of writing book 6 of his *Storia d'Italia* (1537–40). Not only did the discoveries demonstrate that the ancients had been wrong in claiming three of the five zones to be uninhabitable, thereby delivering a body blow to the authority of classical antiquity for his humanist contemporaries, but more alarming still, the authority of scripture, or at least its traditional interpretation, now came into question regarding the message of the apostles having reached the corners of the earth, for it seemed not credible that faith in Christ had existed in these newly discovered lands before present times, nor that so vast a part of the world had ever before been discovered by men from Europe's hemisphere.[71] The abrupt expansion of the scope of the Great Commission and the need to evangelize all mankind before the world's end placed a heavy burden on the missionary effort of the Catholic religious orders as they scrambled to effect this goal in what appeared to many as an eschatological twilight.

In the turmoil of new peoples encountered, plagued, exploited, and massacred, Rome sought to give at least formal recognition to their humanity as well as to their Adamic origin. The papal bull *Sublimis Deus*, the papacy's explicit response to the Indians' outrageous subjection, sought to cast a protective net over all the newly discovered peoples—western, southern, and others (*occidentales et meridionales Indos et alias gentes*)—that had come to papal attention by this time. They were not brute animals (*bruta animalia*) fit for servitude—they were true men (*veros homines*) capable of being won to the Christian faith. Perceiving them as sheep of the Lord to be diligently incorporated into his fold provided an expectable though still simplistic answer to one of the supreme problems facing early modern Europe.[72] As a banner of Christian aspiration it was long overdue; as an effective measure of intercession it never emerged. Because the bull apparently intruded upon the jurisdiction of Castile's Council of the Indies, it was promptly revoked.[73] According to the emerging regalism of European states, Spanish Catholicism rather than its Roman papal counterpart would come to prevail in the Indies. Though cheated in fact, however, Rome in principle preserved and expanded its own claims to universality, now conceived on a global scale in a post-Cratesian and soon post-Ptolemaic earth.

In the first flush of sixteenth-century discoveries, was there ever a moment when a conception existed, other than an ecclesiastical one, of the meaning of *ecumene*? In successive editions of Ptolemy's *Geographia* after 1475, the latest geographic additions placed a strain upon the traditional framework and its *terra habitabilis*, or ecumene. The editor of the second Roman edition (1508) found himself compelled to admit that besides the ecumene of Ptolemy, there was a new one, "deduced from more recent observations" (*ex recentioribus confecta observationibus*). With Pirckheimer's new Latin rendering and Erasmus's Basel edition of 1533, the work attained the status of a classic, a fixed monument, one that faced displacement by accumulated discoveries. In fact, the Renaissance, both a proponent of experience and an advocate of classical authority, saw the supersession of Ptolemy's *Geographia*. From Venice in 1561, Girolamo Ruscelli told his readers that the present version of Ptolemy was the most perfect possible, but the world had changed so much from what existed in his time that the greater part of particular places described by him had been, as it were, annulled (*ad esser come annullata*).[74] The total ecclesiasticization of the meaning of *ecumene*, to the apparent obliteration of any possible secular understanding of the term that might have emerged in the new worlds Europeans were encountering, reflects the effective alignment of Rome's purposes, evinced in global missionary activities yet channeled through Spanish *patronato real* (royal patronage) and its Portuguese counterpart, *padroado real*.

For a moment we may pause to see the cartographic culture of Venice, which had come to focus upon the publication of Ramusio's *Navigations and Voyages*, as possibly foreshadowing a potentially secular understanding of the ecumene. The awareness not just of new lands but also of inhabited lands, of new peoples on a global stage fashioned by a Platonized God, Creator rather than Redeemer, provides a brief moment when such an ecumene of many diverse peoples was perceived. Unquestionably, the total import of Ramusio's volumes served to challenge the Ptolemaic view of the earth's surface, displace it, and present "an image of the earth organized according to homogeneous areas of human occupation" now firmly linked, rather than walled off, by areas of navigable ocean.[75] Is something else being said here? As one historian of Renaissance geography has observed, "In all ways it seems that the revelation of the habitability of the tropics and the antipodes had been more decisive for contemporaries than the discovery of America to which we attach retrospectively so much importance."[76] Not just new lands, nor even new continents, but that they are inhabited—communicable and communicating.

In an earlier report, the "Discourse on Geographical Expanses" ("Discorso sulle spazie"), written in 1547, Ramusio claimed that one of the most admirable and stupendous acts "that a great prince could perform would be to get the people [*uomini*] of our hemisphere to come to know those of the opposite hemisphere," thereby once again surpassing the ancients.[77]

> This could easily be done by dispatching into diverse places of that hemisphere colonies for living there as the Romans did in newly acquired provinces, whereby little by little those parts would come to be opened up, cultivating and introducing there civility [*la civiltà*] and thence to have preached by worthy men the faith of our Lord Jesus Christ; and for domesticating them more easily [such princes] would cause to go every year ships loaded with grain, wine, spices, sugar, and other sorts of merchandise from these our parts.[78]

Thus this interchange of peoples would be a European initiative characterized by settlement, cultural expansion, evangelization, and commerce, with religion figuring as one among several civilizing factors. In short, with his apparent emphasis upon commerce, Ramusio seemed at least momentarily to envisage a preeminently secular rendering of this European enterprise.

Around the same time, in 1547–48, Ramusio entered into discussion with his close friend Gerolamo Fracastoro regarding the reason for the periodic increase in the volume of the Nile River. At one point in his "Discorso," having disposed of an ancient classical argument that depended on the uninhabitability of the middle third of the earth, Ramusio sweeps Fracastoro into his belief, "contrary to the ancients and their erroneous imagination concerning this globe of earth, which is now clearly known to be all inhabited, nor is there any part either hot or cold, discounting deserts and oceans, that is not full of men and animals, that everyone exists there as in a temperate region. I say temperate according to the constitution given to them by nature."[79]

When, nine years later, in 1556, Ramusio came to publish the third volume of his *Navigations and Voyages*, he began with a very revealing "Discorso" addressed again to his friend Fracastoro.[80] After drawing extensively on the *Timaeus*, he cuts through the philosophic debate on the lost Atlantis to advance a crucial argument on the basis of the Platonic principles of plenitude and sufficient reason:

> To Plato—having to write regarding the structure of the universe [*fabrica del mondo*] which he believed to have been made for human arrangement so that man, divine creature [*animal divino*], seeing such ornaments of stars in the heavens and the motion of so stupendous and marvelous luminaries, would know his maker and knowing him would continually praise him—to [Plato] it appeared to be a thing far beyond reason that two parts of this order would be inhabited and the other part deprived of men; and likewise the sun and the stars with their splendor would make half the course vainly and

> fruitlessly, leaving unilluminated seas and places deserted and deprived of animate creatures. . . . Rather the sun makes its course with such order that the inhabitants [at the North Pole] live not as moles buried under the earth but as other creatures who are upon this terrestrial globe, illuminated so that they are able most profitably to maintain and provide for their livelihood. . . . Since rationally it cannot be believed that the maker of such a beautiful and perfect structure as are the heavens, the sun, and the moon had not wanted that, this having been made with such stupendous and marvelous order, the sun illuminate but a fraction of this globe which they call Earth and the rest of its course be in vain over seas, parts with diverse animals and upon the other with man, as patron and lord of all, for whose purpose it has been constructed, having endowed him with that divine and celestial part which is the soul and consequently has disposed and distributed in each place the necessary gifts for living, more or less, according to His divine providence and pleasure. . . . Now, by the matter stated above I think there can be no longer any doubt that beneath the equator and below both poles there is the same multitude of inhabitants that there are in all the other parts of the world . . . [rather than these areas] according to all the ancients . . . being uninhabited, shapeless, and wasted by extreme heat or frost.[81]

Philosophically, Ramusio's remarkable argument for the earth's total habitability, by appealing to the principle of plenitude, reflected the continuity and pervasiveness of a Platonism stretching from Plotinus to Leibniz. The assumed infinity of God's productive potency, arguing for the necessary innumerability of its actual effects, moved in the Renaissance from the relatively well-known level of astronomy to that of biology and geography.[82] More immediately, his argument reflected contemporary mid-sixteenth-century Venetian culture, which was heavily saturated with Platonism and its elaborate derivative, Hermetism.[83] Pietro Bembo, that great paladin of Renaissance Platonism and oracle of literary culture, had specifically addressed the question of habitability. Assuming the rational plenitude of a supreme architect, Bembo attacked the classical notion that only two of the five climatic zones were habitable. He credits Columbus with an address to Ferdinand and Isabella in which he asserts the Macrobian urge: "It would be necessary [to believe] God to have been almost improvident in His having so constituted the universe [*mundum*] that by far the greater part of the earth on account of excessive intemperateness be devoid of humankind and of no human use. [In fact] the globe of the earth is of such a nature that to man has been given the capacity for going through all its parts—achieving their complete accessibility."[84]

The Venetian resort to the Platonic argument of a divine plenitude did not exhaust itself at mid-century with Ramusio and his circle. No less a mind than Giordano Bruno made it central to a philosophy that admitted no unique intrusions or special phenomena, but sang of the infinite power of the divine. In his treatise *On the Infinite Universe and World* (1584), he fiercely rejected the notion that divine power could remain idle or its infinite amplitude frustrated.[85] Although he applied it to infinite worlds rather than to mere continents as evidence of this earth's general habitability, Bruno's assertion reminds us of the astronomical reference of geography within the comprehensive field of cosmography, at the same time giving extreme, radical, even heretical statement to the pervasive Platonism of the day.[86] Ultimately it was Bruno's commitment to the idea of a pervasive uniformity throughout the universe that would ensnare him before the uniqueness of Christ.

Venice's leadership in European cartography and the new science of geography, already evident from Ramusio's publications and the reputation of his close colleague Giacomo Gastaldi, Italy's foremost cartographer, received further expression toward the end of the century with the work of the geographers Girolamo Ruscelli and Gioseppe Rosaccio. At the outset of the *Descrittione della geografia universale* they presented the traditional zonal view of the earth in order to emphasize how since 1492 it had become apparent that all parts of the earth were habitable, that new habitations were found in all parts, that the frigid polar zones were habitable by people, and that the torrid zone, where rules a perpetual spring, was most inhabited. Rather than God, now Benign Nature (*la benigna Natura*) does nothing by chance but provides all things, constituting them according to its own essential character (*la sua qualità*).[87]

The Venetian geographic program, which advanced the idea of the earth's total habitability, proceeded somewhat unevenly on two legs. The first was experience and the empirical—actual navigational encounter with new lands and peoples. The second and apparently the more powerful was philosophical and rational in its belief in a divine Maker whose construction of the world disallowed any unique or special features but promoted a fullness of species in all places. The priority of the conceptual and perceptual over the empirical, a matter familiar enough to historians of science, here needs to be noted as it played itself out in the sixteenth century's reshaping of geography. Twenty years before Columbus sailed to the West Indies, more than one Florentine posited a fourth landmass out there.[88] In 1507, six years before Balboa got his knees wet, and thirteen before Magellan sailed through the straits named after him, the cartographer Martin Waldseemüller, in landlocked Lorraine, already envisaged for the first time a vast ocean west of the emerging American continent. Similarly, it was no *mathematicus* or "scientist," but rather a poet, Giordano Bruno, who was the first, at least in postclassical times, to insist upon the reality of an infinite universe. And with his poetic vision, it was Dante, surpassing Cicero, who provided us with a breathtaking perspective, six and a half centuries before the photograph taken by our astronauts, of "that threshing floor which makes us wax so fierce."[89]

Yet the empirical has the capacity for checking the perceptual, defining the possible, and rendering the actual reality of things. In short, it places salutary restraints upon the flights of the imagination and the urgings of philosophy. Thus, interweaving it with his Platonic argument, Ramusio introduced the evidence provided in 1539 by the archbishop of Uppsala, Olaus Magnus, that Finland, Lapland, and the northernmost reaches of Sweden and Norway were all bubbling with people (*tutta abitata d'infiniti popoli*).[90] Ramusio's commitment to the extensive habitation of Christendom's northernmost reaches (*extrema Aquiloniae christianitatis plaga*) went even further.[91] Since 1539 he had been aware of materials, hitherto considered dubious, but now demonstrably genuine, pertaining to the enterprises of the Zeni brothers, who between 1394 and 1401 had explored the mid-eastern and mid-southern coast of Greenland and then ventured south to Nova Scotia. By letter Fracastoro recognized these lands' habitation, while Ramusio speculated as to whether Europe and America were conjoined.[92] He knew of these Venetian materials and had planned to publish them, but his death and the burning of Giunti's printing shop prevented their appearance until the posthumous second edition of his second volume in 1574.[93] Nor did Ramusio's special preoccupations with northern routes and *nostro polo* of the Arctic end there. In his "Discourse on the Spice Trade," he considered the viability of a northeastern Baltic-Muscovy route to the Indies that might displace those of the Portuguese and Castilians. Likewise he pursued with

Jacques Cartier and Sebastian Cabot the possibility of a northwest passage to Cathay. In the process, "our pole" became conceptually populated and humanized immediately below its northernmost reaches (*sotto la nostra Tramontana*).[94] Enthralled by the Age of Discovery, Ramusio emerged as its veritable secretary.

Ramusio never manifested the same explicit concern regarding the heat of the torrid zone, hitherto believed to constitute a great impassable and uninhabitable belt around the earth. Yet in his writings there are scattered expressions of respect and awe for the Portuguese accomplishments throughout most of the fifteenth century in pushing southward along the western coast of Africa, thereby penetrating to the antipodes and potentially defining a Southern Hemisphere.[95] In reporting on a meeting held at Fracastoro's estate at Cafi, Ramusio spoke of a third presence there, mysterious and imposing, *grandissimo filosofo e mathematico*. It was this person, unknown to us, who gave voice to the stunning achievements of the Portuguese while holding a sphere of the world in his hand.[96] Nevertheless, for an explicit recognition of the habitability of the torrid zone we must wait until the bemused reactions of that otherwise compleat Aristotelian, José de Acosta, who, experiencing the exhilarating coolness in parts of Peru, which according to tradition should have been uninhabitably hot, cannot suppress a somewhat anxious laugh in this particular instance at Aristotle, the ostensible Master of those who know.[97]

But what of the South Pole? Or Antarctica? According to Giunti, Ramusio at the time of his death was planning to produce a fourth volume that would have addressed the matter of the peoples of this great Southern Hemisphere and of Oceania.[98] To believers in the total habitability of the earth's surface, this uncharted area still remained to be empirically verified and defined. Recognizing this need, Ramusio apostrophized any further great prince who would undertake "the other part of the earth toward the Antarctic," hitherto unattempted: "This would truly be the greatest and most glorious enterprise that anyone would be able to imagine, thereby making his name much more eternal and immortal to all future centuries, surpassing that of so many military undertakings which continually occur in Europe among the miserable Christians."[99] In the articulation of this fond aspiration, he was again preceded by Bembo, who saw this task as falling to the lot of Spain and its empire.[100]

The Renaissance imagination seems to have had its negative as well as positive aspects. The fiction of a great southern continent played upon some of the same urges that fashioned flying saucers in our own age: the lure of the still-to-be-explored, the desire for communication with the exotic, the possibilities for exploitation. On the basis of vague reports the great southern continent first came to be cartographically depicted in all its fictitious splendor in the map by Oronce Fine in 1531. Its acceptance by Mercator and Abraham Ortelius (1569–70) had the effect of canonizing the fiction (see fig. 7).[101] Ortelius reports on his own map that Mercator divided the earth into three continents: (1) Europe, Asia, and Africa; (2) America or the West Indies; and (3) the south main or Magellanica. When in 1599 the English cartographer Edward Wright deliberately omitted the last, the general cartographic culture of the day failed to register this advance.[102] Mercator cannot be faulted for his massive inclusion of the southern continent; he was simply following the practice, derived from Marco Polo, of giving graphic expression to places unknown but described.[103] Joseph Hall, later bishop of Exeter, parodied this widespread credulity in his satire of 1606, *Another World and Yet the Same* (*Mundus alter et idem*), wherein he presented a truly upside-down world, especially in its values. Hall has his persona of Beroaldus express indignation with maps that sport TERRA AUSTRALIS INCOGNITA. "For if they know it to be a *continent*, and a *southern* one, how can they call it unknown?"[104] Nevertheless, the presumed unknown continent served to persuade the Vatican to create the Apostolic Prefecture of Terra Australis on July 15, 1681, although the office quietly failed to materialize.[105] Meanwhile, however, this fictitious space would offer generous locations for many a utopia.

One of the crowning ironies in the history of cartography and exploration stems from the Spanish participation in what turned out to be a mirage. Most Iberian cartographers relied almost exclusively on some sort of empirical evidence derived from navigators. Indeed, the instructions of the House of Trade required that pilots report "all entries made on return, but nothing should be inserted that was not properly attested or sworn to"—all in an effort to keep Spain's modular map, the *padrón real*, up to date.[106] Despite their native practicality and their empirical strictures, Spanish navigators carried with them more than enough mythological and biblical ballast in questing for Tarshish, Ophir, and the ultimate resort of King Solomon's ships. Thus, the voyages of Alvaro de Mendaña, who located "the Solomon Islands" in 1567, and those of his pilot in 1595, the Portuguese Pedro Fernández de Quirós, advanced the Spanish knowledge of their lake, our Pacific Ocean, in the last years of the sixteenth century, but did little to establish the elusive southern continent. Quirós suffered from an acute Columbus complex.[107] He pelted Philip III of Spain with memoranda that named the new continent Austrialia [*sic*] in honor of the Habsburg dynasty and world order. In his *Relación* of 1610, first published in Spanish at Pamplona and two years later in Dutch at Amsterdam, he rhapsodized over the huge extent of this fifth [*sic*] part of the terrestrial globe, its riches, and of course its many inhabitants, whom he apparently had seen and whom he reported to be happy and

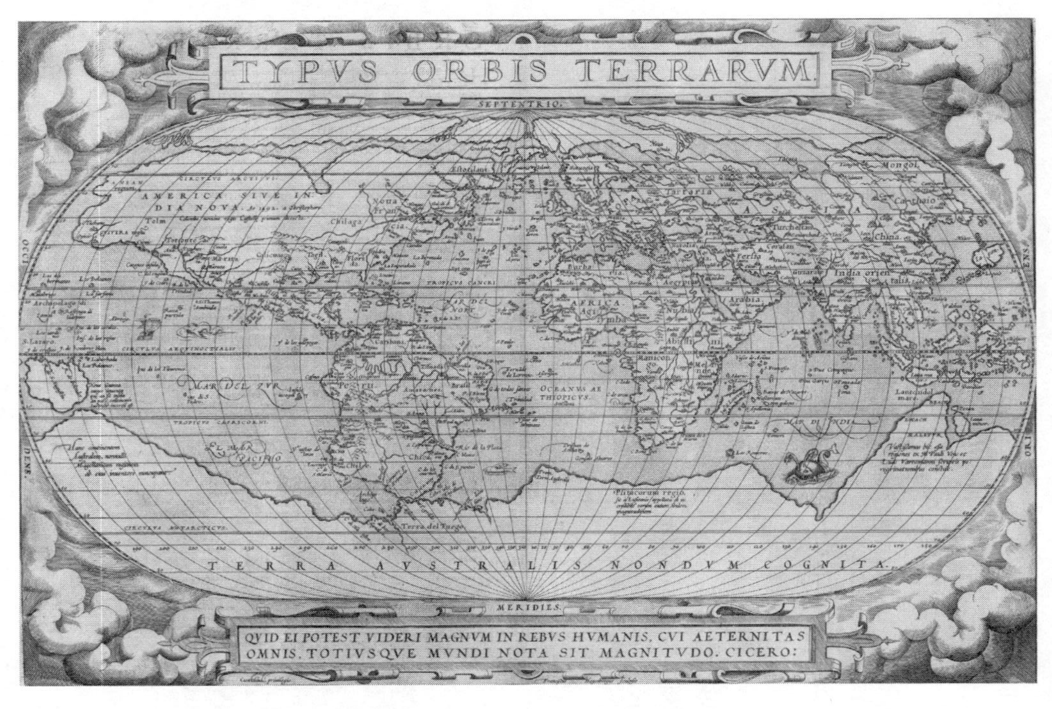

Figure 7. The world map of Ortelius (1570), in which the unknown southern continent of Magellanica figures prominently. One needs to go to later and most especially non-Latin editions for the coloring of such maps because Ortelius himself did not recommend the use of colors. Courtesy of the John Carter Brown Library.

carefree, not sharing "such vexation and torment [as] we here labor to obtain."[108]

The accumulating burden of the sixteenth century's idea of the earth's total habitability seemed to culminate in Juan de Silva during his later career.[109] A distinguished soldier turned Franciscan friar and missionary, de Silva applied his new talents for twenty years in Florida and New Spain before becoming a royal chaplain. In the numerous memoranda with which he bombarded the young King Philip III, we gain a sense of the extent to which he believed the southern continent to be not only populated but teeming with inhabitants: he counters one objection by asserting that while at the convent of San Francisco in Madrid he obtained from the Franciscan vicar general an offer of a hundred religious, all preachers, to go with him for the spiritual conquest of the Austral Lands.[110]

Impelled by Quirós's vision, de Silva evolved the Franciscan missionary plan (1617–27) for the conversion of the natives of the Austral Lands, now ostensibly one vast missionary preserve of the Franciscan order. Although his great memorial to the king did not appear in print until a few months after the king's death early in 1621, Philip III, who had apparently shown uncharacteristic interest in the project during the past six years, read it in manuscript in mid-May 1619. With the new reign and Spain's descent into the maelstrom of global war, the *monarquía* was otherwise engaged in fighting for its life, and de Silva turned in vain to Pope Urban VIII as a sponsor.[111]

In his *Important Notifications* (*Advertencias importantes*), Juan de Silva had exhorted the Spanish monarch: the king's obligation does not limit itself to simple conversion but extends to maintaining the indigenous Amerindians in that conversion in such a way as to make *Christian* and *Spanish* no longer hated terms. Then de Silva turned to consider the innumerable souls in *los Reynos Australes*, the southernmost kingdoms, who were then in the power of Satan.[112] According to the words of the

Psalmist (71:8), that he shall have dominion also from sea to sea, the present king will see in his own lifetime the consummation of that evangelical preaching that will come to all Heathendom (*toda la Gentilidad*) as it came to the Mediterranean lands, the Orient, the Occident, and the southern main (*Medi-odía*)—in what he has referred to as this fifth part of the world (*esta quinta parte del mundo*).[113] This awesome responsibility of the Catholic king warranted de Silva's suggestion that the greatest charge and trust evident in Christ's "Pasce oves meas" (Feed my sheep; John 21:17), which properly pertains to the pope, has been delegated to and has devolved upon the Spanish king, who among Christian princes is as Peter among the apostles. All things support the Spanish king's realization of being lord of all the world (*señor del mundo todo*).[114] To some of those living at the beginning of the seventeenth century, Spain seemed about to realize the world monarchy that had eluded the Romans.[115] Yet the eruption of war prevented Spain's further pursuit of the "Austrialian" mirage as its power began rapidly to decline in the Pacific. Consequently, except for the gradual definition of the Australian subcontinent by the Dutch in the course of the next century, the issue of the great southern continent and its presumed habitability remained suspended until its ultimate resolution by Captain James Cook in the eighteenth century and by Admiral Robert Byrd in the twentieth. Though the ancients had been surpassed, they had not been proved entirely wrong.

In concluding, we must weigh once more Giunti's exclamation about the habitability of the entire globe. All five possible implications of the previously defined resonances seem to pertain. But surpassing all the rest is the last—the celebration of the totally humanized world. The Europeans' awareness of new lands and peoples on a transformed and enlarged terraqueous globe reinforced the cognitive impact of the accomplishment whereby the preconceived yet formidable barriers preventing access to other continents and peoples were dissolved by a rare combination of reason and experience, of Platonist deduction and empirical increments. The machine of discovery, assembled and operated by Europeans—principally Iberians—had produced in "America" not only an immense perceptual challenge and cognitive problem, but also the realization of an almost totally accessible and inhabitable global arena in which to contend with this problem. Once engaged, as it was in Venice by Ramusio and his associates, the continuing reflection upon and account of this ongoing enterprise registered the increasing links of global interconnectedness as Europeans came to know this world. The first stage of this process took five hundred years to play itself out, ending with the dissolution of the motor with which a confident, assertive European civilization had brought about the realization of a global arena. The earth's accessibility and habitability, and the understanding of both, that Giunti's statement proclaims amount to nothing less than humans taking possession of the planet. Indeed, the point seemed clear even in remote Wittenberg, where a Lutheran humanist, Erasmus Schmid, in making an invidious comparison of contemporary knowledge with the geographical ignorance of the ancients, exclaimed in 1616 that such ignorance was not less blameworthy than that of the head of a household who does not know the rooms of his own home.[116]

What was the impact of these events upon the actual reality of the ecumene, so abruptly and astoundingly expanded? The potential dissolution of boundaries effected by encounters between peoples might have led natural reason tentatively to advance a completely new, even secularized ecumene or realized mankind, although will and deep-seated custom pulled another way. The universalizing currents traditional to the West in Stoicism and Christianity, of universal empire and universal church, could and did capitalize on this new global reality and spawned their imperialist challengers among the other nations of Europe in the competitive game of carving up the world. It is thus not surprising that in this still-religious age a shared, balanced secular understanding of the ecumene never developed despite the passing thoughts of a Ramusio or Botero. Such an understanding lacked any institutional or conceptual basis of support at the time; nevertheless, natural law's potentially secular view of mankind inhered in the larger theological construct of the derivation of the entire human race from a single Adamic source and would soon see development. What these relatively tiny European kingdoms lacked in size, they more than compensated for by way of pride and internal organization. Where power asserted itself, as it quickly did despite the fine ideals of formal brotherhood, all peoples might be seen as human, enjoying the common human (*commun et humain*) stamp defined by Montaigne,[117] but—to employ an Orwellian twist—some were obviously more human than others.

Giunti's exclamation, with its cognitive implications, occurred in the first flush of European expansion and exploitation, before the shattering of the monogenetic view of human descent and well before the European motor had spent itself. The process of forging those global interconnections would reveal the ascendancy of technology, the imperatives of power and baser human interests over anthropology and human understanding. At the end of his "Discourse on the Spice Trade," Ramusio reflected upon the immense aggressive force of the European explosion into a larger world:

> From so much variety and changes the men of our age had reasons far exceeding the ancients in enterprise for searching out the world; in not recognizing their natural fragility and weakness, as if they were immortal, they

> did not hesitate before any difficulty, neither the torrid zone nor the two cold, icy zones, from going forth, continually toiling, surging throughout the entire roundness of the earth in order to satiate their immense cupidity and avarice.[118]

The European core would need to burn itself out, and with it the exclusivities of Christianity and a sense of special preeminence, before Europe and its neo-Europes of the periphery might begin the task of bringing peoples together in terms of equality and understanding rather than of superiority and exploitation. We confront here a paradox: the Christian-European civilization that had made possible, at least technologically and theoretically, a single, global world would have to suffer the displacement of its original preeminence before the harmonization of peoples and their respective cultures could be addressed on a basis of equality. And yet it was neither paradoxical nor ironic but, rather, appropriate and even necessary that the same society that would come through its resourcefulness, courage, and, yes, brutal avidity to achieve momentary mastery and domination of the globe should at the same time be struggling to define and promote the idea of a comprehensive human community that might in a different way and a different time address that one world.

Some at the inception of this five-hundred-year period recognized the adjustment that would be required. Shortly after the initial impact of Luther's reform, the radical spiritualist Sebastian Franck compressed within a decade of his own experience the entire gamut of confessional dissent that would convulse the life of Europe for the next century. His rethinking of Christian history and theology led him effectively to expunge all the institutional, sacramental, and hitherto distinguishing features of the church and to claim that since the death of the apostles the church had existed only in the spirit.

From his remove in central Europe he devoted an entire section of his *Weltbuch* (1534) to America. After considering the slaughter, pillage, and rapine effected by the *Hauptmann* Hernán Cortés upon an entire people, he continues:

> There are a small number of pious everywhere. In short what scripture shows, all histories prove: now [God] weighs the number and variety of the world's beliefs; likewise the work of this wonder-working God disposes an impartial kindness, uniform and like-minded toward all peoples, without consideration of persons. For he is gracious toward all who fear, love, invoke him among all peoples, even as his church is strewed in every corner of the world. And he has not fastened his favor upon only one people as Israel, but from the South and North Poles, from the east and the west, he will seek out his elect so that the children of the kingdom, who were considering themselves first, perhaps will [themselves] become rejected.[119]

More immediately, however, and with respect to the inroads that had been made into what was now a truly global arena, the age of European exploration and discovery marked a new level of communication and interchange, howsoever often malign, among the peoples of the earth. In the words of one historian:

> Toward the beginning of the sixteenth century the combined effects of the work accomplished since several centuries by some factors very diverse but convergent, such as the development of international exchange, the opening of new routes both internal and international, the advent of print, the advent of the Reformation, the advent of the public postal service and the intensification of human relations gave to civilization a resonance such

> that life political, economic, intellectual, religious, and social acquired an international and global (*mondial*) character that it had not had up to then.[120]

No wonder that the greatest of the Spanish scholastics, Francisco de Vitoria, would give such prominence to this new consolidation and intensification in his right of communication, of commerce, traffic, wandering, and expanding, the *jus peregrinandi*.[121]

Chapter 2

The Universalizing Principle and the Idea of a Common Humanity

Both the nature and the operation in time and space of a unique feature of Western civilization invite attention—namely, the early identification of the idea of humanity as a single moral collectivity and the often erratic and uncertain, but never entirely abandoned commitment to the realization of that comprehensive ideal. Its imperfect manifestation expressed itself in a religious cast that in the course of the Renaissance passed to a more expansive and diverse secular register, where the more fragile and inevitably more particularistic notion of civilization displaced and frequently disfigured but never entirely lost the ongoing momentum of commitment to a universal jurisdiction of a common, all-inclusive humanity. The early modern period (1500–1800) provides the main context for analyzing the shift in the continuity of this idea from the specifically religious to the secular.

As a single theme among many in our past, the process of universalization unfolds in three stages. The first is the religious, ecclesiastical, and Christian, best manifested in the medieval church and its rendering of Roman law. Next, with the increasing emphasis upon classical, secular elements in the course of the Renaissance, Europe as a distinct, self-conscious civilization matures, ultimately facing down the acknowledged preeminence of Chinese civilization. Then, after 1900, the new construct of consolidated power, which emerged earlier as the nation-state, overwhelms the world as well as itself in a third stage that begins to feature the agency of "the West."[1]

The first section of this chapter addresses the origins and development of the universalizing process in its Christian phase, engulfing the classical as it comes up through the Middle Ages to the Renaissance. At that point increasingly dominant secularizing forces begin to reshape the comprehensiveness previously afforded by Christendom (*Christianitas*) into the fragile notion of Europe, of civilization, and of European civilization. The second section examines this new entity, as it emerges from the late sixteenth century, in terms of natural law as the vehicle for the idea of a common humanity.

As used in this study, the term "universal" connotes that principle inherited from classical antiquity that expresses a potentially comprehensive integration or inclusion of all peoples into a broad community, together with the legal and constitutional issues that this process entailed. The expanding inhabited world or *oikoumene* of the Greek experience, informed by the Stoic notion of cosmopolis, found its practical realization in the Roman Empire and Roman law. Although Cicero defined the "barbarians" and the "provincials" apart from the resulting community, at the same time he extended that community to them. As one scholar expresses it, "The frontier between the world of civil men and that of the barbarians was forever dissolving." Christianity itself provided a further reinforcement and dimension to this universal dynamic, as evinced in the Pauline appeal to a transcendent oneness in Christ Jesus (Galatians 3:28). With the grafting of the Christian church upon the Roman community, the Imperium Christianum partook of and extended this same "simultaneous open exclusiveness," this tension between an apparently narrow identity and a potentially broad inclusion. The Aristotelian-Ciceronian complex served to demarcate the world of civil (urban) civic humanity from the barbarians, provincials, *pagani*, and outsiders, yet opened itself up to their inclusion.[2] Both the fifth-century Christian and the sixteenth-century Spaniard had recourse to this complex mechanism of incorporation.

In the Spanish case only the papacy, not the classical Roman Empire or any of its secular derivatives, possessed anything approaching a true universality. Only the Christian church extended or sought to extend its ecumenical jurisdiction to all humankind, making any independent secular claim to universality essentially rhetorical, unless it somehow informed and validated itself by the more certain ecclesiastical claims and religious aura. In the sixteenth century such a comprehensive role fell to Spain—along with the task of attempting to achieve a measure of coincidence among the overlapping concepts of humanity, Christianity, and classical (urban) civility.

This chapter argues for a unique combination of exceptional elements, intellectual and religious, present at the inception of the Western development. It suggests that at the core of this development is a universalizing principle directed toward the construction of humanity as idea and fact, and that it was not altogether accidental that it fell to a society so conceived and structured to create the global arena for the realization of the universal jurisdiction of humanity, among other better-known and less attractive enterprises. Moreover, the gradual detachment of the features denoting what we understand as civilization from the long nurturing chrysalis of the medieval church—its theology, liturgy, and political structures—becomes decisive for the outward thrust of an essentially moral and religious universalizing principle, its transformation, and its ramifying deployments in the global arena. The detachment served to release the immense existing and to some extent evident energies of a comprehensive, universalizing action upon the peoples of the globe.

The Universalizing Process: From Christendom to the Civilization of Europeans

True law is right reason in agreement with Nature; it is of universal application, unchanging and everlasting; it summons to duty by its commands, and averts from wrong-doing by its prohibitions. . . . And there will not be different laws at Rome and at Athens, or different laws now and in the future, but one eternal and unchangeable law will be valid for all nations and for all times, and there will be one master and one ruler, that is, God, over us all [*quasi magister et imperator omnium deus*] for He is the author of this law, its promulgator, and its enforcing judge.

—Cicero, *De re publica*, III.22

If the intellectual capacity is common to us all, common too is the reason, which makes us rational creatures. If so, that reason also is common which tells us to do or not to do. If so, law also is common. If so, we are citizens. If so, we are fellow-members of an organized community. If so, the Universe is as it were a state—for of what other single polity can the whole race of mankind be said to be fellow-members? . . . Live as on a mountain; for whether it be here or there, matters not provided that, wherever a man live, he live as a citizen of the World-City.

—Marcus Aurelius, *Meditations*, IV.4, X.15

There is but one indivisible humanity and specific essence of all men by which all individual men are men numerically distinct each one from each. The same humanity is that of Christ and of all men, the numerical distinction of individuals remaining unblurred. Hence

> it is clear that the humanity of all men, who in the temporal order came before or after Christ, has in Christ put on immortality . . . But while there is but one humanity of all men, there are various and divers individuating principles which contract that humanity to this or that subject; and in Jesus Christ alone these were most perfect and most powerful and closest to that essential humanity which was united to the divinity.
>
> —Nicholas Cusanus, *On Learned Ignorance*, III.8

In the beginning there was Stoicism. Coming in the wake of the Alexandrian conquests and contributing to the creation of that extraordinarily rich context of the Hellenistic age, Stoicism introduced the principles of interiority and universality that would progressively serve as a corrosive to the polytheism and particularist customs of the ancient city. Although it taught outward respect to such customs, it inevitably created an inner distance from them and prepared the ground and space for another moral, legal, and theological code.[3] In the concomitant crushing and intermixing of peoples subsequent to their conquest, Middle Stoicism, especially as promoted by the new Roman conquerors and aristocracy, refined the notion of "cosmopolis," the universal political community, poorly translated as "world city," whose practical realization the emerging Roman Empire then effected. Ideas of an immanent natural law that bore implications for human rationality and equality were grafted onto the emerging *oikoumene* by Roman law and its extension.

If this almost marvelous preparation of the Roman world for early Christianity does not explain the subsequent convergence of the two, nevertheless it makes such an association in the opinion of one analyst certainly "less improbable." With Paul's separation of Jesus the Christ's message from the synagogue and its transcending of all particular ethnic links in a higher spiritual law, the new religion of Christianity—"the religion for departing from religion"—would open out a new sort of universal highway in its effort to teach all nations of the earth.[4] Concomitantly with the penetration and grafting of the new Christian faith onto the ultimate form of classical culture, we have the supreme knitting together of the two great statements of human universality standing at the ground and the beginning of our civilization. However, the remarkable meshing of the universalism offered by Stoicism in its idea of cosmopolis with the complementary universalism of Christ's Body would never prove a perfect fit. The chief difficulty arose from the fact that Christ had preached a spiritual kingdom, whatever that might be, and although its precise definition was to concern the next two millennia, it managed to create a sacred interior space for the self, its identity and destiny, long after its formal, single, ecclesiastical jurisdiction in the West, paralleling the powers of this earth, had been broken. Yet whatever the hidden incoherencies between the Roman imperial and the Catholic Christian at the end of antiquity, they did not prevent a practical, working identification of the Roman imperial community of civic humanity from coalescing with the Christian humanity embraced by the church. The expansion of Roman citizenship came to coalesce with the new citizenship of Christian baptism to extend itself in what has been called "a simultaneous open exclusiveness" directed toward barbarians and *pagani* alike.[5] Humanity, having been first identified with membership in the civil Roman community, after 380 CE was reinforced by association with the Christian church. The ideals of civility, humanity, and Christianity moved together, simultaneously exclusive in defining the New Society, but open-ended in extending the composite to the rest of humankind as includable in the club.

In this fateful alignment and apparent correspondence Cicero provided the most obvious and attractive link to the Christian and proved most readily accessible to the early church fathers. At least in his political and ethical writings this eclectic came across as a Stoic.[6] In the Latin language's understanding and development of the notion of *humanitas*, the subjective meaning reflecting notions of human nature—namely kindness and philanthropy—became the more frequently encountered sense. The objective sense, denoting mankind as a single biological collective, as the human species—this biological sense would only acquire moral meaning as a later endowment.[7] Nor should we exaggerate Roman citizenship in the period of the Empire as being comparable to the simple uniformity that would be announced at the inception of the French Revolution in the Declaration of the Rights of Man and of the Citizen.[8] Although Stoicism certainly foreshadowed some aspects of Christianity—and their distinctions later blurred toward one another—the two were not identical; Stoic sociability (*oikeiosis*) is not Christian love (*agape*).[9]

For its part, Christianity would have been impossible without Judaic universalism. Paul's exhortation that there be no longer Jew nor Greek, bond nor free, male nor female, but that all be one in Christ Jesus, that former strangers and foreigners now dissolved in a new fellow citizenry (cf. Ephesians 2:19–20) raised scattered universalist tendencies in the prophets and in Deuteronomy (23:3–9) to a formidable pitch. For all its intense particularism, Judaism never lost the larger reference to the *Ethne*, the nations, mankind in general and for whom in the belief of the rabbis the Torah would eventually be destined.[10] The Christian church would now advance its universalist claims and appeal. If exclusivist in dichotomizing the human race eschatologically into believers and unbelievers, saved and damned, in its pastoral performance it took the whole world as its parish.[11]

Yet, as the church entered into the fourth century, its bonds with classical culture were very real. The Christian Cicero,

Lactantius, writing his *Divinae institutiones* two decades before the formulation of the Nicene Creed, both pressed the duty of universal benevolence and liberally quoted Cicero in his affirming right reason or the law of nature as the true law.[12] He defined Christians as "those not knowing war, who preserve concord with all, who are friends even to enemies, who highly prize all men as brothers, who know how to restrain anger and assuage rage with calm moderation [*tranquilla moderatione*] . . . for what else does it mean to maintain kindness [*conservare humanitatem*] than to prize man as such and because we are all the same?"[13] In fact, a new vocabulary, a new language was here in the making. And shortly thereafter in the same century, further to secure the link between Stoic and Christian, an ostensible correspondence emerged between the leading Stoic moral philosopher, Seneca the Younger, and Saint Paul—a forgery, but thus all the more significant in its strivings.

Apparently so high the ideals, so splendid the ends—must they not enlist the means of coercion to hasten and secure their realization and greater inclusion? Indeed, by the end of the fourth century the Constantinean Church had come into being, with its first persecutions and the transformation of the community of love into an enforced uniformity, no matter how clumsily effected. With the collapse of the Roman Empire in the west, circumstances worked to promote a duality of jurisdictions that found expression in Pope Gelasius's famous definition at the end of the fifth century according to which two different, unequal orders ruled the world—one dignified by the moral and spiritual force of *auctoritas*, the Church; the other, in multiple manifestations, endowed with the coercive property of *potestas*, the State—both to direct and rule over humankind. Thus the moral/spiritual directive of open engagement came to be both enforced and skewed by the exclusive impulse to self-identity. Historical circumstance allowed the

Gelasian principle to graft its two jurisdictions onto the operation of this simultaneous open exclusiveness in ways that allowed for shifting degrees of participation in the directive and coercive functions. This unique dualism of jurisdictions, which provided the first step in the Western definition of the secular, presented a tension of internal self-criticism wherein neither spiritual nor secular jurisdiction could ever entirely identify itself with the ultimate, presumed principle, the foundational ideal of this emergent new way, while themselves as two distinct jurisdictions often falling into near catastrophic controversy with each other.[14]

Again we have to appreciate the distinctive break effected by Stoicism from the earlier classical development and the fulfillment it thus achieved in its current Christian Roman/imperial guise. For what Aristotle had intended in his concept of justice as a rational, discriminate apportionment that pertains only among equal citizens and only in the tight little context of the *polis*, the city-state, becomes opened up and out by Cicero and Marcus Aurelius to apply to all peoples, all humanity in a world community. At the end of antiquity it fell to Aurelius Augustinus to achieve the decisive, inherent removal of *justitia* from its traditional classical framework of the *polis* with later restatements in the Roman republic and empire and adjust it to a new, truly universal framework in which the pivot of the whole system lay outside itself, oriented to a divine justice and to an ultimate divine community toward which the hitherto resident aliens of the ancient world, its notable noncitizens, the metics and *peregrini* of humanity, might look forward in their fractured, imperfect citizenship to becoming full citizens. What remained implicit in the Stoic affirmation of and aspiration toward a universal community becomes now explicit in its Christian Augustinian application.[15] In accepting the understanding of justice emerging in Roman law as a rendering unto each his own (*suum cuique*), Augustine had earlier in his greatest writing established the momentous touchstone to Western political thought ever since: "Without justice, what are kingdoms [and all self-proclaimed polities] but great robber bands?"[16] Now he would deny to that monumental Roman edifice that it had ever been a republic, had ever embodied a people, because it lacked a common acknowledgment of a supreme law (*jus*), because it lacked a community of interest, but above all because it lacked that orientation toward the divine law that manifests the admission of a true justice.[17]

This powerful principle of universal inclusion and incorporation emerged as the greatest single legacy from the ruins of the ancient world. In rallying his own generation to this momentous destiny, while contending with the catastrophe of Rome's fall, Augustine gave religious definition to the motor of inclusion and its operation that also allowed for a measure of particularity:

> This heavenly city, then, while it sojourns on earth, calls citizens out of all nations, and gathers together a society of pilgrims of all languages, not scrupling about diversities in the manners, laws, and institutions whereby earthly peace is secured and maintained, but recognising that, however various these are [*quod licet diversum in diversis nationibus*], they all tend to one and the same end of earthly peace. It therefore is so far from rescinding and abolishing these diversities, that it even preserves and adopts them, so long only as no hindrance to the worship of the one supreme and true God is thus introduced.[18]

In contrast and yet as a supplement to Augustine's ecclesiastical understanding of that process, drawing all peoples and societies to the Body of Christ, let us align the more philosophical and specifically religious statement of Nicholas Cusanus a thousand years later in his *On Learned Ignorance*. The union of the divine and the human nature in the person of

Christ, announced in 325 at the First Council of Nicaea and confirmed in 451 at the Council of Chalcedon, allowed Cusanus to recognize in Christ that coincidence of contraries (*coincidentia oppositorum*), of extreme maximum and extreme minimum, that was central to his philosophizing, and therein the universal content of humanity to be enfolded in Christ. The idea of Christ justifies and legitimates the idea of humanity.[19] As manifest in the third epigraph of this chapter, Cusanus perceived both philosophically and religiously the immense import of this double-natured, three-personed God, with his inscription of humanity into the very nature of the godhead. Humanity was not just a spiritual or moral endowment, but rather a total collectivity that nevertheless respected the distinctive attributes of its individual members. In case there could be any doubt as to this second understanding of *humanitas* as a universal community, each of whose particular members was an object of divine solicitude, Cusanus, just earlier, quoted Matthew 25:40 (45): "Inasmuch as ye have done it unto one of the least of these my brethren you have done it unto me."[20] This massive assertion of comprehensive incorporation helped prepare the ground for that uniquely Western spiritual as well as religious commitment to the divinely based reality of all humanity as fact and idea. This powerful religious ingredient, no matter how transformed or metamorphosed, never entirely disappeared in the larger processes of its secular permutations.

The thousand years that elapsed between Augustine and Cusanus saw within the effective structure afforded by the church a consolidation of the process among the peoples at the westernmost extremity of the Eurasian landmass and the definition of Latin Christendom against Islam. During the twelfth century, the most creative in our civilization, yet to which obversely inheres for some the formation of a persecuting society, the internal tension between exclusive enforcement and its critique in an expansive inclusiveness, between *potestas* and *caritas*, power and love, continues. At this time a legal interpretation emerged that proved of paramount consequence for the later missionary thrust of the West and for the peoples of the globe. For in the general recovery of Roman law, the church, which had fashioned itself as an ecclesiastical empire on the model of its Roman predecessor, was better equipped than any of the contemporary motley kingdoms not only to adopt this law for itself in an ecclesiastical rendering of imperial Roman law but also to create in canon law the "First Modern Western Legal System" common to all the western Christian political communities.[21] Thus we need to attend the ruminations of the twelfth-century canonists on the various meanings of that fateful term *jus naturale*, or natural law.

Apart from the most immediate meaning of *jus* as some absolute, higher law of what is right—moral, divine, or immanent in the universe—in a primarily objective sense, a more individual sense surfaced. The twelfth-century canonists began to be sensitive not simply to the just thing itself but to what was justly due someone. They defined *jus* in a subjective sense as a faculty, power, force, or ability pertaining inherently to individuals and proceeded to develop a panoply of such natural rights—among them the ownership of property and the capacity of individuals to form their own government. Thus an inhering universal claim promoted individual, particular expression. Innocent IV in 1250 extended these two rights to infidels and Christians alike; in the course of the century other rights, such as the right to liberty, to self-defense, and the right of the poor to be safeguarded from hunger came to be defined. The marvelous ambivalence of *jus naturale* as meaning both a higher law and the inherent rights defined by that law resonated through the language of the Gregorian decretals, these papal decrees, and their medieval commentaries. This inheritance entered formal political philosophy with

William of Ockham and by 1400 was recapitulated by Jean Gerson—theologian, religious thinker, and chancellor of the University of Paris—in his important definition of *jus* as "a power or faculty belonging to each one in accordance with the dictate of right reason." The great Spanish juristic theologians would usher this rich tradition into the early modern period.[22]

Both complementing and paralleling the late medieval explication of *jus naturale* at the hands of the canon lawyers moved the development of Roman law itself, focused more on the practicalities evident in the *jus gentium*, the law of peoples. Here from the beginning Cicero himself, without renouncing entirely the philosophical implications of the concept of cosmopolis or the metaphysical overtones of Stoicism, rested his case for human community more on reason and on law. For Gaius, the great Roman jurisconsult of the second century, the *jus gentium* is the common law for all men; interestingly, he seemed to admit the existence of savages, as *sylvestres homines*, living outside of normal governance, wherein *jus gentium* could be claimed as the most universal custom of humankind. This law of peoples comes to express an idea of the community of fundamental customs, suggesting that the juridical unity of humankind becomes permanent in the course of the fifteenth century. With Alberico Gentili, Italian humanist yet Protestant, teaching at Cambridge University in the 1580s, a scholar to whom Hugo Grotius silently owed so much, the universality of *jus gentium* appeared as the common law of humanity. Thus, in the work of the Civilians, the expositors of the Roman civil law, there persists this effort to articulate the idea of a common humanity.[23]

The development of later thinking upon natural law and natural rights took a definitive turn following the sixteenth century. Under the dual impact effected by the American Indian on the one hand and the Reformation's political and theological fragmentation of Christendom on the other, the idea of natural rights was explicitly expanded onto a global scale and, most portentously, divested of its religious and ecclesiastical chrysalis. Here the Dutch prodigy Hugo Grotius would prepare the ground. The implicit, if still pending, secularization of the idea not only heralded the theoretical universalization of natural rights and the idea of humanity as a collective reality, but also provided the basis for the detachment of the civilizing from the specifically Christianizing, leading to the articulation of the concept of civilization. The immediate impact of these ideas was lost amidst the development of competing sovereign states and the rerouting of natural law, but several centuries later, in our own age, they augured a rich harvest of opportunity and challenge in a truly global forum. A consideration of natural law and natural rights in the early modern period will occupy us in the subsequent section.

Catholic Christianity's perduring commitment to the universality of the human and the obligations appertaining to it ultimately and inevitably worked to compel that old roué, Pope Paul III, to pronounce on more than just the recently encountered Indians as *veros homines*. With the papal bull *Sublimis Deus* (1537) Rome sought to cast a protective net over all the newly discovered peoples—western, southern, and others (*occidentales et meridionales Indos et alias gentes*). Rather than brute animals fit for servitude, they appeared as true men, rational, and thus capable of being won to the Christian faith.[24] The American Indians, despite whatever Aristotelianly based arguments might be ingeniously advanced for their natural slavery, must remain *veros homines*, open for conversion to Christianity. Although quickly annulled by Charles V's Council of the Indies as an intrusion upon its jurisdiction, the papal bull put Europe and the world on notice that Christianity sought Brotherhood, not Otherhoods, whether other peoples wanted it or not.[25]

Eight years earlier, in exhorting the same emperor, Clement VII had managed once again to couple universal love with its enforcement:

> We trust that, as long as you are on earth, you will compel and with all zeal cause the barbarian nations to come to the knowledge of God, the maker and founder of all things, not only by edicts and admonitions, but also by force and arms, if needful, in order that their souls may partake of the heavenly kingdom.[26]

The immense proselytizing efforts of the religious orders throughout the globe, together with the Spanish colonial enterprise, no matter how awkwardly, even unjustly, realized with respect to the Indian, announced a unique, astounding effort at an open-ended inclusion. Is the Catholic Church in the early modern period to be understood in the work of the newly founded congregation for the Propagation of the Faith (*De Propaganda Fide*, 1622), or that of the Holy Office—of expansive inclusion or enforced, exclusive identity?

In 1539, the mid-thirteenth-century rulings of Innocent IV regarding the rights of infidels to the holding of property and to the determination of their own government were reaffirmed in the explosive context of the Indians by the great Dominican Francisco de Vitoria: "Barbarians are not impeded from being true lords publicly and privately, on account of the sin of infidelity or any other mortal sin." The assertion was more than academic for Vitoria's fellow Dominican Bartolomé de Las Casas. Speaking from the political and evangelical trenches of engagement, he resoundingly rebutted the Aristotelian humanist Juan Gines de Sepúlveda's attitude toward the Indian: "They are our brothers, and Christ gave his life for them." Nor did he limit his outlook to the immediate problem represented by the Amerindian; in fact, he rose to a view that included blacks and Asians as well. Quoting Cicero and significantly appealing to the Stoic idea of a universal brotherhood of man, Las Casas insisted: "All the peoples of the world are humans and there is only one definition of all humans and of each one, that is that are rational. . . . Thus all the races of humankind are one." It can be argued that Las Casas was something of a maverick and that despite his best efforts a new period of racism was dawning. Nevertheless, the very complexity and polyphony of the European intellectual context would never allow the rich universal resonance of humanity to be entirely marginalized or suppressed. With Hugo Grotius, the idea by necessity began to shake itself free from its hitherto protective, nurturing religious shell and to reengage the rational, secular origins of the notion in Stoicism.[27]

By necessity? Yes, because the Reformation had created a complex of warring confessional camps out of the former Latin Christendom, each flourishing its own dogmatic brand and insisting on its own exclusive truth. Grotius felt compelled to construct a system of laws that would carry conviction in an age wherein theological controversy ground against itself and no one doctrinal camp was able to address all Christians in a now disfigured *corpus christianum* (Christian community). Seeking a theory of laws independent of all theological presuppositions, Grotius returned to Aristotle and the optimistic belief in the distinctive sociability of humans, which he erected into an immanent law of nature. He effected this step of potential secularization through the Great Hypothesis appearing in the Prolegomena of his *De jure belli ac pacis* (*On the Law of War and Peace*) of 1625, in which he declared that the law of nature would still apply even if, "which cannot be admitted without utmost wickedness, there is no God or human affairs did not concern him." Enunciated in the midst of the raging Thirty Years' War, the worst religiously inspired war of them all, this extreme measure sought to achieve a deliberate religious neutrality in order to make possible the potential universality of civil procedures and the reign of a Stoic "sociableness."[28] Grotius's fateful step became possible only as part of the long tradition of the alternate meanings of *jus* and its recent rendering of that inherent natural right by the Jesuit Suárez, Vitoria's most distinguished successor in the silver age of Scholasticism: namely, that the capacity to establish communities endowed with political power was innate in humans from their first creation, and that ruling power came into being by the will and the consent of free rights–bearing individuals entering into a compact among themselves to form a political community.[29] Indeed, the rights of a variety of groups, not just political, to self-assembly, procedure, and administration (*jura universitatis*)—this principle had been in practical operation since Innocent III (1198–1216).[30] Here canon law's development achieved a confluence with Roman and Germanic law in manifesting what the great historian of medieval universities, Hastings Rashdall, attributed to the medieval genius, that peculiar power of embodying its ideals in institutional form.[31]

The Renaissance saw a progressive displacement of what had been understood and included in the concept of *Christianitas* (Christendom) by the notion of Europe as a distinct civilizational construct whose material base belonged to that subcontinent. In the course of the fifteenth through the seventeenth centuries, political, moral, and cultural links came to replace the former preeminence of religious and ecclesiastical ones. In late sixteenth-century France, Bodin, Le Roy, Pasquier, and La Popelinière extended the term *civilité* to create at least the idea of civilization.[32] The new importance of navigation and geography heightened the Europeans' self-confidence and their power over other peoples, cultures, and lands. The cosmographers, drawing upon the recovery of Strabo's *Geographia* and, ultimately, upon Hippocrates, claimed that in contrast to Asia, Europe manifested an intense variety and its very harshness produced opposing stimuli promotive of the warlike and the resourceful, of courage and prudence, working for its preeminent vitality and enterprise. To Sebastian Münster in 1544, Europe, although smaller, surpasses the other continents in being more fertile, more cultivated, more populous. The emerging European ascendancy became visually imaged in the title pages to geography books picturing Europe as crowned, cuirassed, armed, and scientifically equipped, while the other continents appeared in varying states of servility and nakedness. In his *Thesaurus geographicus* (1578), Ortelius specifically equated "Christiani" and "Europaei." But as early as 1526, the Spanish humanist J. L. Vives found Europe's very diversity the source of dissension, an increasing danger in this new, quasi-national, multicellular, secular construct; such explosive tensions encouraged him to forsake the traditional term Christendom for Europe.[33] Connoting not just a continent and its people but a superior culture, civility, even civilization, during the late Renaissance, "Europe," in its particular national shapes, unequal bearers of a greater universality, strained outward in pullulating enterprises toward the rest of the globe.

However anachronistic the term for the increasingly global influences of Europe after 1600, "Europeanization" nicely includes the shifting ingredients within that universalizing amalgam of specifically Christian religious and of classical secular origins. The medieval chivalric and courtly tradition, culminating in the ideal courtier of Baldassare Castiglione's most influential book of 1528 and the subsequent books of manners, further enhanced the secular while developing the civil characteristics.[34] The definition of such ingredients and their transforming relationship, seen under the lens of Europe's expansion in America and more precarious penetration in Asia, will serve to extend our inquiry into the seventeenth and eighteenth centuries.

The recovery of Ptolemy's *Geographia*, translated in 1406 and published in 1477, had promoted the practical application of Alexandrian mathematics to the interests of cartography and had supplied the vital intellectual component to the Age of Discovery. Mathematics, the most universalizing of all intellectual disciplines, had provided a grid of coordinates that rendered the globe's surface uniformly homogeneous. America to the west and access to the Indian Ocean basin to the south and east represented the final achievements of the Renaissance and the decisive milestones in the European construction of the global arena. By the end of the sixteenth century, Europe's initial engagement with the peoples of the earth was well advanced. The bitter, brutal realities of that process—epidemic, conquest, enslavement, subjection—are beyond the scope of this analysis. Instead, we now turn to the shifting composition of attitudes regarding Christian conversion that express the universalizing principle. What was the cultural face, in its entirety and in its components, with which Europe intruded at this time upon the peoples of other cultures?

Certainly, among the forces impelling the first half century of the missionary orders in the New World, the expressly religious stood uppermost: the spiritual drive by means of quick baptism to include the newly found children of Adam within the Christian fold before the impending end of time. With the arrival of the Jesuits on the American scene, however, the more explicitly civil, secular dimension of the Europeans' impact on the indigenous populations revealed itself. It had become a matter of missionary policy for the Jesuits, whether evangelizing in the Indies or in those *otras Indias*, such as the back alleys of Naples, first to establish "civility" before attempting baptism and formal conversion.[35] We are reminded of this connection by that notable authority on political geography Giovanni Botero, who wrote in his *Relationi universali* (*Global Reports* [1596]) that there was nothing more alien to evangelical doctrine than unsociableness or wildness (*salvaticchezza*) in our bearing and cruelty of mind, for Christ presented himself as gentle and humble of heart, in which manner it was easier to inform others more effectively as to the meaning of humanity. Botero continues: "We hear the apostle asking us to bear each other's burdens and in another place duly to respect our superiors—behold the sum of civility and of all kindness [*ecco la somma della civiltà, e d'ogni gentilezza*]":

> Thus I consider it the greatest advantage to the introduction of the faith that refinement [*pulitezza*] (whatever it may be) is introduced by government and by rule of the great princes in America, because it removes peoples from rudeness and from harshness, disposing them to the gentleness and pleasantness that so become the life of a Christian.[36]

The classical seems here to inform, promote, and be fulfilled in the Christian. Despite the intimate association, even coalescence, of the classical and the Christian, the Jesuit program reflected the beginnings of a potential disengagement, which becomes evident in the light of an earlier statement on this relationship. In the course of the Middle Ages the two had been so closely identified as to be indistinguishable; only with the Renaissance did the beginnings of a concept of civilization emerge. At the start of the Age of Discovery, the Italian humanist historian Polydore Vergil, in concluding his rambling *De inventoribus rerum* with a section dating from 1521 and titled "The Preeminence of the Christian Commonwealth," identified the civilizing process with the very heart and purpose of Christianity, the reverse of the later Jesuit priority: the civil manners and virtues were the import and consequence of the Christianizing. The mission of Christianity was to civilize the savage and to soften his ferocity with mild-tempered virtues, *pudici mores*:[37] "Thus it is generally recognized that only to the Christian Commonwealth has it been given to promote in the world the most perfect mode of living."[38] It can be argued that although Polydore Vergil conceived of Christianity and civility as a single amalgam, in giving the entirety a secular purpose he went well beyond the later Jesuit program in understanding the relationship between the two and thus their potential separation. At any rate, in the context of Spanish colonialism after 1570, the long-standing practice of the *reducciones*—of resettling the Indians into urban contexts and using this enforced association to instill urban, civil customs of living—came to be extensively applied during the viceroyal administration of Francisco de Toledo in Peru. Exposing the Indian to the regularities and rationalities of the inherited classical *polis* conveyed, it was hoped, that measure of *policía* (political ordering) that embodied what was understood by the later term *civilization*. The broadly held assumption prevailed that living in towns meant becoming Christian and, even more, becoming true men. Implicitly Christianity, civility, and humanity now marched together. And for the Spanish administrator, the greatest of these was civility. Whatever the degree of failure of the civilizing ideal, there can be no doubt as to its presence in the purposes of the *reduccion*, the resettlement, which coexisted with the religious as well as the economic and administrative purposes of the program.[39] Conversion to civility jostled conversion to Christ. If for the sixteenth century the two conditions seemed closely connected and interrelated, for the Enlightenment exactly two centuries later, according to the jaundiced view of civilization's first and foremost critic, "Our missionaries sometimes make Christians of them, but never Civilized men."[40]

Before leaving the Western for the more familiar Eastern Hemisphere, we may well ask ourselves what meaning had

America for enterprising Europe in the first centuries of encounter and contact. Apart from the obvious interests of expansion and exploitation, in more general, abstract terms Europe now came to exercise and enjoy a total monopoly over the development of half the globe for at least three hundred years, a truly unique advantage as well as responsibility; each of Europe's several parts had the opportunity to develop an alternate space in its own image—Spanish, Portuguese, French, Dutch, and finally English—with accompanying tensions and also fruits, both bitter and succulent. Yet a still more comprehensive meaning has been perceived in the recognition that through its discovery of America, Europe had at once pragmatically encountered both the unity and diversity of humankind[41]—the latter as a lingering problem, the former in the immediately to be repeated but unsuccessful efforts to fit the newly encountered into the single Adamic family. If the ready-at-hand religious category proved too narrow and inexplicable, would a more neutral, universal, secular version serve? Although the problem was not to be easily resolved and even today requires continual adjustments, nevertheless it fell to Europe to be forced to contend with this momentous issue, so much in keeping with its own preoccupation regarding the reality of a single common humanity. A new interconnectedness for the globe, a world without walls, hitherto theoretically conceived, was now becoming a glaring, even an embarrassing reality. As J. H. Elliott so clearly discerned, in summing up the premier quincentenary conference on the Columbian impact, "the sense of one interconnected world was establishing itself as a commonplace in the sixteenth century, assisted by the new conceptualization of space made possible by the Renaissance device of the globe."[42] Following upon the recovery of Ptolemy's *Geographia*, Europe had proceeded to cast a net of mathematical coordinates around this sphere, our planet, and through improved cartography and navigation to draw that net ever tighter and more coherently, holding the American hemisphere in its engagement of global interconnectedness and consciousness.

This new emerging sense of global interconnectedness becomes evident in the truly remarkable statement made by the mestizo priest Bartolomé de Alva to his diverse flock and found in his *Confessionario* of 1634. Apparently responding to the news of the 1622 martyrdom of Christians in Nagasaki, he exhorts the fragile faithful of the New World in his native Nahuatl:

> Turn your eyes back (better I should say forward) and look at the nation of the Japanese and others who, being your younger brothers in the faith and very modern and new in it, have left you far behind, being very firm and constant with the acts and demonstrations they have made. They do not have your superstitions and bad habits, . . . and [have] banished from their hearts the idolatry in which they blindly (like you) used to go along.[43]

This exhortation seems remarkable in two respects: first, it manifested a totally new, global interconnectedness and responsive energy; second, in its appeal to "younger brothers," it asserted a Christian community and common humanity that transcended the distance of oceans and the separation of continents. And this from the mouth of one only part European. Also notable is that the exhortation is in the specifically Christian rather than the Stoic register of universalization.

In the Western Hemisphere the rampage of Iberian peoples had rapidly led to the obliteration of at least three pre-Columbian civilizations and the almost breathtaking erection and imposition of a system of Spanish Catholic brotherhood that incorporated the native population both religiously and legally. In the East, however, matters proved very different indeed. There several ancient, well-established civilizations, confident and even complacent in their superior sophistication and maturity, could afford at least for two more centuries to look down upon the barbarian intruders. Hence missionary work in Asia—India and China—could not be a matter of annihilating existing native societies and cultures; rather, missionaries lived on sufferance in toeholds of trading posts and under precarious conditions of ephemeral recognition. Despite the presence of the mendicant and religious orders in Asia, the conditions of coexistence and contacts between the European intruder and the indigenous populations were dictated there more by issues of economics and commerce. Trade, rather than conquest and religious imposition, distinguished these relations. What with the relatively unruffled continuance of great empires—Mughal and Chinese—together with their religions and social systems, the expressly cultural or, more anachronistically, civilizational issue came to the fore, because anything like an American-style Catholic sweep proved quite out of the question. In Europe's reconstitution and transformation of its universalizing features, the initial cultural curiosity and respect of the Europeans would give way ultimately to a growing self-confidence, arrogance, and even disdain.[44] But through the Europeans' cultural confrontation and engagement with China, the expressly secular dimensions of Europe in its civilizational register articulated themselves. All the more ironic that this shift in register from the preeminently religious to the preeminently cultural, technical, and civil should itself have been effected by the foremost religious order of the day—the Jesuits.

If the more explicitly civil, secular aspect of a universalist composite asserted itself at this time, given the different conditions in Asia, how well did Renaissance Europe measure up to the other leading civilizations of the globe—Islamic, Indian, and Chinese? The brilliant analysis of a pervasive parable, shared largely among merchant communities, allows us to recognize and take advantage of this contemporary displacement in the evaluation of two major civilizations and concentrate upon China as the only effective competitor to an aspiring European cultural hegemony.[45] Even those most innocent of Muslim history can justifiably protest the enormous contributions of Muslim culture to Latin Christendom down to 1300—not to mention Islam's rival ecumenical ambitions.[46] After that time, however, not only did Europe's emerging civilization begin to pull ahead technologically, despite the economic contraction following the Black Death in the fourteenth century, but the whole Islamic system, especially Iran, suffered an even worse contraction and dislocations from the Mongol invasions of the thirteenth and fourteenth centuries. Whatever the longstanding cultural preeminence of Islamdom over Christendom during the Middle Ages, it is important to recognize that in the very period 1350–1500, which saw the distinctive cultural revival in the Italian Renaissance, a more or less general decadence and remission befell the world of Islam, stretching from Morocco to India and Southeast Asia.[47] It was in the mirror of China's acknowledged superiority as a civilization that Europe's understanding of itself as a more than viable competitor—a civilization—matured.

To the Venetian Nicolò Conti (ca. 1385–1469), who traveled in Asia for more than thirty-five years, "India" signified the whole of mysterious Asia. In his long sojourn, particularly in the central and southern parts of India proper, this observant traveler made some comparisons that divided "India" into three parts, the third being everything beyond the Ganges, which "excels the others in riches, politeness, and magnificence and is equal to our own country in the style of life and in civili[ty]" (*vita et civili consuetudine nobis aequalis*). Good and bad, civilized and barbarous were determined according to their conformity to European practice: eating at table attested to civilization, eating on a carpet to barbarism. Conti's idealization of what lay beyond the Ganges began to pertain to "Cathay," or China. Although his account of China, based on hearsay, is anachronistic and partly mythical, Conti's Cathay was that of his oriental companions, who included Arab and Persian merchants and sometimes oriental Christians. Focusing upon the European-like civilized model, Conti went on significantly to report: "The natives of 'India' call us Franks, and say that while they call other nations blind, they themselves have two eyes and we have but one, because they consider that they excel all others in prudence." The comparison presented by this proverb recurred repeatedly over the centuries, and a remarkable analysis of the language, circumstances, persons, and contexts strongly argues against simple cases of textual borrowing. J. P. Rubiés argued in his thorough analysis of the recurrence of this proverb in the works of different authors, the use of this visual metaphor for comparing these levels of civilization enjoyed wide support from late medieval and Renaissance European sources on Asia. In his historical-cum-geographical report to Pope Clement V in 1307 regarding central Asia and the Mamluk power of Egypt, Prince Hayton of Armenia spoke of the people of Cathay:

> These people, who are so simple in their faith and in spiritual things, are wiser and subtler than all the other peoples in material works. And the Cathayans say that they alone see with two eyes and that the Latins see with one eye, but of the other nations they say that they are blind. And from this it can be understood that they see the other peoples as thick-witted.

Shortly afterward, the author of the *Book of Sir John Mandeville* appropriated the comparison, claiming for the Chinese, with their two eyes, superior subtlety, malice, and wit, and crediting the Christians with one eye "because they are the most subtle after them; but they say all the other nations do not see at all and that they are blind of science and artistry." In all of this exchange we recognize in the making the cultural criteria of civilization, absent the explicitly religious. *Res* (the substance) long precedes *verbum* (the term itself).

Perhaps the best independent source for this parable of civilizations derives from the account of a Castilian embassy to Timur's court at Samarkand in 1404 that described a display of different goods from various peoples:

> And the goods that are imported into this city from Cathay are the best and most precious of all those brought thither from other parts, and those from Cathay say it themselves, that they are the subtlest people in the whole world; and they say that they see with two eyes, and the Moors are blind, and the Franks have one eye, and that they have an advantage over all the nations of the world in the things that they make.

Most interesting here is the clear distinction among three levels of civilization according to the production of sophisticated commodities and the designation of these other nations as essentially the Moors (that is, Muslims). As a fifth source for the proverb, Iosafa Barbaro, relating in 1487 his embassy to Persia, reported on the king of Persia's allowing that "the world has three eyes, the Cathayans have two, and the Franks one." Barbaro's anecdote has further interest in that it suggests such a view had spread as a result of the devastation produced by the Mongol and Turkish invasions of the late Middle Ages—invasions that rocked Islamdom. The consequent reconfiguration of the earth's peoples revealed a conception of a world that had two main centers of civility at its two extremes—East and West—a view that even had some currency among leading Muslim intellects. In the fourteenth century the great Muslim traveler Ibn Battuta declared that "the Chinese are of all peoples the most skillful in the arts and possessed of the greatest mastery of them," and at the turn of the century Ibn Khaldūn observed, "We further hear now that the philosophical sciences are greatly cultivated in the land of Rome and along the adjacent northern shore of the country of the European Christians."

The proverb about the superior wisdom and civility of the Chinese became common to sixteenth-century Europe. The Portuguese humanist chronicler Joâo de Barros, in the third of his Asian *Décadas* (1563), explained:

> And in the same way as the Greeks thought that in respect of themselves all other nations were barbarian, similarly the Chinese say that they have two eyes of understanding concerning all things, that we Europeans, after they have communicated with us, have one eye, and that all other nations are blind. And truly . . . these gentiles have all those things for which Greeks and Latins are praised.

Remarkable here is the shift of Franks or even Christians to Europeans, or, more exactly, "we from Europe" (*os da Europa*), and the alignment of the Chinese with the ancient Greeks and Romans as a model of civilization. Furthermore, Barros essentially consolidated from the proverb the maturing European appreciation of China as the most civilized kingdom of the world.[48] This attitude was soon to be reaffirmed by Botero himself[49] and persisted in Europe until the eighteenth century: for according to Leibniz, in his *Novissima Sinica* (The Latest Chinese News [1697]), Europe had now managed to acquire a second eye through its superior mathematics.[50]

By the closing decades of the sixteenth century, tiny Europe, having established a network of *carreras*, or maritime highways, throughout the world and thus created the global arena for her further enterprise, was now positioned for a more sustained engagement with the superior Chinese civilization, whether the Middle Kingdom wanted it or not. Although the subsequent contacts were formally conducted by Catholic religious orders, especially Jesuits and Franciscans, it was on the more secular level of a comparable civility and a superior technology, rather than that of the expressly Christian and religious, that the issue of universality was to be contested. And in the Jesuit Matteo Ricci's effort to convert the largest and grandest civilization that history had yet produced by civil means to a Christianity of Catholic renewal, we encounter one of the supreme moments of the human intellect—however impossible—comparable on the historical and social level to Johannes Kepler's contemporaneous charting of the orbit of Mars. Each endeavor was equally universal in its own way and equally expressive of the universalist principle.

Founded in 1540, by 1615 the Society of Jesus had 13,000 members active throughout the world.[51] Indeed, the new Jesuit international announced the coming of the global age. It has been perceptively claimed that "the Jesuits were the first planetary men, the first in whom the world network became, to some degree, a world system."[52] In the Jesuits' vast enterprise of world evangelization, China figured as the preeminent task; in fact, from the Columbian beginnings China had been the express goal, and Francis Xavier, greatest among early Jesuit missionaries to Asia, had early recognized that the conversion of the whole East depended on that of China. So imperative seemed the winning of China that it was to become an obsession of the Jesuits.[53] Yet the Christianization of the most advanced civilization on earth did not present itself as a simple matter of bagging another people and its beliefs for Christ; rather, it raised the most profound and intricate problems. Where and how was one to direct one's efforts? And how far down the road of engagement could one go without losing one's own identity? And then there was the problem of gaining access in the first place to a highly xenophobic Ming China.

From 1583, when he arrived in China from Macao, to 1601, when he reached Peking, Matteo Ricci kept his gaze fixed upon winning the emperor to Christ. It had long been a practice of the Jesuits first to seek out the ruler and make their appeal to the ruling class. Ricci and his associate Michele Ruggieri had initially stumbled in assuming the attributes of Buddhist monks, appealing thereby to the people at large, which quickly led nowhere. Better to direct one's efforts to the mandarin bureaucracy and appear not only as a mandarin dressed in crisp silks and hoisted about in a sedan chair, but also as a most learned mandarin, prepared to extend—in impeccable Chinese—a Christianity laced with the fruits of European science and technology. As a student of the great Clavius at Rome, who had effected the Gregorian calendar, Ricci was supremely well equipped both in natural and in moral philosophy. During a period of eighteen years of careful planning and study that included the sending of such devices as maps, a clavichord, and a clock to Peking, Ricci had to make some fateful decisions. While directing his efforts to winning over the ruling class and insinuating himself into the emperor's palace, Ricci and company had to determine the correct Chinese term for the deity, a notion otherwise lacking to the Chinese. The closest arrived at, but never completely successful, was *tian*, which carried the sense of "Master of Heaven." More formidable was the issue of determining the nature of the rites performed by the Chinese to honor their ancestors, practices deeply ingrained in the entire social matrix. Eschewing the least hint of Christian exclusivity and advancing every effort at accommodation, Ricci fatefully interpreted such practices as signifying a civic rather than a religious cult and proceeded to fortify his tenuous position with an appeal to Probabilism.[54] As a product of the late-sixteenth-century groundswell of Stoic revival in Europe, Ricci also advanced a minimalist brand of Christian Stoicism, more Grotian in its ambitious accommodationalist program than the earlier Christian humanism of Erasmus.[55] As in the beginning, Stoicism recommended itself to the task of comprehensiveness and inclusion. Chinese sensibilities were not to be ruffled by the *scandalon* of a crucified God: Ricci's China mission was reluctant to display the crucifix. Furthermore, in his Chinese catechism, six of the seven sacraments remained unmentioned, only baptism admitted. By reducing Christian teaching to natural reason, Ricci sought to construct a common basis for both civilizations. The most arresting and daring of his intellectual enterprises was to identify and construct from the Chinese past a monotheism that could effectively serve as a preparation for the gospel (*praeparatio evangelica*).[56]

In this huge effort to reveal an inchoate monotheism of indigenous Chinese belief, Ricci fixed on the remote, shadowy figure of the sage Kongzi, otherwise Kong Fuzi, Italianized to "Il Confutio," from which would derive by 1689 the Latinized equivalent Confucius. Ricci envisaged this task as a reduction of China, its civilization, and the main thread of its past to Confucius and the moral philosophy associated with him. *Ru*, the lettered followers of Confucius, tended to become for Ricci the mirror image of the Jesuits. What Ricci took to be the law of the literati (*legge de' letterati*) conformed to natural light (*il lume naturale*) and to Christian truth. Ricci claimed sole legitimacy for his identification and interpretation of the tradition of the *Xianru*, in short, Kongzi's authentic teaching. In proceeding by means of Renaissance philology far across the bridge to an entirely other system of belief, Ricci probably never realized how much of his own he had been forced to relinquish. On the basis of an apparently common rationality and moral philosophy, Chinese and Jesuit, mandarin and missionary seem to metamorphose into each other. He revealed his self-understanding of his own achievement: "We have acquired much by pulling Confutio over to our opinion." By the time of his death in 1610, the authority of the Jesuit interpretation of a primordial monotheistic lettered tradition had been recognized by some Chinese. Succeeding generations of missionaries sustained it, and some of the Jesuit membership, especially Ferdinand Verbiest, director of the Bureau of Astronomy, enjoyed high appointments in the imperial bureaucracy.[57]

The Jesuits proved equally adroit in drawing a European public to their accommodationist achievement. From 1662 to the end of the century, Jesuit translations of Chinese texts disclosing the latent Christianity of the Chinese appeared in European bookstalls. Published in the same year as Newton's *Principia mathematica*, the *Confucius sinarum Philosophus* (*Confucius, Philosopher of the Chinese* [Paris, 1687]) marked the most deliberate statement in that process of selling China to an already supremely Sinophilic European readership. This composite work of many hands coined the term *Confucian*. Through the workings of those tricky Greek suffixes, the "isms," Confucianism came to be progressively reified in the European imagination. Among rulers subscribing to this enthusiastic appropriation of China and the Chinese were Louis XIV and, soon afterward, Frederick William I, King of Prussia; among the intellectual leadership the numbers were legion and included Newton and Leibniz. Nevertheless, the most notable single appropriation of Confucianism by the Enlightenment came with the Amsterdam 1758 edition of Diogenes Laertius's *Lives of the Philosophers*. There amidst the traditional thinkers of classical antiquity could now be found a ninety-page exposition of Confucius and Confucianism.[58] By a simple alignment of the Confucian Chinese with the classical inheritance, a bridge to Chinese civilization had been created in order to include the Chinese in the expansive European civilization on the basis of a shared civility and natural law. Something distinctively new, a new confidence, a new civility long maturing, a new civilization capable of contending with the most ancient and established had in the meantime come into being; its leadership, from Leibniz to Metternich, from Gibbon to Burke, recognized it as a single country, Europe; a single civilization, European.[59]

Contrasting ironically to the apparently huge indifference and xenophobia of China, the xenophilia of Europe had increasingly come to be focused upon and even mesmerized by China. Most immediately this express Sinophilia has been interpreted as working to the benefit of the moderns over the ancients. But more in keeping with the theme of our inquiry here, the European espousal of Confucianism and things Chinese, made possible on the presumption of a common rationality and civility, suggests a further displacement of the expressly Christian from the original amalgam of universality. Yet it is not our intention here to argue for the greater expansion of the universalizing principle to the total evacuation of its religious ingredient, nor for any simple process of secularization. The identifiably Christian component never entirely disappears but is transmuted and continues to exercise a potentially beneficent effect upon the more aggressive, expansive, ramifying manifestations of the universalizing principle. In the restructuring of the universalizing principle, at the expense of the specifically Christian to the enhancement of Europe considered as a self-conscious, coherent civilization, a natural ethic for morals, a natural law in politics, and even a natural religion all afforded to the potential outsider and more immediately to the European insider a relatively neutral ground, appealing to that presumed rationality becoming to a human being.

In many ways Leibniz's *Novissima Sinica* represents the culmination of European Sinophilia. Appearing shortly after the great K'ang-hsi emperor's edict of toleration 1692 for Christians in the Middle Kingdom, it signified the long work and attitude of conciliation on the part of a European philosopher that had included the Christian churches but now extended to different civilizations in the interests of achieving a universal jurisprudence, an overarching practical philosophy, a common civility. Leibniz began by noting in his preface that human cultivation and refinement appeared today to be concentrated at the two extremes of the continent—Europe and China. One vied to learn from and surpass the other.

> In profundity of knowledge and in the theoretical disciplines we are their superiors. For besides logic and metaphysics, and the knowledge of things incorporeal, which we justly claim as peculiarly our province, we excel by far in the understanding of concepts which are abstracted by the mind from the material, i.e., in things mathematical, as is in truth demonstrated when Chinese astronomy comes into competition with our own. The Chinese are thus seen to be ignorant of that great light of the mind, the art of demonstration, and they have remained content with a sort of empirical geometry, which our artisans universally possess. They also yield to us in military science, not so much out of ignorance as by deliberation. For they despise everything which creates or nourishes ferocity in men, and almost in emulation of the higher teachings of Christ (and not, as some wrongly suggest, because of anxiety), they are averse to war. They would be wise indeed if they were alone in the world.[60]

But alone they were not.

Although Europe surpassed China in matters theoretical, mathematical, and especially military, the Chinese proved superior to Europeans in the precepts of civil life—a shameful admission for Leibniz, a Christian, to affirm. Europeans had advanced from a one-eyed condition to the acquisition of another eye for understanding things incorporeal, but the Chinese manifested a superior exercise of practical, civil philosophy. So great and admirable did Chinese civility appear in its idealization by Leibniz that he posited a highly unlikely diaspora of Chinese missionaries to Europe to instruct Europeans in a more perfect manner of living, despite the superior gift of Christian revelation granted to the natives. With Europe slipping daily into ever greater corruption, the Chinese missionary might teach Europeans the use and practice of natural religion and assist in advancing the boundaries of natural law and the jurisprudence of humanity.[61]

While maintaining close relations with the Jesuits, Leibniz sought to arouse Protestant Europe to emulate the Jesuit missions in order to effect the greater good of faith, country, and humankind. He especially placed his hopes in Brandenburg Prussia. In 1700 he wrote to the Elector Frederick III regarding the opportunities awaiting:

> Nowhere among the Protestants has such a foundation been laid as in Berlin for Chinese *literatura et propaganda fide*. Moreover, and with the help of the special dispensation of Providence, the uncommonly good personal relations with the Czar open a wide gate to Great Tartary and to magnificent China. Through this gate not only goods and wares but also light and knowledge may find an entrance into this other civilized world and "Anti-Europe."[62]

In its emperor and the obedience of his people this Anti-Europe,[63] even oriental Europe, this magnificent China, had apparently achieved that sort of mathematics of justice implicit in the Platonic ideal, where justice and mercy are not occasional or arbitrary but eternal truths, like numbers and fixed proportions. Leibniz's thought moved relentlessly to a justice marked by balance, harmony, and a charity of the wise: *justitia est caritas sapientis seu benevolentia universalis* (justice is a knowing love or universal benevolence). In this cosmos of reliable ideals, Christ had become necessary only because humans used their reason poorly. Writing in 1697 to Father Claudio Grimaldi, Leibniz in effect shelved the necessity of Christian revelation and allowed that God aided all those of good will by means of another kind of grace (*alio gratiae*). He could await the unlikely arrival of those Chinese missionaries with the natural religion and universal benevolence that Europeans had apparently lost.[64] Yet in the criticism of his own civilization in the mirror of China's, and in his forsaking of the specifically Christian for a rational charity of universal benevolence, Leibniz had distinguished a quality that came increasingly to characterize the operation of Christianity in the modern world, however offensive it might prove to the Arnaulds and the Augustinians of his and future generations.

In the course of the eighteenth century, Europe's great love affair with China began to wane. A significant change in European values effected this important shift in perceptions from an enthusiastically positive to an increasingly disdainful, negative outlook. Leibniz's view reflected the essentially Jesuit version of China that prevailed in 1700: a well-disciplined, stable society based on the respected authority of parents, tradition, and the emperor. Nevertheless, this traditional, patriarchal order failed to address for Europeans the rising tide of interest in human relations, in creativity and progress. Adherence to the past and its traditions now seemed less admirable and promotive only of stagnation. China came to be judged as wanting in military power, effective government, and technical as well as scientific knowledge. The former principle of civility now seemed to retreat before the Enlightenment's confidence in progress and machines, in science, and the ideal of individual, personal achievement. More specifically, perceptions had soured, especially those of the British, whose rising impatience and arrogance fretted before the apparently blind, obstructive conservatism of the Celestial Empire. By 1778,

Dr. Johnson had delivered himself of a magnificent condemnation of the Chinese as barbarians, allowing them only the single accomplishment of pottery.[65]

The very notion of civilization, long in incubation during the Renaissance, began to surface in the languages of Western Europe only toward the end of the eighteenth century.[66] We first encounter the English term in the sense of a developed or advanced state of human society in an exchange between Boswell and Dr. Johnson, for Monday, March 23, 1772. Boswell reports finding his eminent friend preparing a fourth edition of his dictionary. When pressed to enter the word *civilization,* he would only allow *civility.* Boswell's rejoinder is significant: "I thought civilization, from to civilize, better in the sense opposed to barbarity than civility." As if to reinforce the value of the new coin, Edmund Burke in 1790 drew out its meaning with the statement, "Our manners, our civilization, and all the good things which are connected with manners, and with civilization."[67] Across the channel, first the marquis de Mirabeau, father of the more famous revolutionary orator, at mid-century preceded the English in coining the term for the French language.[68] In a widely and well-received treatise on population, *L'ami des hommes* (The Friend of Men), first published in 1757, Mirabeau introduced the word apparently for the first time with a notably Vichian twist: "Religion is incontestably the first and the most useful rein upon humanity; it is the first expression of civilization, constantly reminding us of fraternal community, sweetening our heart."[69] The roles of religion and civilization have here become reversed: religion is a function of civilization, even though the new concept remains preeminently moral and not yet comprehensive.[70] The Italians seem to have adopted the term later and with greater reluctance, complaining that it was a French contrivance and that the Italian language could be satisfied with its *incivilimento, costume*, *vivere civile*, and *civiltà* (civilizing, manners, living civilly, and civility).[71]

Yet it is hardly accidental that the new term would see its elaboration on the most remote frontiers of European activity—in the dense woods of North America and the wastelands of Siberia. In New Hampshire, a school for missionaries to the Indians had been founded at Dartmouth College in 1769, its seal bearing the fateful words *Vox Clamantis in Deserto* (Isaiah 40:3)—"The Voice of One Crying in the Wilderness." Whatever the energies for proselytizing the infant school may have harbored, they seem to have been quickly lost on the restless, enterprising John Ledyard or, better, transformed into anthropological inquiry. Ledyard early forsook his Christian proselytizing and thenceforth devoted the rest of his short life to the service of English patrons and Thomas Jefferson, who suggested that he traverse the North American continent, west to east, beginning in Siberia and Kamchatka; the project eventually established Ledyard's belief in the common racial stock of American Indians and Asian Mongols.[72] But for our purposes here he provides interesting evidence not only for the extensive use of the term *civilization*, but also, somewhat ominously, of *incivilization*. Writing from Siberia in July 1787, he mused: "When I was at School at Mount Ida [Dartmouth College] there were many Indians there: most of whom gave some hopes of Civilizing: and some were sent forth to preach, but as far as I observed myself and have been since informed that all like the ungained Sow returned to the mire." Then he referred to his present condition among the Tartars: "the nice gradation by which I pass from Civilization to Incivilization appears in everything: their manners, their dress, their Language and particularly that remarkable and important circumstance of *Colour*." A few weeks later he wrote to Thomas Jefferson on his current encounter with the Tartars and how profoundly they resembled the aborigines of America: "The cloak of civilization sits as ill upon them as our American Tartars—they have been a long time Tartars and it will be a long time before they are any other kind of people."[73]

As a sort of herald of a Jeffersonian and republican conception of Continental empire, Ledyard posited an advanced, Enlightenment conception of empire whose benevolence and consensualism contrasted with the similarly Continental but despotic empire of Catherine the Great's Russia.[74] The arrogance and apparent masterful control betray the worm of an incipient racism that also distinguishes this newly self-conscious civilization. This unpleasant emergent reality asserts itself well beyond its earlier religious foundations, or at least that part of them that represents a universal force of comprehensive inclusion working to realize at its best a pervasive benevolence and the recognition of a single humanity. That the condition of a single humanity can ever be realized seems unlikely, but the drive toward this ideal becomes the ultimate merit and meaning of the West in history.

We end this section by returning to the statement of the marquis de Mirabeau and his new term, *civilization*, and to the problem of the relationship of the original religious beginnings of a society to its efflorescence into a civilization. By the time Mirabeau wrote, the roles of religion and civilization had become reversed: religion now appeared as a function of civilization, momentarily foremost, but shortly to be displaced from its central role. For in its long confrontation with the superior two-eyed Chinese civilization, in the mirror of that civilization, Christian efforts at its conversion would seem to have themselves been converted, at least for the rising body of European Sinophiles, into something new and different, itself now a civilization, also twin-eyed, a European civilization, soon with growing confidence and self-assurance, the only civilization. And despite the original coining of the term in the context of religion, the new European civilization, self-conceived as the only civilization, would differ from and face down all other such claimants by the preeminence of its very secularity and express freedom from religious definitions.

What had started as love and community among all humankind had somehow developed by 1800 into the elaboration and deployment of a number of forces into a global context, forces that seemed more expressive of power than of love. Indeed, the Jesuits had been able to extend their tenure in China largely by serving as cannon founders for the war machine of the Qing emperors.[75] The universalizing agent in European civilization, though it had not lost all its original religious focus and momentum, had provided the modern or postmodern world, either directly or indirectly, with two universalizing forces: the one political, broadly conceived not in terms of dominance or express forms of government but rather in the workings of human equality, rationality, and dignity, and affecting moral practices and law; and the other expressly intellectual and scientific, affirming a rational, sovereign Legislator whose physical universe could be decoded by his rational creatures, as evinced in the technological and scientific current shaping the present world. The second reality, broadly recognized, needs no further exposition.

The first of these two universalizing forces, here treated at length in its moral, political, and legal dimensions, unifies the picture presented and, though often forgotten and poorly expressed, represents the most attractive feature of the Western universalizing principle: the extension of a rule of law in programs of human rights to all the peoples of the earth, born of the belief in an essentially uniform and rationally disposed humanity—or, as Second Isaiah announced in another register with a culture-transcending resonance, *vox clamantis in deserto*.

The Career of Natural Rights in the Early Modern Period

The exposure to and the engagement with China and its advanced civilization worked to heighten the civil, the secular, in the traditional amalgam of the classical/Christian complex; a common natural light seemed to offer access to and agreement with the *legge de' letterati*. While Ricci still lived, important steps occurred in the process of natural law's secularization and hence the effective removal from a theological and expressly Christian framework. It would fall to the Spanish theologian-jurists of the sixteenth century, in their utterly novel experience of contending with the problem of the American Indian, that this process developed and found its completion with Hugo Grotius and his followers. This shedding of natural law's specifically religious framework, this secularization of the concept, will prove to be of decisive importance, for it made any program of human rights and the vision of a single humanity religiously neutral and hence potentially more open to other cultures, preparing the ground for its true universality. That this development began within possibly the most coherent, sustained theological tradition from medieval High Scholasticism, namely that of the Spanish theologian-jurists, and was advanced in an Aristotelianized Protestantism representative of the Reformation's dissent made the resulting statement all the more effective and authoritative. By their own contribution, the Spanish moral theologians have been frequently represented as crossing a bridge from the medieval to the modern.[76]

Much of what constituted this later Scholasticism or School of Salamanca, which was to produce such luminaries as the Dominicans Domingo de Soto and Melchor Cano, and later, derivatively, the Jesuits Francisco Suárez and Luis de Molina, can be attributed to its brilliant founder, Francisco de Vitoria, who had first studied and taught at Paris from 1509 to 1523. His intellectual career rewards attention. Returning to Spain, he became professor of theology and director of studies at the College of San Gregorio, Valladolid, until elected in 1526 to the prime chair of theology at the University of Salamanca, where he taught for the rest of his life. Though he published nothing himself, Vitoria became enormously influential through his lectures and his posthumously published lecture notes, which were of two sorts: those on Aquinas's *Summa theologica* and Peter Lombard's *Sentences*, and then a series of *relationes* (lectures). With the first it would prove crucial to his own development that he should at the outset place Saint Thomas at the center of all his future thought, and vital for later Catholicism that this centering of Aquinas would contribute to a displacement of Lombard as the textbook for subsequent Catholic theology. In this conscious reappropriation of Aquinas, Vitoria engaged the familiar features identifying the Thomistic system: the full, confident appropriation of Aristotle's empiricism with its dignification of the natural and the human as a distinct order of reality but its clear subordination at every point to *gratia*, grace; for God, as in all that is associated with the theological and religious, does not annihilate but rather perfects and fulfills the natural and the human.

Regarding the second category of his lectures, there is something momentous in his breaking with the traditional procedure in the medieval university of always expositing a specific, received text and shifting rather to broad subjects such as the civil power or the prominent issues shaping his day. Such a departure led in 1539 to Vitoria's *De Indis* or *On the American Indians*, the hottest Iberian issue for the early sixteenth century and one that most immediately concerned the legitimacy of Spaniards in the New World.[77]

It is important to appreciate that Vitoria came to his treatment of the Amerindian problem through his own earlier understanding of Aquinas. On Vitoria's effective remobilization of *jus naturale* (natural law) in its subjective sense, the question arises as to whether Aquinas himself entertained such a view that distinguishes between the objective and the subjective understanding of the term. The most prudent assessment finds that the great Scholastic understood by *jus naturale* only "the just thing itself" or "the object of justice," in short, the words in their objective reference. Nevertheless it is impossible to believe that Aquinas was ignorant of the other sense coming down from the twelfth-century Decretists and thus must have deliberately excluded it. Vitoria, however, in response to the apparent pressures within Aquinas's texts, especially on the issue of restitution, seemed driven to elicit from them the term in its subjective sense. More significantly, he was receptive to the canonical tradition subsequent to Jean Gerson, with its understanding of *jus* as a power or faculty for acting.[78] Most recently this issue had been examined exhaustively by the German moral theologian, Conrad Summenhart, who, in material available to Vitoria, defended the view that the terms *jus* and *dominium*, right and ownership, meant the same thing and went on to consider Gerson's *jus* as a liberty, a freedom of action in relation to other persons and things.[79] Vitoria's recovery of and identification with this late medieval tradition, this endowment of *jus* in its subjective sense as a possession, a liberty, now partly clothed in the authority of Aquinas, constituted the crucial link in the rooting of the later modern theory of natural rights with its distinctly medieval canonical origins. Spain's unique experience in the New World now shaped Vitoria's thinking.

In his inquiry Vitoria proceeded to dismantle any claim that emperor or pope might mount in terms of lordship over the world or possession of any sort over Indians. In fact, whatever their apparently inferior intelligence, "before the arrival of the Spaniards these barbarians possessed true dominion both in public and private affairs."[80] Significantly, he resorted to Innocent IV's commentary on Innocent III's judicial determination *Quod super his*, along with Aquinas, to establish that unbelievers in their present state could not be forced to recognize any papal dominion nor be despoiled of their goods on this pretext.[81] It is important to note that at the inception of Europe's exegesis of natural law Vitoria in effect returned to invoking the two original rights Innocent IV had elicited three centuries earlier: the right to property together with the capacity to form one's own government. Having removed all rightful claims to Spanish intrusion upon the Indian, however, Vitoria appealed to one: the *jus peregrinandi*, the right of worldwide commerce or traffic so much in keeping with Dominicans as the Order of Preachers. What allowed the Spaniard ultimately to move from diligent preaching to outright plunder and enslavement could only be the result of the Indians moving from resistance to outright violence, wherein the rights of war would obtain. But had all peaceful means to conversion been exhausted? Vitoria doubted it. In encountering continued, violent resistance to the propagation of the gospel and working for the conversion of the Indians even against their will, the Spanish resort to force may have served only to obstruct rather than encourage conversion; thus some other method was required. Yet Vitoria continued to doubt that such a new practice had been exercised with moderation.[82]

If there had been any question about adherence to *jus* in its subjective, individual sense coming down from Ockham and Gerson and entering the sixteenth century with such significant Scholastics as Jacques Almain and John Mair at Paris, it was certainly to be reaffirmed by the greatest of Vitoria's Scholastic followers, Francisco Suárez, in his *Laws and God the Lawgiver* (1612). In an early chapter entitled "The Meaning of *Jus*," Suárez called for discriminating between the two terms, *jus* and *lex* (law). *Jus* referred to more than just "that which is right," we are told: it also could be used to signify "a certain moral capacity which everyone possesses." *Jus* thus meant not simply rightness but rights. Among them, and innate in humans from their creation, Suárez claimed their ability to institute political communities, completely apart from any special divine act or intervention.[83] And in his further involvement with Britain's James I and the furor over the Oath of Allegiance—fomenting one of the great growth industries in Catholic theology at the beginning of the seventeenth century—he came to assert over James's threatened depredations the right to preserve one's life, a right of self-defense that does not fall short of resisting the prince, even to the ruler's assassination. For when the life of the community as a whole is threatened, then it is legitimate to resort to such extreme measures.[84]

Again in his *De legibus* Suárez provides us with a definition and understanding of humanity now in its objective, collective sense, rather than as a personal virtue. More than just a biological collectivity, humanity came to be perceived as a political and moral community:

> Humankind [*Humanum genus*], howsoever divided into various peoples and kingdoms, always has some measure of unity not only specific but even as it were political and moral, indicating a natural sense of mutual love and compassion [*misericordiae*] that is extended to all, even to strangers and to whatever nation. Wherefore, granted each city, state, or kingdom may be a complete community to itself . . . and remain firm among its members, nonetheless each of them is ever a member in some way belonging to this whole [*huius universi*] as far as it pertains to the human race.[85]

Inaugurated in Spain during the course of the sixteenth century, the revamping of Catholic Scholasticism as it came to northern Europe and most specifically to the Netherlands toward the century's end was to encounter another fateful revival. Christianity had always borne elements of ancient philosophy, perhaps most prominently Platonic, at least with respect to its metaphysics and mysticism. But for ethics and politics Stoicism enjoyed prominence. The great resurgence of Stoicism in the course of the sixteenth and seventeenth centuries has considerable significance not simply for the ethos of the individual Christian and his piety but for natural law as well. For the emerging Iron Age of confessional strife and bloody religious wars, the Age of Confessionalism and Confessionalization, natural law offered a neutral common ground, no matter how dimly resonant its higher cosmopolitanism in an age of emerging territorial states and their rivalries. Although Renaissance philology might provide the intellectual tools for dismantling the happy mythology of a correspondence between Seneca and Saint Paul, "Sancte Seneca, ora pro nobis" (Holy Seneca, pray for us) became common recourse on both sides of confessional divides. Preceding Grotius, yet associated with him, the Dutch humanist Justus Lipsius was responsible for the revival of a specific Stoicism: with his *On Constancy* (*De constantia*) of 1584 and his *Six Books on Politics* (*Politicorum libri sex*) of 1589 running into myriad editions, the influence of the Stoa would pervade the age, becoming the philosophy, even the religion, of educated Europe. This development within Dutch humanism decisively shaped the background of Hugo Grotius.[86] In Lipsius's terse, staccato style one message was coming through, free from all biblical and theological entanglements: Follow reason, curb one's natural instincts.[87]

Among the leading evidence for this conscious revival of Stoicism, beginning toward the end of the sixteenth century and thus providing the intellectual grammar for the young Grotius, was the appearance in 1634–35 of the edition of Marcus Aurelius's *Meditations* by the distinguished humanist

Meric Casaubon. By then in Caroline England, prior to the civil war, the Stoic had reengaged the Christian, Grotian sociableness that had become associated with Christian love; Casaubon presented Marcus as an advocate of a sociable charity, linking charity and sociability in his translation and notes on the Stoic emperor.[88] Nor was this link to Stoicism accidental or transient but continuous and substantive, expressive of a current in contemporary thought that would in its moral philosophy implicitly support and nourish the explicit development of human rights in the early modern period. By the mid-eighteenth century, Adam Smith could quote with approval Marcus Aurelius in his calling all of humanity into that greater community as citizens of the world.[89]

Grotius partook of a Dutch Protestant humanism that was currently receptive to this revised Stoicism. In fact, he would make his own its cardinal principle—that of human sociability, the natural drive of the human creature toward communication and community. Yet he had early to learn to speak to a new world and its audience of an expanding Europe, indicative of greater competitive, consolidated power as its members flexed themselves into new problems of overseas empire and colonialism. Grotius's first legal assignment came in 1604 from the Dutch East Indies Company: he was enjoined to write in defense of the Dutch taking of a Portuguese prize in the East Indies. Only the twelfth chapter of this *De jure praedae* (*The Law of Plunder*) would be published, as *Mare liberum* (*Freedom of the Seas*), and only in 1609, too late to affect the establishment of the Twelve Year Truce with Spain. Yet Grotius had to negotiate with the English in London within two years and again at The Hague in 1613, now arguing almost for the reverse of what he had so eloquently defended in *Mare liberum*. The practicalities of the expanding Dutch maritime interests in the context of the long war against Spain and Portugal were to refine a tough international lawyer. Little wonder that in this transformed world of competitive, expanding states his views on natural rights, law, contract, and property would be drawn away from Vitoria and the Spanish Catholic theologians, yet without entirely forsaking them, into the changed language of imperialistic states and their extra-European interests.[90]

Grotius's great achievement would lie not in political thought but in the field of jurisprudence, in rationalizing and moderating the new system of emerging territorial, dynamic states in Europe. An inevitably politicized theological controversy would fracture his own life as a Calvinist moderate, sending him to life imprisonment from which he would early escape into permanent exile. In Paris he published in 1625 his great *De jure belli ac pacis*. In its prologue or prolegomena we encounter at the outset the author's declaration that the welfare of mankind cries for a comprehensive ordering and correction of that confusion present in respect to law; the need becomes all the greater and more urgent, given the marked lack of restraint prevailing presently within the Christian world to a degree that would shock barbarian peoples regarding the general disrespect for all law divine and human.[91] To this grotesque and most lamentable confusion Grotius's immense erudition and legal talent bring an Erasmian reasonableness and proportionality.

In his resort to the corpus of Roman law, beyond the expressly Stoic element, the Aristotelian, Thomistic, and Spanish scholastic strands play their part. Grotius departs from the Roman lawyers in their belief, shared with the ancient Greek Skeptic Carneades, in defining the natural as that which human beings share with all animals. For Grotius man is an animal, but of a very special sort. In fact humanity is sufficiently different from the bestial: to oppose Carneades's claim that all animate beings seek only their own benefit, presumably at the expense of others, Grotius has recourse to Stoic doctrine.[92] He finds the common characteristic of all humans to be an impelling desire for society (*apetitus societatis*). Furthermore, with the second edition of the *De jure belli*, the *socialitas* of Stoicism would be lengthened by recourse to its notion of *oikeosis*, a fellowship or community with a rational order,[93] for human nature itself is the mother of natural law.[94] Having begun with Cicero and later appealing to an even more explicit Stoic in Chrysippus, Grotius claims that the origin of this law, which makes impossible that man among the animals only seeks his own, could only be that *Jus* of Jupiter himself, despite a lurking presence of self-interest.[95] There intruded the notorious *etiamsi daremus* ("even if we were to suppose") hypothesis—that natural law, the established rational order of things, would pertain and prevail, even if God and his providence did not exist.[96] Nevertheless, God remains, as does the rationality of a theologically neutral law.

In advocating Aristotle's man as a political animal in the larger sense of a totally social being, Grotius derives the informing principle of his understanding of natural law. He finds three meanings conveyed by the critical word *jus*: (1) the Aristotelian-Thomist meaning of that which is just; (2) its rendering as a subjective right whereby "*jus* is a moral quality of a person, enabling him to have or do something justly"; and finally, (3) as a law, "a rule of moral action obliging us to what is right." On the second of these, *jus* conceived as a subjective right, Grotius here picked up on a rich tradition dating from Ockham and Gerson down to the Spanish jurists Suárez and Vázquez.[97]

If rights are derivative from natural law, natural law is itself derivative from human nature in its sociableness. Less evident and more implicit than this overriding moral sense that amounts to a faculty, power, or subjective right are those of self-preservation and of property. More clearly in his earlier *De jure praedae* Grotius states that all such rights pertain to several precepts of the law of nature, that allow for the defense of one's life and the acquisition of useful possessions.[98]

For his own age and its needs, Grotius modernizes and simplifies natural rights by making them more prominently subjective and universal to the human condition, distinguished as a caring for society. Right becomes the faculty of acting with regard to society as a social, rational animal. For Grotius obligation is the defining feature of law. For his younger contemporary, Thomas Hobbes, a more radical modernizer, self-preservation will resoundingly distinguish the new basis of natural right.[99]

The secularization of natural law is usually attributed to Grotius. Yet the famous *etiamsi daremus*, hypothetically posited as a possible condition imagined, suddenly presented a path Grotius never effectively entered upon, with its evacuations of the moral and rational implications of the traditional understanding of natural law. Although in a sense they advance in parallel, Grotius and Hobbes do not share the same horizon.[100] With Hobbes, of course, the path is seized upon and all metaphysical or ontological references or possible attachments are forsaken in order to construct from a new and irreducible basis, found in "The Natural Condition of Mankind," to be identified shortly by Locke as the notorious "state of nature," that Mortal God that distinguishes the new polity of the State in its artificial rather than natural construction (1.13).[101] Hobbes effects a ruthless reduction that inverts the understanding of natural law so radically as to leave its later, great expositor, Otto Gierke, breathless: "Such Natural Law was no law at all: it only sailed under the name of law like a ship under false colors, to conceal the base piratical idea of power."[102] In chapters 14 and 15 of Hobbes's *Leviathan*, the old natural law suffers dissolution in an analysis that distinguishes the single overriding right of nature, "which writers commonly call *jus naturale*," as the preservation of oneself in the war of all against all. The laws of nature become so many precepts "found out by reason," or prudential rules for best effecting that preservation. The two are quite different: Right, *jus*, consists in liberty to do whatever is needed to effect one's preservation, whereas law breathes obligation, duty.[103] After the enumeration of nineteen of these moral theorems, such as justice, gratitude, modesty, equity, and mercy, we are finally informed that these dictates of reason are not laws at all, "but conclusions or theorems concerning what conduceth to the conservation and defense of themselves."[104] Although Hobbes's ruthless inversion and reduction created a new trajectory for the development of natural law, his successors would never be so radical as to forsake entirely the moral and rational overtones of the concept.

Insofar as natural law would survive at all in a changed environment, it would be responsive to human needs and material conditions rather than to grand principles and ideals. Mathematics assists the great departure, bringing a new absolute, a new certainty to human matters—its advent revealed in the new science of natural philosophy. One needs to recall the impact of contemporary science, of Cartesianism and mathematical abstractions, in the mid-seventeenth century. In his *Ethics Demonstrated in the Geometric Manner,* Hobbes's younger contemporary, Baruch Spinoza, certainly carried out his threat that he would treat man's laws and practices mathematically, as so many geometrical solids. For in his effort to reduce all human emotions and ways to the common laws of nature, Spinoza sets out in his preface to part 3 of the *Ethics* his intention of applying as elsewhere the *mos geometricus* (the geometrical practice): "I shall discuss human actions and appetites just as if the inquiry concerned lines, planes, or bodies."[105] Hobbes, a kindred spirit, found the idea appealing in its very abstraction. While rummaging through a private library on his continental tour, he stumbled upon a copy of Euclid and immediately became captive.[106] Euclid afforded him the opportunity to transcend the uncertainty of words and to draw near to the reality of geometrical solids and mathematical uniformities. More largely, Euclid would preside over a new precision in the thinking and language of the period. Natural law became transformed into the natural condition of mankind.[107] Political existence was no longer natural but "artificial" and contractual. The hypothetical, pre-civil condition of man revealed a single right, uniformly present and common to all men—the right to self-preservation. Natural right comes to supplant natural law in the new environment of uniformity. Hobbes's successors retained the vocabulary of natural law, but any sort of organic endowment of the notion of natural law, such as that later evinced by Edmund Burke, was stripped away in the new world of rights in order to advance the abstraction of a basic equality inhering to the human condition.[108] This very equality presents in its universality a uniformity in keeping with the current assumptions of physics regarding the natural world. The motor of this vast process, equality, which would come to reshape the life of the planet, was characterized by the principles of universality and uniformity, and the motor itself was driven by the inexorable logic of these principles. For if the idea of equality has a structure, that structure is such as to effect the universal application of its content. In a way impossible for any idea of freedom, equality lends itself to mathematization in its drive to universality and uniformity.

In the new context of seventeenth-century northern Europe, natural law and rights became transformed. Whatever transcendence natural law seemed to possess in its capacity to obligate as well as to evoke universality would appear evacuated. These positions, insofar as they were recognized at all, came to be occupied by the more subjective side of natural law as being common and universal to all humans. To some extent, with some thinkers such as Hobbes the laws of nature, because they conveyed obligation rather than liberty, were rendered into so many moral theorems for human behavior. The state of nature was devised and advanced as a preparation for the necessity of the civil state, providing thereby a legal fiction not without current references; upon its reductive anvil would be hammered out the minimal absolute rights of the human condition, namely the natural liberty expressed in that single human right to do anything for one's self-preservation.

Though natural law finds its obvious and ready reception as well as its application in the process of the internal consolidation and organization of the territorial state—that is, in individual national, political contexts—we need to consider all this rationalization from a more abstract, Olympian perspective in accordance with how the intellectual enterprise advances through ideas or impulses of universality and equality. The fundamental unity of mankind in one common human nature becomes the prime consideration. The great legacy of our civilization appears to be less in its science and technology and more in the unifying force and challenge, the aspiration to a comprehensive political community that cuts through the myriad instances of localism and tribalism that clutter the geodetic surface. It is this aspiration that has the capacity to transcend the culturally specific in the creation of a world citizenry, if not a world governance.

In its capacity to dissolve the legal and political structures intervening between ruler and subjects, natural law worked to effect the ever-greater consolidation of each of these territorial states toward their becoming the modern national states. Our task here is not to explore the great philosophic systems of the age but to consider those specific thinkers who significantly promoted natural law in terms of natural, human rights, explicated under the modes, or principles, of universality and equality. Here, rights are understood explicitly in reference to the context of the individual absolutist state, and not to a universal commonwealth or single human community. Yet those of the school of natural law always claim for themselves to be dealing with the true nature of human beings, wherever they are on the earth's surface. Any a priori understanding of natural law receded before the more empirical practice announced by Grotius in his Prolegomena to the *De jure belli ac pacis*[109] that "the very nature of man"—at least as perceived—"is the mother of the law of nature"; therein reason itself assumed a less ontological, more interpretive role. In this continuing elucidation of the generic nature of the human, the rising appeal to and evocations of "mankind" had to be tested for their inherent sense of universality as well as of equality.

Samuel Pufendorf assumes importance for the present purpose of understanding the advancement of an idea of a common humanity. His political contribution proved crucial in freeing the civil from any transcendent moral or religious reference and allowing it to breathe in its unimpaired secularity; the political and civil were decisively uncoupled from any moral or religious purposes.[110] He denied the Aristotelian state as nature's vehicle for realizing human virtue, seeing it instead only as an instrument for providing security.[111] Emerging in the decades following the Westphalian settlement (1648) and the hyperactive confessional activities that had produced bloody religious wars, Pufendorf effectively wrote to get the state out of the business of piety and enforced virtue. He claimed that it mattered not to the prince whether his subjects held the same religious belief as himself, so long as they performed their duties as subjects. In probably his most extreme statement, at the end of his life he averred that polytheism, paganism, idolatry, and even devil worship were permissible, if kept within one's thoughts and not expressed in public or outward action.[112] After all, Hobbes had allowed perfect religious freedom within one's own skull just as long as one remained externally in step.

Pufendorf's influence would prove enormous over the next century. That his works captured the attention of the Founding Fathers[113] and, on the other side of the globe, as a political alphabet, informed the Petrine pulpits and academies of the reforming czar[114] suggest his wide extra-European influence; while Madison and Jefferson readily approved the removal of the religious from state purposes and the privatization of religion, the czar delighted in the removal, even subjugation, of the church for the greater freedom of the autocratic state. And, in the more immediate European context, the library of John Locke had a notable number of Pufendorf's works.[115]

In his rise to prominence, Pufendorf became the first to hold a chair in international law as well as in natural law created for him at the University of Heidelberg (1660–63). His range as a jurisconsult expanded over a career that included the role of political and legal councilor at the courts of Sweden (1677–87) and Brandenburg-Prussia (1688–92). His desacralization of law and politics came to be best expressed in his main works, *De jure naturae et gentium* (On the Law of Nature and of Peoples [1672]) and its famous epitome of the following year, *De officio hominis et civis juxta legem naturalem* (On the Office of Man and the Citizen According to Natural Law).[116] In many ways the arena of Pufendorf's philosophical endeavor can be seen as the effort to reconcile Grotius with Hobbes in order to preserve Grotius's sociability as a fact of societies against Hobbes's notion that sociability was simply a pragmatic calculus of the individual. In this endeavor it is worth noting Pufendorf's conscious departure from Aristotelian doctrine for the espousal of Stoicism, which he referred to as a sacred inheritance: in fact, 310 major references to Stoic authors have been noted in his principal work. Whatever his admissions to Hobbes, he never renounced the centrality of promoting and preserving "a peaceful sociableness with others, agreeable to the main end and disposition of the human race in general."[117]

For Pufendorf, natural law was not that law which realized man's essentially sociable nature as a goal, but rather that which consisted of the rules whereof man constructs and imposes sociability on himself as a prudential means of attaining his own security.[118] Such rules are called the laws of nature that come to reinforce and be identified with the current laws of human society. He was both indebted and took exception to Thomas Hobbes. He essentially adhered to an Epicurean view of man's basic animal and primitive traits, but he took issue with Hobbes regarding the nature and operation of the Englishman's construct of the state of nature. In the first place, he saw this state less in terms of perpetual warfare and more as a condition of relative sociability. He understood the process from such a state to that of civil society in terms of two successive contracts, not one. With the first contract one moves from a state of natural liberties to an association of moral individuals. With such a moral relationship established, natural law becomes operative, and state power becomes grounded in contract. The second contract, that of subjection rather than association, amounts to an identifying and defining of specific authority and government. This double process seeks to ensure the moral consent justifying the powers of the sovereign. At a third level, reciprocal commitments occur between a ruling person or assembly and those who have made the choice. Thus, natural law and the law of nations became identified and existing positive laws were read back into the natural law. Pufendorf's understanding of the state of nature served less to remind the ruler of the original rights of subjects—a point that would soon bear correction—and more to induce the people to submission.[119]

Pufendorf reconstructed natural law as a secular civil ethic. In two ways the two agreed: first, the purpose of natural law, sociable existence, was achieved "most fully in the state governed by laws of a civil sovereign"; and second, "the stability and tranquility of the state are enhanced if its citizens act in accordance with the natural law of sociability." Thus, natural laws could be enforced as civil law, thereby closing the gap between natural and positive law; the religious uses of the law were crowded out, for the end of natural law concurred with that of the civil state in realizing security.[120] Through a peaceful sociability natural law became the moral form of natural liberty, whereby natural rights were transformed into correlative natural duties to God and to other men. Such honoring of God pertained little to salvation but served rather as a reinforcement of political and social purposes in emphasizing a fundamental authority. Natural law further prescribed the universal duties of each to oneself that assumed the general form of a more perfect integration of a person into society. The final set pertained to our duties toward one another, as prescribed by natural law—among them that each should recognize the natural equality of men and act accordingly.[121] Man is a social animal less by nature than by prudential choice. His self-love out of a sense of weakness and vulnerability turns to *socialitas,* which derives from this awareness, thereby combining Hobbes and Grotius.[122] Rather than claiming any natural virtue for humans, Pufendorf sought to construct a civil discipline in order to create the good citizen.[123] Despite its important reinforcement of natural law in a secular key, Pufendorf's teaching pertained to the increasingly consolidated territorial states of seventeenth-century Europe. He showed little interest in the development of natural rights as a universal reality, however implicit that application may be; rather, he sought to identify natural law with the existing order of things.

Eighteen years after the initial publication of the *De officio hominis et civis,* its English translation, by Andrew Tooke, appeared in London as *The Whole Duty of Man According to Natural Law.* It had two further editions in 1698 and 1705 before considerable revision and additions in 1716; a fifth edition of 1735 included some of the modifications effected by Jean Barbeyrac for his French version of *The Whole Duty*. The odyssey of the English version reflected the difference in milieu from German princely absolutism to English parliamentarianism, requiring such changes of crucial terms as *state* from *civitas* and *sovereignty* from *summum imperium*.[124] Or again, Tooke's translation speaks of municipal law, rather than Pufendorf's actual imposition of the state, as setting limits to private ownership of property.[125]

It seems not altogether fortuitous that England should provide the political environment to the fateful development of natural rights embedded in natural law. For with its long tradition of the Common Law and the seventeenth-century struggle between king and Parliament, which promoted a sense of political rights vested collectively in Parliament as being the birthright of every Englishman, such developments within a single state's territorial law afforded a most auspicious basis for the decisive promotion of natural rights, now as the fulfillment of the right peculiar to all men. Nevertheless it can be argued with greater validity that the English Common Law tradition represented such a fundamentally different view regarding the law's origin, nature, and development from the hyperrational, almost mathematical features of what natural law had become that together the two appear to confront the observer as polar opposites. As two fundamentally different types of law in a field wherein no third seemed possible, their coexistence during the advance of human rights and liberties would in fact reveal this essential difference at the end of the century and of this inquiry.

A consideration of what has been called the Common Law Mind affords an opportunity at this point to appreciate the radical, revolutionary nature regarding the direction taken by natural law. It has been effectively shown that David Hume, no innocent to the study of law, which preoccupied him from 1725 to 1729, gave philosophical statement to the Common Law especially as represented by Sir Matthew Hale, one of its most distinguished seventeenth-century expositors. Hale conveniently provides us with the image of the Argonauts' ship, which in returning home was perceived to be the same one that had set out, although through successive patchings it actually retained none of its former materials. The metaphor, enunciated by John Selden, pertained to the development of English law over a period of six hundred years. Though seen in the present as immemorial, the law's validity rested not in any immemoriality, nor in any claim to a remote, antique origin, but rather in the fact that it enjoyed present wide acceptance, a shared conviction in the law's continuity. Both Hale and Hume had this sense as well as the medieval belief that law was not made but rather announced or declared. Hume proceeded to construct a view of humans in society as being radically interdependent, implicitly undercutting any abstract individuality. Present society represented the product of a myriad of micronic, complex alterations. Yet such a view, nearer to the nature of Common Law, did not prevent the two systems from interacting, the Common Law experiencing some of the allure of natural law. In the early seventeenth century Sir Edward Coke, England's greatest jurist, manifested interest in Francis Bacon's aspirations to systematize the Common Law. Thus it is hardly surprising that in the mid-eighteenth century, the heyday of natural law, William Blackstone in his famous *Commentaries* talked something of the language of natural law and wrote of reason in a way suggestive of natural reason, but in fact remained true to the Common Law sense of slowly accumulated tradition through which reason runs. The point is, as Edmund Burke would argue, that such "naturalness" and "reasonableness" were immanent in a law that looked to no transcendent source for validation.[126]

In England's seventeenth-century constitutional development, during the venture into republicanism at mid-century, among the Levellers, the most politically articulate group among the radicals, Richard Overton, a Leveller pamphleteer himself, defined property significantly as having elements both egalitarian and universal. His statement has particular interest in the way the Protestant Reformation further intrudes upon our problem:

> To every individual in nature is given an individual property by nature not to be invaded or usurped by any. For every one, as he is himself, so he has a self-propriety, else could he not *be* himself; and of this no second may presume to deprive any of without manifest violation and affront to the very principles of nature and of the rules of equity and justice between man and man. Mine and thine cannot be, except this be. No man has power over my rights and liberties, and I over no man's. I may be but an individual, enjoy my self and my self-propriety and may right myself no more than my self or presume any further; if I do, I am an encroacher and an invader upon another man's right—to which I have no right. For by natural birth all men are equally and alike born to like propriety, liberty and freedom; and as we are delivered of God by the hand of nature into this world, every one with a natural, innate freedom and propriety . . . every man by nature being a king, priest and prophet in his own natural circuit and compass, whereof no second may partake but by deputation, commission, and free consent from him whose natural right and freedom it is.[127]

Though such a radical statement of the individual person as self-property cannot be claimed to have had any direct influence upon the future John Locke, it nevertheless marks a most fateful coming of age in the passage of natural law onto the more practical and manageable track of natural rights. One discovers in England's experiment with republicanism in the 1650s a new, intense interest in natural rights rather than natural law, as evinced in the thinking not only of the Levellers, but also of the Diggers, another radical group of the Interregnum, and the Putney Debates, which would argue the basic rudiments of modern democratic order.[128] Indeed, is it possible that, with the decline of feudal practices and some hierarchical structures in a post-medieval Europe and the centralizing, equalizing, leveling tendencies of the new territorial state, the time had come to make good on and give coherent expression to those rights that had already been adumbrated five hundred years earlier in canon law and later Scholasticism and now more recently reworked by Grotius and Hobbes? And in the England most especially of the Interregnum, the brief advent of republicanism gave abrupt and timely, relevant support to the political incorporation of these rights as a prominent intellectual concern.

One may first turn to the less-read *First Treatise* of Locke for his opposition to the royalist political writer Robert Filmer's *Patriarcha* and its exegesis of Genesis 28. Therein Locke sees the setting of mankind above animal creatures as God's giving "to Man, the whole species of men," dominion over other creatures. In rejecting Filmer's claim that God gave Adam monarchical absolute powers over other men, or sole Property and Private Dominion, Locke instead understands and asserts a confirmation of the original community of all things among the sons of man, thus snapping any further link in the continuance of a private possession that would make Adam proprietor of the whole world and deny all the rest of mankind the materials of life.[129]

In his longest and last chapter of *The First Treatise* "Who Heir?" Locke examines a revealing statement by Filmer (whose actual words are here italicized):

> *Most of the civillest Nations of the Earth, labour to fetch their Original from some of the Sons or Nephews* of Noah, p. 14 [58]. How many do most of the civillest Nations amount to? and who are they? I fear the *Chineses*, a very great and civil People, as well as several other People of the *East, West, North,* and *South,* trouble not themselves much about this matter. All that believe in the Bible, which I believe are our *A[uthor]'s most of the civillest Nations*, must necessarily derive themselves from *Noah*, but for the rest of the World, they think little of his Sons or Nephews. . . . Beyond these they look not, nor consider who they were Heirs to, but look on them as such as raised themselves by their own Virtue to a Degree that would give a Lustre to those, who in future Ages could pretend to derive themselves from them. But if it were *Ogygis, Hercules, Brama, Tamberlain, Pharamond*; nay, if *Jupiter* and *Saturn* were the Names, from whence divers Races of Man, both Ancient and Modern, have labour'd to derive their Original; will that prove that those Men *enjoyed the Lordship of Adam, by right descending to them?* If not, this is but a flourish of our *A's* to mislead his Reader, that in it self signifies nothing.
>
> To as much purpose, is, what he tells us, p. 15 [59] concerning this Division of the World, *That some say it was by lot, and others that* Noah *sail'd round the* Mediterranean *in Ten Years, and divided the World into* Asia, Afric *and* Europe, Portions for his three sons. *America* then, it seems, was left to be his that could catch it.[130]

Locke, in determining what is properly and most immediately one's own, could build upon what Overton had announced as a "self-propriety" and present property in both a general and specific usage. Regarding the former, property is identified with the rights to life, liberty, and estate. More specifically, and more notoriously, it is explicated in terms of this last—estate. Here he engages natural law, the state of nature, and what belongs to all men in a way that permits us to inquire into his understanding of mankind, a term and notion that will increasingly be on the quills of the later eighteenth century. To what extent is it to be understood restrictively to pertain to Adam's inheritance, or does it consciously include other peoples than those readily included among the heirs of Shem as well as even Ham and Japheth? Are other distinctly different organized peoples of the world appearing, quite outside the original Judaic tradition? And, of course, regarding that new continent, it fell to Europe and those Europeans to catch America and establish a European monopoly that produced in the course of the eighteenth century an Atlantic world, which shortly came to displace the long economic and cultural hegemony enjoyed by the civilizations of East Asia.

Locke broke with the Noachic inheritance. Thus, by the time he got to the *Second Treatise*, in a detailed treatment of property Locke could announce most emphatically that God had given the world not to Adam and his inheritance but "to the children of man, given it to Mankind in common," a point to be repeated. Then:

> God, who hath given the World to Men in common, hath also given them reason to make use of it to the best advantage of Life, and convenience. The Earth, and all that is therein, is given to Men for the Support and Comfort of their being. And though all the Fruits it naturally produces, and Beasts it feeds, belong to Mankind in common, as they are produced by the spontaneous hand of Nature; and no body has originally a private Dominion, exclusive of the rest of Mankind, in any of them, as they are thus in their natural state.[131]

Scriptural exegesis must give way to an analysis guided by natural law: that all mankind, common humanity, rather than just Adam and his heirs, had possession both lifted the argument from its Scriptural (tribal) hinges, placing it in a natural-law framework, and gave it a new, true or truer resonance and intent to signify a mankind that extended beyond just the enterprising Europeans.

What did require reiteration and reinforcement was the intention and direction of the analysis that has been pursued. Locke would have to admit to the difficulties in the practicalities of natural rights' application. Continuing in his inquiry into Paternal Power, he states: "Though I have said above, Chap. II, That all men by nature are equal, I cannot be supposed to understand all sorts of Equality." He then admits such determinants as age, virtue, birth, and connections as factors that depart from and complicate that basic, original equality.[132] Locke's hesitations and apparent equivocations were well founded for an age that continued in its fear of King Mob, democracy, and anything like the full implications of equality. Furthermore, a generation earlier James Harrington, the notable political thinker and author of *Oceana,* in his efforts to preserve a balance between aristocratic leadership and popular decision for the creation of an "equal commonwealth," had actually drawn out dimensions of traditional meaning and concern from the bald notion of equality. Harrington's understanding here sought wider without complete participation of most groups, always in the interest of stability and an intricately constituted order. According to a recent astute analysis, Harrington's "equal commonwealth" thus "assumed a society of hierarchical inequality articulated in terms of property, ability, eminence and deference."[133]

In this light it becomes easier to sympathize with Locke's difficulties and to appreciate the dangers of imposing a post-Enlightenment understanding of egalitarianism upon a seventeenth-century context. And yet an inquiry into the foundations of Locke's egalitarianism reveals a sense of morality, law, and religion that transcends the multitude of nagging, obstinate inequalities belonging to seventeenth-century hierarchical society. For a philosopher who would later claim that the removal of God dissolves all, it has been persuasively argued that human equality finds its support in the natural law and morality of Christ's teachings. Locke affirms the certainty that by Jesus Christ a positive, common law from heaven has been provided to all mankind. A basic egalitarianism inheres to his philosophy; moral responsibility and human equality require this elementary theistic premise.[134]

On Locke's hesitant qualifications regarding equality and possible degrees of same, scholarship has noted, in pursuing leads elsewhere in his writings, that simple common sense dictated not all could attain the higher degrees of rationality and consequent accomplishment in which the world had apparently been given over to the industrious and rational.[135] Locke appears to argue for a natural "Preheminency": "but all men seem equal till some one's eminent virtues, or any other advantages," lead to his advancement.[136] In another explanation of the differences in degree and kind, Locke recognized that whatever their natural equality, not all people made proper use of their faculties, thus leaving room for inequalities in performance. For if the law of nature might be known by the light of nature, the latter depended upon individual capacities.[137]

A less charitable and more specific handling of the passage at issue can be found in the monumental study *Adamo e il nuovo mondo*, by Giuliano Gliozzi, whose Marxist eye has ferreted out from the *Essay Concerning Human Understanding* the fleeting observation in the context of the vast variety of species that "there are some Brutes that seem to have as much knowledge and Reason as some that are called men."[138] If Locke cannot be made a "racist" on such slender evidence, nevertheless he seems to qualify for a generation of Englishmen exposed to colonial affairs and prone to making distinctions among the ramifying peoples of the earth now coming into view. What is seen here as an alignment between commercial and slave ideology "typical of bourgeois thought" (*tipica del pensiero borghese*), a discrepancy between law and fact, on a rising tide of racial distinctions and prejudice, admittedly introduces a sour note into the proclamation of universal equality and liberty being pursued by the contemporary school of natural law.

Unquestionably the foundations in the defining of racial distinctions were being laid in the course of the later seventeenth century. Locke's contemporary Sir William Petty, a man of wide curiosity with a cast of mind that invaded new areas, creating new subjects, such as political arithmetic, had in 1676–77 begun to distinguish the races of mankind, differentiating human species as to their capacity for memory, intelligence, judgment, and external senses. He seemed encouraged in such a pursuit by the growing disintegration of the Adamic-monogenetic understanding of human origins in response to the pluralist views of multiple origins most explosively asserted by Giordano Bruno as well as by the more recent pre-Adamite view of human origins offered by La Peyrère.[139] Although himself a monogenetic biblicist, a traditionalist of sorts, who was attempting to be faithful to the account in Genesis, Petty had fatefully created a new division for mankind based upon kinds of humans rather than on nations. Into his scale of calibration, a great chain of being comprising all species, but now in time endowed with progressive change, he introduced the savage.[140] Of giants and dwarfs he hazarded that races of each existed, generations for each of whom the individuals remained unknown. Skirting the pre-Adamite, polygenetic alternatives, Petty advanced a racial distinction that would later mature in Voltaire's aspersion that saw the intellect of the black either as another species or as one much inferior to the European, a distinction that he extended to the indigenous of the New World as opposed to those of the Old. But Petty's entering wedge did not have to wait until 1734 to have its implications recognized and authoritatively aired. As early as April 24, 1684, shortly before Petty's death, a brief essay appeared in the influential *Journal des sçavans*, a French journal and voice for the new scientific learning and culture; probably written by François Bernier, an Indic scholar, the essay charted five races according to their skin colors: (1) the European, which curiously included the Egyptians and the East Indians by understanding their brown color as "accidental"; (2) the African, whose darkness was seen as essential; (3) the Chinese; (4) the Japanese; and (5) the Americans.[141] In the confused yet necessary effort to define and distinguish among the new peoples encountered, Europeans, like peoples of any other civilization, manifested ethnic prejudices which would in a later and different context provide some of the ingredients for racist theory.

In contending with the anomaly of sorts of equality, Locke reveals a central attribute in the development of natural law. The exposition of natural law as it proceeded through the seventeenth and eighteenth centuries had come to pursue a more empirical procedure insofar as it became a continuing elucidation of the generic nature of man—in short, those attributes or qualities that were believed to be common to all peoples. The principles of equality and universality threatened to become the obvious precipitates of that endeavor, Europe's most prominent, each with explosive implications. And although the glib use of the terms *humanity* and *mankind* as a total moral and biological collectivity all too frequently appears in the literature and philosophizing of the eighteenth century, where the great words of rhetoric strain beyond knowledge and actual fact, nevertheless there remains an irreducible element pointing with inexorable logic toward a greater fulfillment in the fundamental unity of humankind and the idea of a common humanity, whatever the embarrassing discrepancies and lapses.

Our civilization's entertainment of the doctrine of natural rights in its universal and egalitarian registers seems doomed to contain the worm of a practical exclusion or an inability to comprehend and include all, despite the implacable logic of the ideal. For nineteenth-century liberalism this exclusionary feature has been progressively identified with a practice of introducing specific, if changing, cultural and psychological conditions as requirements that effectively raise the bar to the otherwise universal inclusion.[142] Yet in a less sophisticated sense, witness the Levellers of the 1650s, who advanced the natural rights of the franchise for all men, yet did not include the women in their very midst, nor servants and beggars.[143] A century later Montesquieu would note that Grotius and Pufendorf failed to extend the same rights to slaves as to freemen.[144] And shortly thereafter, in 1776, a slaveholder society proudly proclaimed that all men are created equal. This self-contradiction and discrepancy between the ideal and the practice, a discrepancy that in the American instance encountered the acid irony of Dr. Johnson, perhaps can best be understood in terms of the marvelous absurdity advanced by George Orwell: that yes, all are equal, but some are more equal than others. Yet increasingly operating over time, the apparent absurdity of this statement and its terrible irony will be drained away by the effective historical reality of an imperfect equality. Given the force and logic of the ideal, an immortal spur upon the conscience, death-transcendent, there would always be someone far down the track who actually takes the principle seriously and is in a position to correct the injustice or move the process nearer to its logical comprehensive inclusion. For thus would Lincoln take the necessary step Jefferson found impossible to take. Yet before that moment Lincoln, speaking prior to his presidency on the Dred Scott decision, would shine some light on our present dilemma:

> I think the authors of that notable instrument [the *Declaration of Independence*] intended to include *all* men, but they did not intend to declare all men equal *in all respects*. They did not mean to say that all were equal in colour, size, intellect, moral development or social capacity. They defined with tolerable distinctness in what respects they did consider all men created equal—"equal in certain inalienable rights, among which are life, liberty and the pursuit of happiness." This they said, and this meant. They did not mean to assert the obvious untruth that all were then actually enjoying that equality, nor yet that they were about to confer it immediately upon them. In fact, they had no power to confer such a boon. They meant simply to declare the right, so that the enforcement of it might follow as fast as circumstances should permit.[145]

Beginning with Locke, one notes the increasing, easy recourse to references to mankind. In this respect Locke can refer to mankind very generally regarding the Ocean as "that great and still remaining common of Mankind,"[146] but again, with the most specific philosophic import, associating it with that very natural right of the individual to his or her self-preservation. For he repeatedly links the preservation of Mankind to the preservation of oneself as integral to the Law of Nature and as incorporated into prime purposes of "Politick Society."[147] The growing practice on the part of contemporary thinkers and *philosophes* to invoke mankind posits the issue of an emerging sense of the expressly human, the human race, the nature of humanity and of the earth's common humanity. The pursuit of natural law itself necessarily commits one to a universalist perspective. Significantly, at the turn of the seventeenth century Giambattista Vico would refer to Grotius as "the jurisconsult of mankind."[148] What precisely was being understood or intended by the word? Did it mean anything more than a reference to all Europeans generally known and immediately present? To what extent did it even specifically include or intend the Chinese, or the Jews, or blacks, or, even more remote and less likely, that other half of humanity, women? Or were the latter to be considered as subsumed under the designation of mankind? In a wonderful statement to the Scottish historian of America, William Robertson, in June 1777 Edmund Burke opened the contemporary door of awareness and of speculation upon the problem. The European engagement of the globe with the diverse peoples of the world was seen as having gone so far that one no longer needed to depend upon rummaging about in history books, for "now the Great Map of Mankind is unrolled at once; and there is no state or gradation of barbarian and no mode of refinement which we have not at the same instant under one view."[149] Certainly by 1800 Asia—meaning, for the most part, the Middle East, India, and China—had succumbed to ordinary human dimensions in the eyes of an increasingly confident, enterprising, expanding Europe. No creditable *philosophe* could theorize regarding man's nature without some judicious reference to the American Indian or the African black.[150]

Because sub-Saharan Africa still remained quite unknown and would continue in Europe's basic ignorance for another century, any notion of a common humanity suffered from reports and experiences regarding the indigenous population as being repugnant not only to European values and sensibilities but also to Europe's own best sense of a single humanity. Indeed, the description of local kinglets, each with the interior of his domicile decorated by skulls, seemed to precede the opposing constructions of Joseph Conrad a century later.[151] As early as 1684, in his article for the *Journal des sçavans*, François Bernier could accept the Amerindian as being of the same species as Europeans, although at an earlier stage of development; but he proved reluctant to accept the black. Nevertheless, whatever the physical differences, he did not himself draw invidious mental distinctions from such variants, nor apply biblical or climatic reasons—practices to which English Protestant travelers since the early seventeenth century had become more accustomed.[152] If the black man belonged in the club, his membership was of an inferior kind. For a human race that was being inevitably defined by Europeans living in temperate latitudes, the climate of Africa seemed to defy the progress of human society.[153] Yet earlier, at mid-century, Jean Jacques Rousseau had claimed, in a most revealing and extended footnote to his *Discourse on the Origin and Foundations of Inequality among Men*, after pressing a sort of preliminary anthropological inquiry that left Voltaire according to his own admission on all fours, that ignorance still prevailed regarding an awareness of the earth's several peoples:

> For the three or four hundred years since the inhabitants of Europe have inundated the other parts of the world, and continually published new collections of voyages and reports, I am persuaded that we know no other men except the Europeans; furthermore, it appears, from the ridiculous prejudices which have not died out even among Men of Letters, that under the pompous name of the study of man everyone does hardly anything except study the men of his country. . . . All of Africa and its numerous inhabitants, as distinctive in character as in color, are still to be examined; the whole of the earth is covered by the Nations of which we know only the names—yet we dabble in judging the human race![154]

Posited at mid-century, 1756, this challenging statement remained essentially true at the century's end. Notwithstanding the aspiration persisted.

In case there had been any doubt after Grotius and Hobbes regarding the new ascendancy of natural rights, the impact of Locke worked to transform the whole issue of natural law into the more immediate issue of natural rights. Locke's understanding of law renounced any view of the law as an objective order of norms from which rights derived; rather, the rights of the individual were prior, and from them resulted whatever order that must follow. The concept of natural law had thus become transformed from some transcendent reality enjoying metaphysical dignity into a political theory committed to a number of political changes.[155] Except for Locke, the English tended to define rights in terms of the traditional rights of Englishmen—the birthrights associated with the liberties of Parliament. It would be first in an American, then in a French context that rights would be redefined in the last third of the eighteenth century in more explosive, even universal terms, potentially accessible to all. The rights included in the British case of the Declaration of Rights (1688) did not attain that fundamental, distinctive level of universality evident in the American instance of the Declaration of Independence.[156]

In France *droit naturel*, as with the Latin *jus naturale*, had the meaning of both natural law and natural right. In fact Bishop Bossuet, Louis XIV's mouthpiece on such matters, conformed natural right to the manner in which the soul went to heaven. In the course of the eighteenth century the Enlightenment usage came to reflect a right given by nature and thus applicable to all men.[157] Denis Diderot, in his *Encyclopédie* article on natural law (1755), saw man as being endowed with a natural right to everything that was not disputed by the rest of the species. He proceeded to align the individual with the general will that bespeaks the public interest. His exhortation to repeat to oneself, "I am a man and I have no other true inalienable rights than those of humanity," breathes the wonderful poetry of the Roman playwright Terence two thousand years earlier in his much-quoted "Nothing human is alien to me."[158] In each instance towered the firm recognition of a common humanness in an all-inclusive humanity, but during the interim humanity had been reconstructed in terms of universally held human rights. Diderot's article affirmed natural law as a familiar idea on account of its basis in reason and common human feeling and proceeded to represent the general will not only as the foundation of social and political duties, but as the source for determining natural rights.[159]

The universality distinguishing the late eighteenth century's program of human rights was not lost to contemporaries on both sides of the Atlantic. The Virginia Bill of Rights, itself a model for those of other American states, and the Declaration of Independence asserted the rights of all men, not just Virginians or Americans. Copies of the new constitutions of those American states soon became current in France; as early as 1778 their French translation, with a dedication to Benjamin Franklin, had appeared in Switzerland, followed by another at Franklin's own initiative in 1783.[160] Such materials were available to the marquis de Lafayette, close friend of Jefferson and participant in the American upheaval, who provided the impetus for a similar move, expressive of universal human rights, but now on the European continent. On July 11, 1789, in an Estates General transformed into the National Assembly, Lafayette advanced the first proposal for a declaration of rights as preamble to a comprehensive constitution for France. At a most national turning point, the dynamics of the moment, consciously transcending all earthly parochialism, nevertheless drove toward the universality of statement. According to the exhortation of the duke Mathieu de Montmorency, "[The Americans] have set a great example in the new hemisphere;

let us give one to the universe." Thus, in keeping with the American precedent, the French Declaration of the Rights of Man and the Citizen reaffirmed the intention of universality in the language of "the natural, inalienable and sacred rights of man."[161]

In the European reception of the declarations and their respective revolutions, the Germanies presented notable instances of their meaning. The leading political publicist, A. L. Schlözer, in 1791 hailed the French declaration, despite its lapses, as "the codex of all European humanity through universal civilization now nearing its maturity."[162] Immanuel Kant, the preeminent heavyweight among European thinkers, a philosopher who would never entirely renounce his hopes for and adherence to the French Revolution, allowed its moral and juristic impact in 1793 to drive his political and ethical thinking to a new level of pronouncement. Thus, men's civil condition he claimed to be based a priori on three principles without which the establishment of no state is possible. Regarding the first, freedom, none can be coerced by another into an alien form of happiness, but each may seek that happiness according to his own lights. Here Kant could draw upon the rich development of eighteenth-century European thinking, specifically Christian Thomasius on the new passion of happiness, without having to have recourse to Jefferson's significant replacement of Locke's third inherent right, estate, with a pursuit of happiness. Regarding the second principle, equality, "each member of a commonwealth has coercive rights against every other . . . and is subjected to coercive right equally with all the other members of the commonwealth." The third principle, independence, in which every member of the commonwealth is conceived as a citizen subject to law, seemed now to reinforce politically the other two.[163]

Not only for his principle of freedom but even more so for the massive drive of his philosophy, and most especially his ethics, toward universality, Kant provides the necessary conclusion to an inquiry pertaining to the early modern period that addresses the globalization of mankind and, more largely, the universalizing principle and progress that distinguishes our civilization. Schlözer's statement, quoted here, speaks of a maturing of a European humanity (*europäische Menschheit*) and betrays the faulting, the incompleteness in the principle's realization. But up to Kant and along the way, hints abound as to a necessary breaking out from this narrow encampment and realizing a more total, comprehensive view of humankind where not only in France Protestants and Jews were included in 1791 but even, *mirabile dictu,* women would be considered for full entry into the club.[164] Regarding the extra-European populations of the earth, they remained in a condition, with shifting degrees, of what can be referred to as unequal equality. With Kant, however, a new effort prevailed to plumb the depths of human universality in the elaboration of his ethics. Perhaps the most notable and certainly the most immediately understood idea deriving from his *Groundwork of the Metaphysics of Morals* was the categorical imperative: "Act as if the maxim of your action were to become by your will a universal law of nature";[165] or, restated, "Act in accordance with maxims that can at the same time have as their object themselves as universal laws of nature."[166]

In his *Toward Perpetual Peace,* Kant presented a picture of empty or inhospitable spaces of the earth's surface and its peoples being reassembled into an ever more consolidated network of inevitably economic and political, commercial and cultural interaction, yet not without injustices. In what would appear to be the fulfillment of Macrobius's and Ramusio's dreams, ultimately distant parts of the world would be brought into relationship with one another and thus "bring the human race ever closer to a cosmopolitan constitution."[167] Nature here became quietly aligned, even informed with a sort of providence, in that Kant, by endowing nature with purpose, claimed it had provided that all the surfaces of the world be inhabited; that by war people had been driven everywhere, settling even in the most inhospitable places; and that again by war they had been compelled to enter into more or less lawful relations productive of an increasing connectedness and extension of habitability.[168] This curious association of providence with nature, which strikes any reader of Kant's political writings, has been perceptively identified with a characteristic Stoic notion of nature's providential design wherein Kant consciously sought the support of Stoic providential religion.[169] Continuing to endow nature with purpose and intent, Kant made war the agent of closer connections, especially with remote peoples; yet, even in his semi-anthropological sweep, war served as the instrument first for populating otherwise deserted spaces and in its wake promoting the need for the constraint provided by public laws. Kant urged an assemblage of nations, each with republican constitutions, although he admitted the difficulties of constituting a republican government, even perhaps requiring angels rather than humans for its realization.[170] The unlikelihood of angels in politics reminds one of the healthy skepticism of republican statesmen who had just completed their work of constructing a new nation across the Atlantic Ocean.

Kant conveys the awareness of a vast, comprehensive movement harbored by Europe, pressing outward to embrace and construct the rest of the world in an association of constitutional republics for the nurturing and support of human rationality and moral community. Here in an extended footnote he attempts to define that veritable motor of this comprehensive process by identifying a mechanism of nature, understood largely in terms of human rationality and moral endowment (*Sinnenwesen*), with a divine providence, a divine *concursus*, even enlisting Augustine's *providential conditrix* as a predetermining cause. God is mentioned later in this passage. But if we ask ourselves the hard question whether this process is to be understood as immanent, its own endowment driving it to a greater development, or as outwardly guided by some external providential agent, the answer would have to be the former—that this cosmopolitan movement of global application is immanent.[171] For ultimately in his imparting of this global vision, the actual motor would appear to be human nature itself as defined over a decade earlier in its being inwardly conflicted, agonistic in its individualistic yet socializing instincts.[172] Kant best expresses the accumulated energies of this Europe, which he refers to as "our continent" (*unseres Weltteils*) over against others, toward which it ambivalently extends itself, potentially in initial violence, for later harmony.[173] At its best this expansion purports to define a process of ultimate meaning for the world, tenuously constructed in terms of an admittedly unstable association of constitutional republics to achieve what has nicely been described as "a growing moral community made up by the humanity of all human beings."[174] In that it pertains to an achievement of the entire human species Kant here reiterates what Dante had adumbrated five hundred years earlier in his notion of *humana civilitas*.[175]

Despite differences of language and religion, with increasing commerce and the experience of greater agreement in principles an equilibrium of lively competition would prevail. Interestingly, Kant specifically rejected universal monarchy, whose very overextension leads to the extinction of law.[176] Only a practice based on the empirical principles of human nature could provide a sound political edifice built on the maxims derived therein, one that couples a concept of right with politics.[177] Somewhat irreverently, he enjoined, "Seek ye first the kingdom of pure practical reason and its justice, and your end (the blessing of perpetual peace) will come to you of itself."[178] He saw the course of world events as justifying this nature-based providence, wherein, despite terrible setbacks, yet with the moral principle in corrupt men never extinguished and with reason building upon the advance of civilization, the process established rightful ideas and legal principles.[179] Nevertheless, Kant is willing to confront and admit the injustices, even horrors, of European expansion.[180] He offered the nice proposition, painfully relevant, as the transcendent formula of public right: "All actions relating to the rights of others are wrong if their maxim is incompatible with publicity."[181]

Kant was sufficiently the tough realist to recognize that such a principle, when applied to the international sphere of cosmopolitan right, proved incompatible, thereby revealing the inherent disagreement of politics and morals. Yet elsewhere he carried his hope further. In his "On the Common Saying" of 1793, he had already enunciated "that from nature, or rather from providence since supreme wisdom is required . . . can we expect an outcome that is directed to the whole and from it to the parts."[182] In the *Metaphysics of Morals* (1797) he admitted that perpetual peace, the ultimate goal of the whole right or legal component of nations, was actually an unachievable idea, but the continual approximation to it is not.[183] And finally, in the *Strife of the Faculties*, to his old question—Is the human race constantly progressing?—he affirmed this idea of a sustained moral and legal effort at approximation. He concluded the work with a prophetic history of humanity, wherein he proposed "that there must be something moral, which reason presents as pure; but because of its great and epoch-making influence, reason must present it as the acknowledged duty of the human soul, concerning mankind as a whole [*non singularum, sed universarum*]."[184] A further proposition, practically commendable, defied all skeptics:

> The human race has always been in progress toward the better and will continue to be so henceforth. To him who does not consider what happens in just some one nation but also has regard to the whole scope of all the peoples on earth who will gradually come to participate in progress, this reveals the prospect of an immeasurable time.[185]

And then his final statement in this late work: "the painful consequence of the present war can compel the political prophet to confess a very imminent turn of humanity toward the better that is even now in prospect."[186]

Kant's former student Johann Gottfried Herder, in his *Ideen zur Philosophie der Geschichte der Menschheit* (1784–91), pursued many issues current at the end of the eighteenth century: nation, race, humanity, humankind, civilization, Europe. In turning away from the cosmological reflections and historicophilosophical generalities of his masterpiece's first six books,[187] Herder began book 7 by disposing of race as an instrument for distinguishing the human species. He preferred nation as a more effective concept, each nation being conceived as one people. Given the sense of identity and uniqueness presented here and elsewhere in his total work during a period of rising national consciousness and the formation of nations, it is hardly surprising that Herder's influence became identified with a new particularism. Yet in advancing the reality of the *Volk,* he never lost sight of the *Einheit des Menschengeschlechts,* the unity of the human species.[188] Indeed, he found particularism and universalism to be so closely associated as to constitute a peculiar synthesis.[189] Wary of the cosmopolitan worldview that all too often serves as a pretext for exporting one's own views, Herder understood by *Menschheit* all human beings collectively, by *Humanität* the moral ends to which all humans need to aspire and which are not yet formed. Admitting variety and diversity, he found the ties of humanity that constitute bonds of sociability intrinsic to the human condition. He imputed a rational sociability to human nature. In fact, he here invented the term *Einfühlung*, whence the English *empathy*, to suggest this sympathetic identification among humans, capable of transcending cultural barriers of apparent difference and commiserating with one's fellow human beings *as* human.[190] This understanding of humanity moves in the register of the moral and subjective as an ideal that he defined as reason and equity in all conditions. The human race was conceived as proceeding through various stages of civilization (*Kultur*), with reason (*Vernunft*) and equity (*Billigkeit*) as their enduring reality.[191] In this internal disposition to regard humanity as being as universal as human nature itself,[192] Herder seemed to resolve the ambiguity inherent in the Latin term *humanitas*, understood subjectively as a universal moral capacity common to all humans, but also understood objectively as a comprehensive biological collectivity: the sense of humanity insofar as it informs all human creatures both creates and reinforces the unity of humankind as a single moral and biological collectivity.

Pursuant to Kant's dark observation in *Toward Perpetual Peace* that a whole continent feeling itself superior to another one would not hesitate to plunder or actually impose its rule,[193] Herder himself sensed the expansionist forces of his age that were moving toward the Europeanization of the world. Similarly, in his own understanding of this event, Providence and Nature were associated, becoming cooperative.

> [Providence] has wonderfully separated nations, not only by woods and mountains, seas and deserts, rivers and climates, but more particularly by languages, inclinations, and characters; that the work of subjugating despotism might be rendered more difficult, that all the four quarters of the Globe might not be crammed into

> the belly of a wooden horse. No Nimrod has yet been able to drive all the inhabitants of the World into one park for himself and his successors; and though it has been for centuries the object of united Europe, to erect herself into a despot, compelling all the nations of the Earth to be happy in her way, this happiness-dispensing deity is yet far from having obtained her end. . . . Ye men of all the quarters of the Globe, who have perished in the lapse of ages, ye have not lived and enriched the Earth with your ashes, that at the end of time your posterity should be made happy by European civilization: is not a proud thought of this kind treason against the majesty of Nature?[194]

Noble words. Noble thoughts. And yet is not the very capacity for self-criticism and review a thoroughly European attribute, as are the insatiable curiosity, the restlessness, the drive to reduce the entire planet to a complete knowledge, a total use that Herder now imputes mistakenly to all humans, to humankind in general, in his universalizing efforts?

> [M]en must learn to know one another; for collectively they are but one family, on one planet of no great extent. It is a melancholy reflection, that every where they first learned to know one another as enemies, and beheld each other with astonishment as so many wolves. . . . Man, while he continues man, will not cease from wandering over his planet, till it is completely known to him: from this neither storms nor shipwreck, nor those vast mountains of ice, nor all the perils of either pole, will deter him; no more than they have deterred him from the first most difficult attempts, even when navigation was very defective. The incentive to all these enterprises lies in his own breast, lies in man's nature. Curiosity, and the insatiable desire of wealth, fame, discovery, and increase

> of strength, and even new wants and discontents, inseparable from the present course of things, will impel him; and they by whom dangers have been surmounted in former times, his celebrated and successful predecessors, will animate him. Thus the will of providence will be promoted both by good and bad incentives, till man knows and acts upon the whole of his species. To him the Earth is given; and he will not desist, till it is wholly his own, at least as far as regards knowledge and use. Are we not already ashamed, that one hemisphere of our planet remained for so long a time as unknown to us, as if it had been the other side of the Moon?[195]

For an analysis of natural law and human rights that seeks to penetrate to the very vortex of the revolutions at the century's end, Thomas Paine affords a suitable conclusion and assessment to the present effort. A man without any formal education, a common man writing for the common man, Paine is truly remarkable. His *Rights of Man*, Part 1, published in 1791 as a refutation of Edmund Burke's *Reflections on the Revolution in France*, and Part 2, appearing in February 1792[196] as a radical revamping of the English tax system, qualified its author for expulsion from England, later election to the National Convention in France, and then a year's imprisonment under the shadow of the guillotine during the heyday of Robespierre. His *Rights of Man* achieved in many ways a transformation of political language in the interests of a deeper understanding of human rights. Constitution, revolution, toleration, civilization—each attains a new level of resonance, not always to be maintained. Although richer in biblical references than Burke,[197] Paine strove to be deliberately unsectarian in rooting the rights of man in the creation of man itself. Only the abruption of upstart governments, presumptuously intervening to unmake man, had disrupted the succession of generations.[198]

He claimed that every account of the creation, if differing in particulars, agreed on one point: "the unity of man; by which I mean, that men are all of one degree, and consequently that all men are born equal and with equal natural rights, in the same manner as if posterity had been continued by creation instead of generation."[199] Something very important and absolutely fundamental to Paine's whole position, especially over against Burke, is occurring here: somehow history as the experience of generations must be circumvented so that each of us may have the original experience of Creation—no matter how mathematical! Thus, at the outset, doctrinal succession, inevitably historical (for the word belongs to the present author, not to Paine), stands opposed to an original, natural condition not always recoverable in time. This overwhelming sense of the immediacy and directness of equality in natural human rights was surpassed only by his sense of the enormity of despotic intervention everywhere effected—except in France.

Part 1 became an extended refutation of Burke's judgment on the French Revolution, which leads at one point to a comparison of the constitution of France with that of the English. To Paine a constitution was antecedent to a government, which was always the creature of its constitution. It provided for the total organization of civil government, its actions, its limits.[200] Such a view imparted a specific statement of rights, whereas the English version was an expression in historical time of hereditary succession and the despotism of government interventions that had arisen repeatedly ever since the Norman Conquest, wherein despotism is understood as the preclusion of consent. Rather than emerging out of society, constitution, subject to constant modifications, emerged over the people, constantly constituting its own process and becoming the cant word of Parliament. Because the present people of England did not make the government, by a constitutional reformation similar to that in France, it should come into their hands.[201] Here Paine's attack upon the English conception of constitution is reminiscent of its very advocacy, earlier, by Hale and Hume, when each recognized that England had indeed seen several different constitutions since pre-Norman times.[202]

Whereas revolutions heretofore merely registered local changes, now with those in America and France the word signifies for Paine "a renovation of the natural order of things, a system of principles as universal as truth and the existence of man"—in effect, a recovery of the Creation. The second of his three principles warrants quotation: "the end of all political associations is the preservation of the natural and imprescriptable rights of man; and these rights are liberty, property, security and resistance of oppression."[203] In its new dignity, revolution signifies a regeneration of man.[204]

More arresting is Paine's understanding of the charmed term *toleration*, which figures in the currents of human rights:

> Toleration is not the *opposite* of Intolerance, but it is the *counterfeit* of it. Both are despotisms. The one assumes to itself the right of with-holding Liberty of Conscience, and the other of granting it. The one is the pope armed with fire and faggot, and the other is the pope selling or granting indulgences. The former is church and state, and the latter is church and traffic.[205]

In fact, the young James Madison had preceded Paine on the inadequacies of the idea of toleration. Most fatefully, he departed in this one respect from George Mason's draft of article 16 of the Virginia Bill of Rights of 1776, which was to provide the model for all later bills of rights. Madison struck out the word toleration and rooted religious liberty in the very nature of man as a right of human conscience. The point is important: toleration suggested the granting of a privilege, a civil right, by a superior to an inferior, and was thus revocable; rather than a benevolence, it now became something inalienable, in the very "nature of things," an imperative endowment.[206]

Paine's agitation of the term *civilization* demonstrates how it had come into a broader parlance in the closing decades of the eighteenth century. He credits civilization with being, if not yet the total cultural and institutional framework of a people, at least something more comprehensive and objective than simply good manners, refinement, *politesse*. He sees it as an extension and fulfillment of society, made possible by man as being so naturally a creature of society. It provides a sort of internal gyroscope that takes over when government is in abeyance, as was evident to Paine in many American states for a few years at the beginning of the Revolution. From this belief he hazarded the notion, dear to the early nineteenth-century liberal, that the more perfect civilization is, the less need has it for government, because the more it regulates its own affairs and government itself.[207] Except for France, all European governments were constructed not upon the principle of "universal civilization," but rather had ingrafted their barbarism, especially in the form of financial oppression of the poor, upon "the internal civilization" of a country, thereby creating the prevailing condition of "uncivilization." The mutual expense of perpetual warfare among the nations of Europe prevented the general felicity associated with civilization.[208]

Continuing his thoughts further on this issue, Paine saw revolutions as bringing about a change in the moral condition of a government, with the consequence of a more equitable public tax system, to the benefit of a civilization marked by abundance. Venturing into the field of commerce, he identified himself as a friend of its effects: in short, "it is a pacific system, operating to cordialize mankind by rendering nations, as well as individuals, useful to each other."[209] Though the statement by no means exhausts Paine's understanding of commerce, it marks the possible minting of a neologism, *to cor-*

dialize, quite unrecognized by Webster, and with only a single and later example (1817) being cited by the *Oxford English Dictionary.*

For all its awkwardness, even barbarism, the idea of "the cordialization of mankind," which presumed in all their precariousness the universality of human rights and the extension of civilization, marked the telos of Paine's argument as well as that of the present inquiry.

Chapter 3

The Emergence of Politically Constituted Dissent in the European World

The exercise of arbitrary power is least possible, not in a democracy, but in a very complicated form of government. The philosophy of "checks" has become a little old-fashioned, and the modern protest against it was timely. Checks cannot be created *e nihilo*, they cannot be transplanted to foreign lands—they are only valuable when they are the outcome of opinions of right; but when all has been said on the other side, the fact remains that we owe our freedom from arbitrary restraints to that elaborate constitutional theory into which our opinions of right have, through long ages, been crystallizing.

—Frederic William Maitland, *A Historical Sketch of Liberty and Equality* (2000)

I confess that I am not satisfied with the Constitutions which have hitherto been formed by the different States of America. It is with reason that you reproach the State of Pennsylvania with exacting a religious test from those who become members of the body of Representatives. There are much worse tests in the States; and there is one (I believe the Jerseys) which requires a declaration of faith in the *Divinity* of Jesus Christ—I observe that by most of them the customs of England are imitated, without any particular motive. Instead of

> collecting all authority into one center, that of the nation, they have established different bodies; a body of representatives, a council, and a Governor, because there is in England a House of Commons, a House of Lords, and a King. They endeavor to balance these different powers, as if this equilibrium, which in *England* may be a necessary check to enormous influence of royalty, could be of any use in Republics founded upon the equality of all Citizens. . . .
>
> It is impossible not to wish ardently that this people may attain to all the prosperity of which they are capable. They are the *hope* of the world [*genre humain*]. They may become a *model* to it. . . . I wish indeed that the blood which has been spilt, and which will continue for some time to be spilt in this contest, may not be without its use to the human race.
>
> —M. Turgot to Dr. Richard Price, March 22, 1778

Although the idea of a common humanity pertains properly to intellectual history, even the history of ideas, the creation of constitutional democracy, with its necessary recognition of dissent, faction, and division, belongs more to the contingencies of political history as the expression and experience of a practical principle. Broadly, however, it returns to the fold of intellectual history, not as a distinct idea but as drawing upon law and contemporary political thought in the tensions and debates of the age. This peculiar use of dissent remains a contingency of the European historical development but is limited here in its original and proper definition to the English and American experience, both peoples enjoying a protective isolation for a critical period. This last of our three unique developments characterizing Western civilization presents immense conceptual difficulties and provides us with the present problem here: the definition and historical emergence of institutions, practices, and habits of mind in which conflict—dissent—is not only admitted and recognized but positively constructed for the survival and amelioration of society.

Perhaps the most immediately notable example of this third principal strand of the Western exception is the idea of His Majesty's [Most Loyal] Opposition. It manages abruptly to bring into focus the modern constitutional democracy, wherein the practice is not to imprison, exile, or exterminate one's opponent, but rather to integrate such opposition into a system of ongoing constitutionalized criticism and control that inevitably modifies the brunt of the temporary majority. The "immediate purpose of opposition criticism is to check, prevent, and rectify any abuses of which government may be guilty."[1] Although the actual term does not seem to have been used until 1826—and then, as with so much else English, in a moment of absentmindedness—it points up a long, tenuous, and uniquely insular parliamentary development that culminated in the eighteenth century.

Yet the culture of self-criticism has a deeper root in Plato's dialogues, medieval Scholasticism, the growth of philosophical skepticism, and the first shoots of toleration, which appeared in the early modern period. Even more prominently, a unique and quite distinctive feature operative from the beginnings of Western civilization is the twofold jurisdiction, spiritual and temporal, of ecclesiastical authority and secular power, in tense and tenuous accord. This is evident with Saint Augustine but definitely enunciated by Pope Gelasius I in 494: the moral/spiritual authority (*auctoritas*) of the bishops and the political power (*potestas*) of kings that presented the first defining and delimitation of the secular. Although during the next thousand years the spiritual realm achieved an ideal legal unity in a veritable reconstitution of the Roman Empire (now, in ecclesiastical guise, the Medieval Church), the secular, political realm was shaped by the *Völkerwanderungen*, the migrations of peoples, that brought down the former Roman Empire and constituted the emerging nations of Europe. By the time of the High Renaissance, after 1500, the notion that came to dominate European political life was that of universal monarchy, which actually referred to the predominance of one power, in this instance the Habsburg emperor Charles V and his son Philip II. Associated with a declining Spanish *monarquía*, the term "universal monarchy" lingered on, used less as a reality in the seventeenth century and more as a propagandistic flail to swat the threatened predominance of a neighboring state.[2] Yet, as late as 1734, Montesquieu understood Louis XIV in these terms.[3] A new principle for political conceptualization, long in the making and derived from Renaissance Italy, had come to prevail for all Europe in the eighteenth century: the balance of power among a congeries of states. So long as European weaponry remained relatively limited and unsophisticated, the intrinsic feuding and competition between European states would serve to bear out Hume's happy assessment that such rivalry, in the form of "emulation," would prove more stimulating and constructive than destructive, even suicidal.[4] The question remained, and remains still: to what extent could dissent, the recognition of diverse parts and parties, be admitted within these ever more consolidated political units, the states of modern Europe?

This question is one of measuring and accounting for a civilization that has come not only to admit but even to court the realities of difference, diversity, pluralism, and fragmentation. This effort, imperfectly and inadequately cultivated but furthered by what later developed as a relatively free press, the process of judicial review, and respect for the rights of the minority, collectively constitutes the present arena of self-criticism and review.

Although respect for the relative, the probable, and the subjective characterizes and informs the modern mentality and all have a clear beginning in Europe's early modern period, the cultural realization and actual institutionalizing of these elements had to await the Enlightenment, the French Revolution, and nineteenth-century liberalism. Our problem more narrowly becomes one of determining what the early modern period, 1500–1800, contributed to the unique Western capacity for contending constructively with the facts of division, diversity, and dissent. Because dissent as a fundamental principle has been authoritatively associated with Protestantism, the answer seems to begin with the Reformation, and most specifically with Martin Luther at Worms.[5] For it was the Protestant Reformation that delivered to this medieval world the decisive and necessary blow—decisive and necessary in that the expression of dissent needed to be theological and religious in nature, with broad ecclesiastical implications, if it was to prove effective and resonant in a still comprehensive society, theologically shaped, religiously penetrated, and ecclesiastically constructed.

In this inquiry into the emerging European practice of politics in a post-Hobbesian world and its exceptional features, one leaves behind Plato and the Stoics, the classics and their recovery in the Renaissance, in order to enter upon the new, unique world of the Western experience shaped by the Gelasian principle with its preliminary definition of the secular; the firm, continuous development of law; and the sanctity of the individual. As with the previous chapter and its issue, our inquiry comprises a period running from the Reformation to the French Revolution. In a memorial written in 1791, the year following his *Reflections*, Edmund Burke saw a certain bracketing of the European experience effected by the two movements. Each he recognized as a "Revolution of doctrine and theoretic dogma"—in short, ideological before the appearance of the term, thereby promoting proselytism and faction and "introduc[ing] other interests into all countries, than those which arose from their locality and natural circumstances." In fact the trajectory of "Justification by Faith or by Works" had barely exhausted itself before the new infection, "the French Rights of Man," and its leveling sovereignty would convulse Europe.[6]

The Initial Constituting of Political Dissent: Thomas More's Horrific Vision

The actions of Luther's friends, the accusations of his enemies, and succeeding ages have understood his expression of conscience—his Great Witness at Worms—in the context of the triumph of private judgment. Such was not Luther's understanding at all. He did not conceive of conscience as free-floating and autonomous but claimed his own to be bound to the objective authority of the Word of God. He never gave conscience any autonomous authority in determining the meaning of Christian faith.[7] In other words, he constructed a new, different framework for it from that of the medieval church and its broad consensus. He claimed for this new authority that it was objective and immediately perceptive to all. The difficulty arose from the fact that his own interpretation of scripture was neither objective nor absolute—there proved to be many others. Luther's own special linking of conscience with the Word of God—no matter how splendidly understood and laid bare by him—gave rise almost immediately to divergent interpretations. In the process, however, Luther had created the critical and prophetic principle of Protestantism, derived and recovered from the Hebrew prophets, that nothing in this world can claim for itself an inherently divine sanction.

After the Edict of Worms in 1521, the story of the Reformation became one of continuous dissent, from which the West has never turned back. Later perceptions of Luther's Witness increasingly dissociated the act of defiance from its specifically religious or doctrinal commitment. And though there is no direct path from Luther's captive conscience to modern private judgment, the subsequent fragmentation of religious life and interpretation, the rationalizing and secularizing forces, all brought the apparent authority and sanctity of private judgment into being in a way Luther would neither recognize nor sanction. Within a decade a number of exotic sects had proliferated, including two new major expressions of Christianity: Lutheranism and Zwinglianism.

But how and where do we encounter the effort to construct the coexistence of dissenting groups? Consider a statement from one who had earlier established his credentials as a leading Christian humanist. For ten years he had been embroiled in savage polemic and theological controversy in the service of Catholic prosecution of heretics, and within less than three years of this statement he suffered martyrdom for his traditional Christian faith:

> And yet, son Roper, I pray God, that some of us, high as we seem to sit upon the mountains treading heretics under our feet like ants, live not in the day that we gladly would wish to be at a league and composition with them to let them have their churches quietly to themselves, so that they would be content to let us have ours quietly to ourselves.[8]

Thomas More's statement, as reported by his son-in-law, William Roper, throws into relief the unraveling of a hierarchically organized unity into a community founded upon the coexistence of differing churches, apparently defanged by religious pluralism, doctrinal indifference, disestablishment, and tolerance. More's terrible vision bespoke the total subversion of the entire thousand-year-old traditional order in which compulsory religious uniformity was conceived as absolutely essential to social and political stability. It has been said that to early modern Europe pluralism was unacceptable—certainly a modest understatement.[9] Ever since the closing decades of the fourth century, when the late Roman emperors made Christianity the one religion of the empire, religious unity came to be considered the necessary foundation for political unity, ethical behavior, and social order.

Reeling backward in horror and disgust, More projected forward almost five centuries to our own day, to that religious neutrality that has made possible liberal democracy and the secular, sovereign state. Enunciated at the beginning of what became more than one hundred years of bloody religious strife, the former Lord Chancellor identified the *telos* and the long-range meaning of the whole event of the Reformation: that the truly revolutionary import of the movement was to be found less in the ambiguous workings of the newly heightened evangelical conscience and the new depths of the individual human's complexity—real enough though they were—than in the enforced departure from at least a formal unity and the creation of that nasty, unwanted context of rival confessional camps, of churchlets equally Constantinean—the coexistence of opposites. From the perspective of confessionalization the period of religious wars can be seen more positively as affording Europe a unique experience in the horrors of religious fundamentalism; under the operative pressures of practical necessity the Reformation in its course and effect reluctantly provided the primordial experience of a constituted dissent. It was neither in the England of the Clarendon Code and emerging Dissent, nor in that France moving toward the

Revocation of the Edict of Nantes, that one might discover the establishment of a functional ecclesiastical parity and the balanced coexistence of opposing groups. Rather, it was in the Germanies, with the Augsburg settlement of 1555, that one first finds the coexistence of two, then three religious groups dissenting from each other, all within a constructed order, strengthened over time by the rising tide of skepticism, toleration, and the appeal to a natural law.

Somehow the scene had radically changed: what for an entire millennium had been the most necessary constitutive and unifying force—religion—had become the social and political order's most divisive and destabilizing threat. The emerging problem had to be addressed.

Among the most prominent in the required rethinking of political order was the Dutch humanist Hugo Grotius, who obliquely advanced our understanding of this thorny problem of religious pluralism and the coexistence of dissenting groups: obliquely, because Grotius was really less an apostle of toleration as coexistence than an advocate of a broad assimilation—*concordia* or consensus—by means of irenic practices and the deliberate ignoring of the most critical doctrinal differences.[10] His well-known work on this subject is the *De veritate religionis christianae* (On the Truth of Christian Religion) of 1622. However, in a work written in 1611 but discovered only in 1984 and published in 1988, he presented what amounts to being the first exposition of his broad religious persuasion. In advocating a *concordia* not significantly different from the irenic practices charted by that preeminent Christian humanist Desiderius Erasmus almost a century earlier, Grotius nevertheless appealed to a historical condition that represented not *concordia*—that is, the amalgamation of different confessional groups to preserve a basic unity by means of overlooking their doctrinal distinctions and by compromise—but rather the political and practical acceptance of an earlier standoff between opposing religious camps. He directly draws upon the work of the fifth-century presbyter Salvian of Marseilles, who described the new presence in Gaul of the barbarians, who are Christian but of the wrong persuasion—Arians. Reaching back a thousand years, Grotius quotes from Salvian:

> Granted they are heretics, but they are so unwittingly. That is to say that they are heretics in our eyes, but not in theirs. For they so much believe themselves to be Catholics that they bring us into disrepute by calling us heretics. So what they are in our eyes, we are in theirs. . . . We have the truth, but they presume they have it. We honour God, but they are convinced that their creed is the right way to honour God. They do not observe their religious duties, but to them this is the highest religious duty. They are impious, but they think theirs is the true piety. So they do err, but they do so in good faith, not out of hatred of God but out of love for him, convinced that they honour and love the Lord. Although they do not have the right faith, yet they consider this the perfect love for God. Nobody except the Judge can know in what way they are to be punished for this erroneous belief on Judgment Day. I think that until that time God is patient with them, since he sees that though they do not have the right belief, their error results from a sincere conviction.[11]

The passage is especially interesting not only because Grotius ends his work on this note as his final resolution to the problem of religious fragmentation, but also because the passage circulated widely in the religious controversies of the post-Reformation era. It serves here to reinforce the dilemma whose essential outcome had earlier alarmed Thomas More.

Salvian's statement arises from the disintegration of the late Roman world in the West, where a sort of standoff had developed between the two major forms of the Christian religion—

between the conquering Arian Christian barbarians and the largely Catholic Romano-Gallic population. The situation dictated a practical observance of toleration as a wary coexistence; only in North Africa was the native population persecuted at the hands of the Arian Vandals. Neither reunion nor *concordia* figured here. Grotius was apparently unable to deal intellectually with the new actualities of toleration as the peaceful, if strained, coexistence of opposing religious groups. Five years later in his discourse to the magistrates of Amsterdam, wherein he addressed the issue of the emerging breach between the two divisions of the Calvinist church, the Remonstrants and the Contra-Remonstrants, Grotius appealed again to the principle of concord and of a toleration shaped by I Corinthians II:19—that it is fitting to suffer heretics and differences.[12] Here tolerance becomes an attitude of forbearance within a single system—not to suffering the existence of two or more separate, distinct systems. Grotius's religious thinking, moving in the grooves of an all-embracing, if loose, consensus, remained that of an irenicist—one capable of compromise to maintain a traditional unity. But Grotius could hardly be blamed for failing to appreciate the distinctive features of a political arrangement a thousand years removed into the past. Nevertheless, during his own lifetime, between 1555 and 1648, another formidable instance of tolerance, painfully exercised in the interests of coexistence and somewhat reminiscent of its fifth-century predecessor, was to be experienced in the Holy Roman Empire.

The general textbook presentation of the Peace of Augsburg in 1555, beyond affirming the fact of two legally recognized religions, emphasizes the limiting of freedom of religion to the members of the imperial estates and the resulting right of each ruler to determine the religion of his territory. Princely authority and the enhancement of sovereignty in the myriad of microstates seem to be the winners, for is not the clue to German history—and, for that matter, European history—the consolidation of political power in the rise of the territorial sovereign state that will later explain the glaring reality of the modern nation-state? Only partly—and one hopes its dominance in historiography would be of limited duration. Such a reading has long obscured the gradual emergence of a German constitutionalism at the center, the Reichstag or imperial diet, and not among the separate territorial parts, in each of which prevailed, supposedly, a single established church conjoined with the state apparatus. For all its idiosyncrasies and archaisms, this awkwardly functioning constitutionalism in the chief federal institution of the Reichstag presented the first example of restraint exercised to allow for the coexistence of differing confessional camps. It is an achievement largely ignored.

Twenty years ago the German historian Martin Heckel thoroughly analyzed the forced relations of Catholics and Lutherans as hostile, rival, but ultimately collaborative religious parties during the period identified as the Confessional Age. His *Deutschland im konfessionellen Zeitalter* (Germany in the Confessional Age) provided a clarification whose meaning we seek to extend beyond German history itself.[13] Heckel presented a matchless analysis of the political and constitutional operation of the Reich, the confederated empire, at the level of the imperial estates in their convening in successive Reichstags (or imperial diets). The strained cooperation between religious parties has remained obscure and essentially unattended, yet it warrants not only attention but profound appreciation both in the immediate context of German history and in assessing the unique achievement of European civilization in general. The painfully crafted and long sustained experience of constituted dissent and difference, achieved and shortly thereafter philosophically packaged appropriately, came to distinguish Europe as much as the precarious idea of humanity. The magnitude of this achievement, namely the defusing of religious fundamentalism at the highest, traditionally most prestigious political level, that of the Holy Roman Empire, would be eventually complemented by the passage of religion from the public sphere to the private experience. Thus, in its long-range workings the Reformation can be credited with assisting the creation of conditions that led to a constitutionally recognized dissent.

The interim arrangement of this system of dual opposing confessional camps, its intentionally provisional nature, first appeared at the Diet of Speyer in 1529, was refashioned in 1555, and came to fruition in 1648 in the Peace of Westphalia through the realization of that essential principle of parity in the procedural formulas of the *itio in partes*—the formal separation of the diet into two bodies whenever a religious issue appeared, as set forth in article 5, section 52 of the Osnabrück Instrument of Peace.[14]

The Peace of Augsburg in 1555 had begun a peculiar century-long controversy between both confessional groups now acting as religious parties within a mutually agreed-upon framework of parity. Based on the understanding that it was an interim, provisional arrangement, the peace settlement possessed sufficient flexibility to allow different interpretations by each party, whereby the more material aspects of religious questions came to be politically negotiated. Each party, Catholic and Lutheran, understood itself as in possession of the sole theological truth and the other as fraudulent and a lie, in a standoff eerily reminiscent of what Salvian a thousand years earlier had described as prevailing between the Catholics and the Arians. In the later case, however, what staved off a seemingly inevitable breakdown into armed hostilities was the rudiments of the understanding, later formulated in the *itio in partes* clauses of Westphalia's article 5, section 52, whereby each confession defined its own religious questions for itself and negotiated as a unit with the other. Even in the apparent breakdown evinced during the opening stages of the so-called Thirty Years' War—a war as much politically internal as confessional and increasingly fueled by European power politics, intensified in its horrors by undisciplined soldiery and the methods of recruiting then current—neither religious party wanted to abandon the substance and ideal of religious peace. And at the high watermark of Catholic triumph, the Edict of Restitution of March 1629, which saw a huge transfer of hitherto Protestant ecclesiastical property back to the Catholic side, the extermination of Protestantism in its Lutheran form did not present itself as an option in the emerging routine of negotiation.[15] Increasingly experienced by themselves in secular terms, the two confessions could be considered part of the political landscape. As Corpus Evangelicorum and Corpus Catholicorum they represented the domestication of the earlier Protestant Union and Catholic League—a foreshadowing of later political parties. The *de corpore ad corpus* (from one body to the other) procedure of the confessional groups—namely, negotiation between the two confessional bodies—instead of the usual deliberation within each of the individual curias or colleges of the imperial estates had developed not only out of the ground of the Westphalian settlement but was already carried out in the earlier settlements of 1532, 1539, 1541, 1544, and 1552 as well as in the Peace of Augsburg. Article 5, section 52 merely confirmed and better instituted the practice of insulating theological and religious discord from the sphere of political negotiation. The empire's constitution provided a refuge wherein the confessions could dissent yet not be assaulted by religious and theological enmity, so that the empire, in spite of its religious division, remained politically viable. The majority principle operated only within the separate curias or assemblies of the imperial estates, where common domestic issues justified negotiation; between the different curias, the majority principle was dropped for *de corpore ad corpus* negotiation, which meant that the interests of the minority Protestants were respected. A friendly settlement, *amicabilis compositio*, remained the goal of such negotiating.[16]

Although the contemporary intellectual currents of neo-Stoicism and natural law, previously considered, undoubtedly eased and confirmed this process of secularization, the existing historical contingencies and political necessity itself, rather than the incursion of any grand philosophy or even a redirection in thought, account for the achievement of the politically operative coexistence observed by the two—and, after 1648, following the recognition of Calvinism, three—confessions. Indeed, only one element is lacking from the largely constitutional, juridical, and political picture Heckel provides, and it never receives due credit: the salutary presence of the Turk, representing the dreadful specter of Moslem engulfment, which impelled the estates to collaborate to some degree in order to raise troops to oppose the long-standing Ottoman threat.[17] The Reformation may here be seen as an abruption that in the context of the Holy Roman Empire created the political necessity of religious coexistence among the major confessions—a new and unwanted experience, nonetheless salutary, indeed essential.

More largely and beyond the peculiar circumstances traced here, political necessity alone could never have effected that broader and deeper change but required a true redirection in thought created by a considerable intellectual effort—"one that reflected a complex mixture of spiritual, theological, ecclesiological, epistemological, ethical, political as well as pragmatic arguments."[18] Such a major transposition of public attitudes and thought would best be advanced by the Savoyard Sebastian Castellio in the course of the sixteenth century and consolidated by John Locke in the seventeenth.

The form of toleration that came to advance the coexistence of effectively constituted opposing groups, inimical on the most decisive and basic issue for the sixteenth century, is but one aspect of the multifarious history of the development of toleration. The resolution achieved in the Holy Roman Empire represents a distinct feature in the development of toleration. The larger picture throughout the individual territories of the empire remained one of limited and piecemeal toleration.[19] While the Reformation's *libertas conscientiae* and *libertas religionis* (liberty of conscience and liberty of religion) were worked out philosophically and legally in the European political literature regarding toleration, within the empire the constitutional and political implications revealed themselves in the operations of successive imperial diets stemming from the Peace of Augsburg. Amidst the religious fragmentation produced by the Reformation, the creation of conditions of coexistence among the supremely sensitive confessional camps was a unique achievement. The empire, through the practices of its diet, was inching away from religious confrontation to long-range habits of collaboration and respectful coexistence. Such processes eventually worked to the attenuation and demise of the Confessional Age. And in a larger perspective, they constituted a significant step toward the controlled admission of dissent in the Western experience and toward the realization of Thomas More's fearful prospect.

The present argument has sought to disclose the intrinsically revolutionary long-range impact and effect of the Protestant Reformation by affirming and giving positive weight to its negative results and most disastrous features, at least as they seemed at the time: ecclesiastical fragmentation and the consequent wars of religion. But we see here that this resulting period of terrible bloodshed can justify a positive interpretation. Indeed, the explosive nature of religious division applied to politics, the century-long bloodbath created by religious fundamentalism would provide this very special civilization with a most precious warning as well as opportunity. Europe, its civilization, the West learned from its own unique and structured experience regarding the horrors of religious conflict. Political necessity and genuine religious exhaustion presented the first case of a constituted political dissent in a system of practical, tolerated coexistence.[20] The much-maligned Old Reich provided the necessary context in its own time and fell mercifully short of any ruthless national consolidation or *Gleichschaltung*.

The magnitude of the achievement for containing religious dissent, however strained and precarious, may be better appreciated by comparing it with a more narrowly political consideration of the problem at the hands of a notorious contemporary thinker. Simultaneously with Luther's challenge, Machiavelli had in the opening chapters of his *Discorsi* boldly inquired how a republic or any political system could endure such inner conflict as that evinced by the Roman republic, but also presented in the cases offered by ancient Sparta and contemporary Venice. He noted, however, that a prince, a nobility, and the power of the people provided a system of reciprocal checks (1:2). Machiavelli acclaimed the adroit introduction of the tribunes at Rome for guarding the interests of the populace and Roman liberty. Admitting some bloodshed and cases of disorder, he deemed the value of liberty to outweigh the costs of some inevitable violence (1:4). In Sparta and Venice he found a deliberate limitation and even extinction of access for the populace at large to political deliberation (1:6). He argued for the necessity of organizing a republic in such a way that it could withstand the destabilizing forces that disrupt a state, for, lacking such a legal safety valve, to vent ill-humors the masses would resort to illegal means with upsetting effects (1:7).[21] Yet, by way of comparison, the confessional issue, with its dangerous religious overtones, posited a more absolute, totally pervasive, and fundamental threat of disruption, transcending the ordinary social and economic tensions of a political community. With the confessional issues diminished, those political contexts would prove themselves more amenable to later formal, abstract programs of constitutional checks such as those considered by James Harrington or John Locke and subsequently perceived by Montesquieu as emergent in English political life.

The issue of the practical, tolerated coexistence of hostile religious groups is so central that we need to linger further in order to listen to the greatest juristic and political mind of the sixteenth century in his judgment of the Peace of Augsburg's import. Writing twenty years later from the holocaust of the French religious wars, Jean Bodin urged the prohibition of any further religious dispute:

> [The prohibition of public disputations of religion] after long civil war was by the estates and princes of the German empire provided for, and a decree made, that the princes should with mutual consent defend both the Roman and Saxon religion: whereunto that was also joined, That no man should upon pain of death dispute of the religions. Which severe punishments, after that the German magistrates had inflicted upon diverse, all Germany was afterwards at good quiet & rest: no man daring more to dispute of matters of religion.[22]

Rome for good reason could not share Bodin's enthusiasm for the Augsburg settlement and indeed never accepted it. The Catholic Church remained most sensitive to the apparent viability of otherwise hostile religions. Nevertheless, by the end of the century one of its least faithful, least confessionally driven members could speculate as to the possible virtues of extensive fragmentation of belief for advancing civil peace and political stability. In his sympathetic reconsideration of the last pagan Roman emperor, Julian the Apostate, Michel de Montaigne weighed the odds in the countenancing of factions promoted by freedom of conscience:

> It may be said, on the one hand, that to give factions a loose rein to entertain their own opinions is to scatter and sow division. . . . But on the other hand, one could also say that to give factions a loose rein to entertain their own opinions is to soften and relax them through facility and ease, and to dull the point, which is sharpened by rarity, novelty, and difficulty.[23]

Such a horrendous idea—namely, the balance achieved by building on a faction and admitting its contrasts and diversity—had to wait two more centuries before being worked into a comprehensive general constitution. In that case, it was for a new nation in a new world.

This constituting as parties two groups that were mutually hostile on the most sensitive issue of the century, religion, had no direct follow-up in German or European history: even in the Netherlands and Poland, one party, one religion, came to prevail over the others. The line of development that leads from British constitutionalism to Montesquieu and Madison seems quite innocent of the development described here. Yet, second, the German achievement alerts us to a forgotten but pioneering example of politically constituted coexistence and dissent. Admittedly, the solution at the time did not include sectarians, Jews, or, of course, atheists. The German case was a sort of harbinger for a new stage in our own unique civilization, a new and distinctly Western experience: we are reminded that no matter how limited and imperfectly realized at the time, the realities of difference, diversity, pluralism, fragmentation, and dissent can only survive and operate constructively within the recognized commonality of a mutually accepted and respected constitutional framework.

Finally, none of this outcome, the product of unintended consequences, could have been perceived or sought at the time. Insofar as it was perceived at all, its utterly strange features proved to be a source of grave distress to one prescient contemporary. In 1533, during the second decade of what would later be designated the Reformation, this man's gaze either assumed or passed beyond the period during which religious parties became culturally as well as politically entrenched in that stage known as confessionalization. Rather, his mind came to fix upon a more distant scene constituted by a plurality of churches existing through reciprocal respect, mutual recognition, and political neutrality, all made possible by the pervasive relativity of truth. Such a world transformed constituted Thomas More's horrific vision.

Party and Opposition in the Eighteenth-Century Anglo-American Experience

The fact of party in its essential role of opposition to an otherwise runaway executive and the incorporation of a constituted dissent into a political system are less the result of a luminous idea minted by some great mind or momentous intellectual abruption than the uncertain product of a practice that evolved from the complexities of continuous political engagement. In the European context, the English Parliament provided the arena for this political engagement following the Revolution Settlement of 1688–89. This unique experiment in the development of government would have been impossible without the Reformation's disrupting the traditional, comprehensive unity provided by canon law and cracking the medieval church's religious and ecclesiastical shell, an event that initially recentered and magnified the religious but led in time to its weakening through fragmentation and intellectual erosion. By the resulting promotion of dissenting bodies, the Reformation effected a displacement of the Catholic monopoly with its unquestioned appeal to custom, tradition, and arguments from time immemorial, all sanctified by the Holy Spirit. In the resulting adjustments, political opportunity—whether it was the uneasy parity produced in the Holy Roman Empire by the Peace of Augsburg or the currents of monarchical centralization—served to promote a new and significant measure of secularity.

Apart from the secularizing, dissenting elements precipitated by the Reformation, a second feature distinguishes the unique development here studied: namely, the protection afforded by England's surrounding waters, which necessitated effective control of the seas. The insular nature of the English experiment, freed from the immediacy of military pressure so evident on the Continent, permitted the development of a different sort of politics; liberties here were less threatened by a necessarily authoritarian government, and its own justification of a standing army, which in England became a focus of criticism and distrust. This last point, the unique advantage of a relative security in the European context made possible by the waters of the English Channel, played itself out on a grander scale, at least until 2001, in the oceanic buffering of the United States of America.

In order to accent the preliminary yet basic role of the Protestant Reformation in creating a new context and its problems for the advent of politically constituted dissent, the first section addressed the most august, if archaic, system, the Holy Roman Empire. The second examines the evolution of the British constitution in the eighteenth century. The development of party will be examined, not so much for the details of party formation but more in the growing consciousness that parties were no longer seen as evil or even just tolerable, but acceptable and indeed necessary for responsible constitutional government. Dissent had come of age. It had now become integral to the effective political process and no longer required exile, incarceration, or extermination.

Only by a conscious effort can we situate our thinking prior to Montesquieu, with his artificial divisions and separations, in order to see a political entity according to its original intention and nature. Before 1640 in England it was all quite different. The origin of parliaments belongs to the history of European estates general as medieval assemblies designed primarily not to provide "supply," the financial needs of the ruler, but rather to broaden discussion, consideration, and agreement in order to lend greater weight to the ultimate will of the king. The English Parliament was at first not a legislative body at all, but a court that received petitions; apparent legislative and administrative acts were couched in a judicial idiom.[24] As the highest court of the land, its preeminent task remained the formation of a single will that expressed consensus. Its procedure, which emphasized the primacy of debate and the unanimity of resolutions, manifested a rhetoric that excluded faction and special interest in order to attain consensus. The consensual nature of medieval politics was reinforced by the fact that the king was himself a member of Parliament, a situation that made internal opposition and the presence of parties impossible. That Parliament consisted of king, lords, and commoners made the subsequent civil war all the more unnatural and dreadful. The events of 1641—the ultimatum of the Grand Remonstrance, the Triennial Act, and the Act Against Dissolution all exponentially enhancing the powers of parliament—transformed this occasional medieval assembly into Parliament, now endowed with a peculiar immortality, according to the momentous perception of the Earl of Leicester: no longer a tenant at the will of its lord but a never-dying corporation. During the Interregnum the opportunity for opposition and parties developed only slightly in fact and even less so in self-understanding.[25] Throughout the later seventeenth century the idea of an opposition as a party remained tenuous, and the sense of the word *party* itself as pejorative, connoting faction and unwanted division, persisted.

With the advent of civil war and the breakdown of the constitution into open warfare, the emerging party divisions were transformed into a military opposition and only with the Restoration returned to a fully political register. Yet in this early stage of our inquiry we occasionally encounter the sense of opposite sides and, even more significantly, of the salutary nature of effective opposition as providing a necessary balance and equilibrium. In 1667, the poet Andrew Marvell, who over a twenty-year period served for Hull, saw "the old gang" as "the Court" and the Presbyterians as "the Country," comparing their contest to a game of chess or backgammon. More instructive, by 1684 an anonymous pamphleteer urged the king to balance factions and encourage emulation among them:

> Besides when a prince has several factions, whether religious or civil in his dominions, as protestant and papal, guelf and gibelline, which he cannot easily reconcile, in his interest, by employing them indifferently according to their parts and loyalty to keep the balance as equallibration [*sic*]: that while they are at enmity among themselves, they shall have no aversion to him . . . and shall strive to outdo each other in service.[26]

The seventeenth-century crisis of constitution was resolved in the settlement of 1688–89 with the extraordinarily fortunate departure of James II from the scene. However, the possibilities of an overextended royal prerogative still needed paring. For as long as the king had the right to punish critics in Parliament, a constitutional opposition in the modern sense would have to await the early nineteenth century.[27] The immediately subsequent period even into the first years of the Hanoverians provides evidence for the currency of the belief in the merits of two parties that were counterweights to each other. John Shute, later Viscount Barrington, a friend of Locke, published first in 1701, then in 1703 and 1705, two tracts on religious liberty and the interest of Protestant Dissenters. In them he supported the current idea of a *concordia discors* (concord with managed discord) whereby the Church of England might retain its strength by promoting competition among other churches rather than by suppressing them.[28] Although this happy notion appeared unlikely, nevertheless it promoted the concept of balance transferred consciously from the world of diplomatic practice to domestic politics.

> The constitution of England consists in a balance of parties as the libertys of Europe do in a Ballance of power. . . . But as when we suffer any power in Europe to become exorbitant, and out of reach of the rest, we destroy the liberties of Europe; so when we allow one of the parties in England to be above the check of the other, we bid farewell to its liberties too.[29]

Indeed, the image of a tense, contested, shifting balance pertained to more than just the world of external state relations and the diplomacy of Europe; it had an internal counterpart as well. Shortly afterward, in a second tract, Barrington added:

> [W]henever the power in England shall be put into the hands of one party, all the prerogative of the Crown and the liberties of the people, will be swallowed by that party; the will of that party must be then instead of the sovereign's prerogative, and their interest must come into the room of the general good of the people.[30]

Barrington's argument that religious freedom in the specific form of relaxing the persecution of Dissenters would promote a more effective national unity than any imposed conformity appeared too subtle, given the need for English unity in the rough-and-tumble of European politics. By associating too closely the diplomatic balance of Europe with the domestic, internal balance of English parties, he hampered the acceptance of his idea of an effective opposing party to the existing administration.

Yet the idea did not disappear from the literature of the period that saw the last years of Anne and the coming of the Hanoverian dynasty in 1714. Indeed, the violence of the Tory recovery and abruption in 1710, marked by Bolingbroke's leading England out of war with Louis XIV and the settlement of Utrecht, occasioned the label of "fury" for the Tories in Paul de Rapin-Thoyras's *Dissertation on the Whigs and Tories* (1717). A French Huguenot of Savoyard background, long resident in The Hague, he had come over to England in the baggage of William III. Rapin-Thoyras produced a history of England that may have later provoked the disdain of David Hume, yet at the time enjoyed wide reading and favorable reception. Rapin-Thoyras characterized the Tories as being led by their most arbitrary and rigid members in defense of passive obedience toward the sovereign and the support of episcopacy and hierarchy. He saw Whig leadership since the Long Parliament as being in the hands of moderates, significantly less violent, although capable of being shaken by those members in support of the Presbyterians. In this contested territory regarding church government, Rapin-Thoyras asserted that "it is not to the interest of the kingdom that one of the parties should become so superior as to meet with no contradiction." If so, the Tories would dispose of Parliament, and the Whigs would establish a republic. The extreme leadership of either required the tempering of each: "It will always be safer for the State that the division should continue as it is at present than that one of the parties should enjoy a superiority." Rapin-Thoyras seemed to conclude by affirming the balance of opposites. But he accepted this situation as a practical faute de mieux, while appealing "to the prudence of a just and equitable king, moderate in his desires, of few passions, a lover of the Protestant religion"[31]—in fact the present incumbent, George I—as a sort of patriot king who would manage to raise politics from its present distressful condition.

Indeed, with Bolingbroke's *Idea of a Patriot King* (written in 1738) and even more with his earlier *Dissertation upon Parties*, published as editorial letters in *The Craftsman* between October 1733 and January 1734, the fanciful idea of counterpoised parties retreated, without entirely disappearing, before the traditional notion of "party" as pejorative. The reasons for this turn were both political and intellectual: the Whig dominance beginning in 1714, made possible by its close association with the new Hanoverian dynasty's successfully expelling the Tories, tainted by their lingering adherence to the Stuarts in Jacobitism; and the eminence of Bolingbroke's prose in support of a single party that would extinguish all parties and all need for partisanship.[32]

Henry St. John, Viscount Bolingbroke, had been among the Tory leaders who were riding high in the last years of Anne's reign. With her death and the advent of a new dynasty, all fell apart for the Tories. Impeached by Parliament in 1715, though pardoned in 1723, yet not released from the Act of Attainder until 1725, and never allowed to recover his seat in the House of Lords,[33] Bolingbroke remained long in exile, both imposed and self-chosen. This single instance in the modern Western experience of the exile of a political loser was as recent as the early eighteenth century. Although the fall of Robert Walpole in 1742 occasioned desire of some Tory extremists for the former minister's head quite unmetaphorically on a platter, a realistic moderation henceforth entered the political life of England. The case of Bolingbroke and the deprivations suffered by the Tory leadership in 1715 present us with the last instance of political proscription in English history.[34] Such a removal of extermination or even imprisonment from the table of negotiation moved politics in the direction of a greater moderation.

Upon returning to England, Bolingbroke founded a journal, *The Craftsman*, with the express intent of opposing Walpole and the moneyed interests of the Court Whigs. His Country platform for countering Walpole's management of Parliament by adroit patronage sought a reciprocal relationship between Crown and the people for the defense of British liberties in the face of Walpolean "corruption." Montesquieu, who was then visiting England (1729–31), saw Bolingbroke in the role of a sort of "anti-Minister." From numbers 202, 208, and 219 of *The Craftsman*, published in the later part of June and mid-September 1730, Montesquieu acquired Bolingbroke's commitment to a government based on the separation of powers as being that most free from tyranny.[35] Indeed, Bolingbroke's effective recourse to the press at this time appears to have been instrumental not only for the early definition of an opposition, but also for the beginnings of a public sphere for intellectual exchange, occasioned by the increasing freedom of the press.[36]

Bolingbroke tried to argue for the unconstitutional nature of Walpole's regime. Having failed, he returned to France, where he struck the pose of the retired philosopher-statesman—Seneca and Cato, or, more recently, Bacon and Clarendon. In the *Dissertation upon Parties* he relied largely on history, resorting not only to English history but notably to continental European events.[37] In his analysis Court and Country replaced Whig and Tory. The recent revolution introduced for all sides a new era. For the Country party the settlement amounted to a new Magna Carta, defining new interests and principles of government.[38] One notable item was a definition of a constitution in the modern sense, which preceded that of Emeric de

Vattel's work on international law (1758) and the coining of the term unconstitutional.[39] In 1688 the Whigs had purged themselves of republican aspirations, as had the Tories the suspicion of popery and arbitrary power; each thus unloaded its most objectionable ballast. Only the names remained.[40] The work conveyed the anxiety of regarding a swollen executive in the Crown and its controlling patronage of Parliament. In its apparent quest for balance and moderation, the work ended on the note that Country and Court parties had become constitutionalist and anticonstitutionalist, respectively. Indeed, agreement on the nature of the constitution made moderation possible.[41] Balance is here conceived less in terms of an effective opposition party and more in terms of a Polybian mixed government of monarchical, aristocratic, and democratic elements.

Later in the 1730s Bolingbroke clarified his position on party. As prelude, his *Letter on the Spirit of Protestantism* (1736) leveled against Walpole's system the criticism "that the opposition . . . is not an opposition only to bad government and public affairs" but also opposed one that supported itself by corrupt, unconstitutional means.[42] As with any Western European monarchy of the eighteenth century, the obvious focus of any opposition was on the heir-apparent to the throne: in this case, Frederick, Prince of Wales. With him in mind Bolingbroke composed in 1738 his most famous and definitive work, *The Idea of a Patriot King* (1749). In it, he constructed a virtuous prince who would now transcend party, not espousing any party "but to govern like the common father of his people." Otherwise to govern by party must always result in the government of a faction:

> For faction is to party what the superlative is to the positive; party is a political evil, and faction is the worst of all parties. The true image of a free people, governed by a Patriot King, is that of a patriarchal family, where the

> head and all the members are united by one common interest and animated by one common spirit.[43]

In an England whose political life was ridden by the factions of venturesome politicians, Bolingbroke had solved the problem, at least for himself, by means of transcendence in the apparent realization of the spirit of the nation. His doctrine was eschatological in that its success would lead to the extinction of opposition, which, significantly, he did not conceive of as a continuing and beneficent institution.[44]

If the appreciation of party as an effective counterweight to an existing regime conflicted with Bolingbroke's intent, the recognition of an opposition party as salutary surfaced during these same years and same sources of journalistic exchange, although in a quite different context. Political life in the American colonies was differently structured and became peculiarly receptive to and shaped by the numerous critical writers of the period. Among the strident voices of criticism none had as much influence as John Trenchard and Thomas Gordon, who collaborated in 144 pieces appearing in the *London Journal* and *British Journal* during 1720–23, to be later collected in a book called *Cato's Letters* which would carry greater weight in America than in England during these years. In actual fact, Bolingbroke availed himself of their ammunition shortly afterward in *The Craftsmen* with his focus on Walpole and the English scene. For their part the colonists avidly absorbed this literature of critical dissent with its mentality of opposition to current English political practices.[45]

In their reflections upon party, neither Bolingbroke nor in later decades Edmund Burke arrived at a notion of its salutary effectiveness as a counterweight to the existing regime. What proved impossible at the time in the English context gained notable recognition in the American colonies well before their rebellion. In 1730, prior to the famous Zenger case over a free press, someone writing in the *New York Gazette* broke through to the new ground in formulating the intrinsic worth of an effective opposition party:

> A free government cannot but be subject to *parties, cabals,* and *intrigues*. . . . I may venture to say that some opposition, though it proceed not entirely from a public spirit, is not only necessary in free governments but of a great service to the public. Parties are a check upon one another, and by keeping the ambition of one another within bounds, serve to maintain the public liberty. Opposition is the life and soul of public zeal which, without it, would flag and decay for want of an opportunity to exert itself.

And five years later, from Pennsylvania, came the statement "there can be no liberty without faction, for the latter cannot be suppressed without introducing slavery in the place of the former."[46]

In the England of Bolingbroke and Hume, the turbulence and discord of conflicting factions and parties emitted fragmentary notions of political liberty. Such notions provided some compensation for this lamentable discord: a factious liberty was to be preferred to a settled tyranny.[47] But again from America by 1752 a greater clarity was forthcoming. The Presbyterian William Livingstone, inspired by Trenchard and Gordon's *Independent Whig,* sought in New York to establish a journal in opposition to the government. Therein he came to voice the key notion that in the understanding of politics as a conflict of interests, the state itself operated as a faction or party involved like any other party in the struggle for power.[48]

The period from the time of Bolingbroke in the 1730s to that of Edmund Burke in the final third of the century introduces us to the fissiparous and kaleidoscope nature of British party politics following the collapse of the Walpole hegemony. The historian Sir Lewis Namier, intimidating authority on the workings of eighteenth-century politics, mapped out the terrain as one dominated more by men than by measures and thus subject to no great principles. It is of course a picture that Namier wished to extend to the entire eighteenth-century British political scene. Amidst the shifting coalitions led by aristocrat politicians of passing prominence, one can discern traces for the advancement of opposition both as a conscious practice and as an idea. Almost to the end of the century, party was looked upon as basically evil. Yet parties pullulated. Hume could sigh that in a free country parties had probably to be tolerated, but there is a difference between toleration of parties and a belief in the respectability of party.[49] If the "great parties," presumably those of the 1680s, were gone and well gone, leaving reasonable and tolerable parties, the new situation had been understood by Bolingbroke and his contemporaries that society had somehow to be organized in a nonpolitical way.[50] His thought shaped the thinking and practices of the political world in which Burke later moved.[51]

A murky notion of opposition and its practices began to emerge in mid-century. Even earlier, Leicester House, the residence of the Prince of Wales, served as a locus for four generations of shifting oppositions. As early as 1722 the government-owned *London Journal* denounced the idea expressed by its own "Britannicus" author that steady, deliberate opposition was a duty and that participation therein presented the criterion for true loyalty.[52] At this time opposition connoted the act of opposition, not the opposers themselves as a group, for which old Stuart terms prevailed—Country, malcontents, grumbletonians.[53] About 1731, contemporary journalism began to settle upon the body of anti-Courtiers as "the opposition." Probably the most consolidating event for any future effective opposition came after 1742, when its members were seated in the benches of the House to the left of the speaker.[54] Basic agreement on the fundamentals, now *constitution*, a term that was appearing in an expanding context of mutual restraint, allowed Britons to perceive a divided house as normal or at least acceptable.[55]

Expectably, the world of print and political thought provided greater, if possibly misleading, clarity than that of practical contemporary politics. Among the political tracts of the 1740s and 1750s, two are notable in this respect: the first, by Lord Percival, later Earl of Egmont, *Faction Detected by the Evidence of Facts*; and the second, by Thomas Pownall, *Principles of Polity*. Percival's, published in 1743, distinguished party from faction in terms of whether the leaders were guided by principles or by self-interest. The former constituted an opposition; the latter, a faction.[56] In the development of his argument he seeks to daub Tories with the taint of excessive Jacobitism, exaggerating and polemicizing against their dangerous affinity for a French rather than Austrian alliance on the Continent—Tory being too easily associated with faction, as Whig was with party.[57] Terms that appear frequently are *moderate* or *moderation* and *constitution*, sometimes reciprocally linked.[58] Percival concluded that "the Opposition of this Time is not an Opposition, but a faction; and that of the most dangerous kind to this Nation."[59]

The somewhat tangled perceptions of Thomas Pownall provide us with our second sounding of the political waters and currents in the mid-eighteenth century. Widely experienced in the workings of the burgeoning imperial system—he served as governor of Massachusetts from 1757 to 1760[60] and was sympathetic and sensitive to colonial matters both American and Indian—Pownall brought considerable knowledge to the political life of his day. His *Principles of Polity* (1752) assumes the form of a dialogue between the two personae of Quintus Scaevola and Lucius Crassus, both notable experts in the law during the Roman republican period. Pownall alerts his reader in a prologue that he has modeled his dialogue upon

Ciceronian methods wherein the author's views are not to be identified with either person but "in the balance of the whole." Within the context of a Polybian notion of mixed government—democratic, aristocratic, monarchical—he advances through Scaevola a different notion of opposition and its necessary presence.

> Can any party support itself unless it hath a Power sufficient to enforce its Influence? and if it hath actually such Power as to be capable to enforce its Acts, it may exert an illegal or undue Influence; and must not this be contrary to the Interest of any other that is connected with it? Therefore any Constitution explained from this Idea must consist not only of different, but contrary Parties, and consequently of Opposition. . . . Thus it becomes the Interest of the Democratic Part, to be a constant Clog and Check upon the Measures of the administrating Power, and to oppose themselves to every new Exertion of its Influence. Here then there are two different Parties whose Interest is essentially contrary, and who can alone subsist by the Struggle of Opposition.[61]

Clearly opposition has shifted from being identified with a group, outside of and resistant to the ministerial party in office, and has become rather the tension, the conflict itself, between two different parties. Crassus will have none of it. He cites Bolingbroke's *Dissertation upon Parties*: "Oppositions become the virtuous support of Liberty and of a noble watchful Care for the common Interest of Mankind."[62] He rejects all talk of balance and counterbalance—"of one Power being constitutionally a check upon another; and that it is constitutionally the duty of these to pull different Ways, even when there is not real Matter of Difference yet to preserve the Equilibrium of Power."[63] He denounces the artful author of the *Dissertation* for having established "the invidious and mischievous Distinction of Court and Country Interest."[64] That Crassus would crush all party and faction and advocate some sort of Polybian-Harringtonian balance need not concern us. Rather, whatever the exact balance of the matter, the idea of party and opposition as a tense equilibrium had been advanced.

With the coming of George III to the throne in 1760 a new period opened: the king made a bid to enter politics more directly by seeking to rule through a favorite—though an unpopular and incompetent one, Lord Bute. The Court now appeared to be the motor for the corruption by royal patronage of members of Parliament, which seemed to submerge the public in a myriad of private interests. For the definition of party in a context wherein the ideal of a patriot king faltered, the political thought and activities of Edmund Burke during the next two decades proved central. In 1770 Burke brought out his significant inquiry into party, *Thoughts on the Cause of the Present Discontents*, in which for the first time the idea of party itself became respectable. But the further step of asserting it as a permanent feature of balance and control within the overall constitution of Britain was not taken. As with Bolingbroke, the "eschatological" understanding of party appeared to prevail.[65] Yet such an understanding would be a misleading simplification. For Burke struggled to articulate a notion of party expressive of a public, principled interest, more principled than interest ridden, as a means of consolidating and effectuating the more public purposes of a concerted group of public, principled men. Increasingly conceived as a permanent feature of the political landscape, although not as a counterweight, such a concerted group makes Burke appear as possibly the first partisan of a two-party or even a multiparty system.[66]

Burke's *Thoughts* became a massive indictment of Court practices at the expense of the public and national good. Burke argued that the discretionary powers vested in the monarch ought to be exercised for public principles and national interests rather than for advancing the prejudices of a Court.[67] As a sort of cabal of royal favorites without any relation to public interest, a cabal at the Court had come to dominate the state.[68] The Crown had dwindled in proportion to the unnaturally grotesque growth, this "double cabinet" upon the Court, which operated outside of and beyond the confidence of the people without any public principle.[69] Burke claimed that the king had been enslaved by a faction and made a prisoner in his closet; abandoning the traditional fortress of prerogative, his favorites had come to lodge in Parliament itself.[70] In fact, the distemper of the monarchy, which provided the great issues for redress in the previous century, had now been replaced by the distemper of Parliament.[71] Thus understood, the situation called for the association of principled members acting in the interests of the people and presumably as a corrective counterweight. "When bad men combine, the good must associate":[72]

> If the reader believes that there really exists such a Faction as I have described; a Faction ruling by the private inclinations of a Court, against the general sense of the people; and that this faction, whilst it pursues a scheme for undermining all the foundations of our freedom, weakens (for the present at least) all the powers of executory government, rendering us abroad contemptible, and at home distracted; he will believe also, that nothing but a firm combination of public men against this body, and that, too, supported by the hearty concurrence of the people at large, possibly get the better of it. The people will see the necessity of restoring public men to an attention to the public opinion, and of restoring the constitution to its original principles.[73]

Burke's emerging notion of party as "a body of men united for promoting by their joint endeavors the national interest upon some particular principle in which they are all agreed"[74]—his summons to the public interest over the factionalism of the private advantage—was not new to the political literature of the mid-century. But it was now placed in the context of a necessary tug toward party unity and solidarity that soon made the Rockingham Whigs the most significant group on the political stage.[75]

Burke's own political career in Parliament and as the directive force within the would-be party of the Rockingham Whigs attests to the creation of something new in the political life of the British people. First taken into the group as Rockingham's private secretary, he soon became recognized as not simply the marquis's "right hand but both his hands."[76] Unfortunately for Burke's higher purposes, the Rockingham Whigs remained a small group lacking any other political energies than those provided by Burke and the steady support of Rockingham's trust. The group lacked any significant base in the House of Commons and, worse still, royal favor. The two instances in which it came to exercise power, as government and ministry, were moments of crisis: in 1765–66, when the party repealed the Stamp Act, and in 1782, when entry into the royal service required the acceptance of American independence, so unpalatable to the king. But most notable in 1782 were the greater steadiness and resolution of the Rockinghamites than any previous opposition. They were indeed unique in attacking not simply an overly swollen minister, Lord North, but the whole ministry and its policy. The party seemed to have come of age not simply with a momentary eighty strong in the House of Commons but also with Rockingham's own understanding and intent to establish party hegemony within any new ministry.[77] Yet Lord Rockingham's untimely death revealed the fragility of this accomplishment. In the process of breaking down the king's resistance to the policy of accepting American independence—the price of the ministry's government—a British triumph such as the taking of Charleston in

1782 only threatened to subvert Burke and Rockingham's case for the necessity of recognizing the American states.[78] One can well appreciate, in the twenty-first century, the politically paralyzing effect upon a party when it understands its own interests to be best advanced by a military reversal abroad.

With the co-opting of the ministry of the younger Pitt, the king's political recovery led to a new level of stability in the emergence and success of the first Pitt ministry. Against the background of a riveting issue, namely the French Revolution, now Tory against Whig, Pitt versus Fox, provided a new reality to political conflict, but within the moderating influence of an accepted, practical constitution. As early as 1788, several ministerial statements appear that respect the presence and workings of an effective opposition as something "of a great service to the country when conducted on public principles." Lord Camden continued: "An Opposition awed ministers and kept them vigilant. It checked their career, put them upon their guard, taught them where error lay, and how to correct it."[79] Henry MacKenzie, a Pittite pamphleteer, recognized the opposition as a sort of public body: "The province of this ex-official body, when it acts in a manner salutary to the state, is to watch with jealousy over the conduct of the administration; to correct the abuses and to resist the corruptions of its power; to restrain whatever may be excessive, to moderate what may be inconsiderate, and to supply what may be defective in its measures." Important in both statements are an appreciation of opposition as exercising effective criticism and even modification of the policies stemming from the ministry and its party in their leadership and direction of the government. The earliest imagery of balance and equilibrium, suggestive of possible deadlock, had been displaced by the national dynamics of political life. The Pittites came to allow the opposition to be a body, a party, granting it a semiofficial status as an alternate government.[80]

Political conflict had not only become tamed but was now profitably used in a way that proved completely constitutional—as "the ventilator of the Constitution," a safety valve rather than an explosive.[81] Strengthened and enhanced by heightened party recognition, loyalty, and discipline, Whigs and Tories, soon to be renamed and rethought as Liberals and Conservatives, moved to that most significant enunciation of "His Majesty's Opposition" in 1826. This almost offhand pronouncement marked the culmination of principles and practices that had already been set in motion and were coalescing to create the reality of incorporating one's political opponent within the rules and context of a mutually accepted game.[82]

Opposition came of age in Great Britain's party government in the late 1820s. At the same moment, it also became a reality in the political functioning of the new American republic. In what had been a larger British political world that shared a common stock of ideas, laws, and literature, after the rebellion of its American colonies a very different political society and its machinery had emerged, "a transformed version of a quasi-republican alternative to parliamentary monarchy" latent in the English tradition since the seventeenth century.[83] Following the rebellion came the real revolution: the making of a formal constitution, which, together with the gifted personalities involved, introduced a *novus ordo secularum*, a new world order, in its bold understanding of the human animal and of political community.

The tense, uncertain beginnings of the new republic had two notable features. First, it owed an intellectual debt as much to David Hume and Viscount Bolingbroke as to Locke and to Montesquieu (who was now actually circumvented by the new republicanism, though his misunderstanding of the English constitution as being one of checks and balances had been incorporated into the American). Second, in the furious exchanges, often swelled by accusations of treason, that marked the initial conflicts and partisanship of American political life, institutional and temperamental moderating controls proved sufficient to avoid the cropping of heads that had distinguished the English political scene of the seventeenth century as well as the contemporary scene in France. In America, amidst the shouts, political opponents learned to talk to each other.

The French statesman Talleyrand, a shrewd, perceptive judge of men and times, at one point identified Alexander Hamilton, rather than William Pitt the Younger or Napoleon Bonaparte, as the greatest person of the age.[84] It can be argued, however, that he erred in overlooking James Madison, who would solve the riddle of the political Sphinx in his transcendence of Polybian mixed government and his new appreciation of a republican form of government applicable to American conditions. Although formally Madison remained deeply opposed to party and party government, paradoxically, he contributed decisively to its foundations. Prior to political parties or factions there had been sects, philosophical in the ancient world, then religious more recently. Growing up in colonial Virginia in the shadow of Anglican orthodoxy, young Madison developed a healthy respect and concern for religious pluralism; the coexistence of diverse religious groups in relative peace offered itself as a model for political pluralism and for a deliberately pluralist society. In his readings at Princeton he stumbled upon Voltaire's wonderful observation in the *Letters philosophiques* (I.74.vi): "If one religion were allowed in England there would be reason to fear despotism; if there were but two, the people would cut one another's throats; but as there are thirty, they all live happy and in peace." The statement accented the viability of restraint and peaceful coexistence in numbers and diversity:[85] the very numbers and their diversity would neutralize one another.

When, as the principal architect of the new Constitution, Madison came to its defense in the *Federalist Papers*, he brought with him the deep-seated notion of party as evil and as synonymous with faction. In Number 10, Madison directly addressed the problem of faction as something endemic to any free political life. Because it could not be expunged without extinguishing liberty itself, it needed to be controlled. At the root of his thinking on political life as expressive of the naturally violent divisiveness of politics was the early-won conviction that every man, however good personally, if politically considered could best be deemed a knave, an insight culled from his reading of Hume's *Essays*.[86] But even more momentous was the analysis that allowed him to transcend the objection of Montesquieu on the matter of republics' being viable only for small political units such as cities or small territories. In Hume's "Idea of a Perfect Commonwealth" Madison found encouragement for the application of republican government on a continental scale:

> Though it is more difficult to form a republican government in an extensive territory than in a city; there is more facility, when once it is formed, of preserving it steady and uniform, without tumult and faction. . . . In a large government, which is modeled with masterly skill, there is compass and room enough to refine the democracy, from the lower people, who may be admitted into the first elections or first concoction of the commonwealth, to the higher magistrates, who direct all the movements. At the same time, the parts are so distant and remote, that it is very difficult, either by intrigue, prejudice, or passion, to hurry them into any measures against the public interest.[87]

Madison followed Hume on factions, compressing the latter's analysis in "Parties in General" and "The Parties of Great Britain." In some places he showed that he had already arrived independently at Hume's position on humankind's overwhelming propensity for factionalism, faction being a function of liberty. Representation and the greater space in an extended republic could serve as a cure for the dangers of faction in what distinguished a republic from a democracy: "first the delegation of the government to a small number of citizens elected by the rest; secondly the greater number of citizens," and, comparably, the greater extent of the country. The federal structure distinguished the national from the more local state interests, channeling and controlling the interest and the competence of the representative. But it is the greater extent of the republic that Madison had in mind and in fact that militated most against the evils of faction. By a combination of representation with federal distribution, and of greater numbers buffered by spatial removal, a greater pool of worthy candidates less attracted to local interests and prejudices created a new context: "Extend the sphere and you take on a greater variety of parties and interests; you make it less probable that a majority of the whole will have a common motive to invade the rights of other citizens."[88] The ultimate constitution seemed to be one that had found safety from faction in the very number and variety of factions, parties, and interests, which achieved their neutralization.

In Madison's arrival at a positive construction of faction, Voltaire's observation regarding the virtues of dissent having multiple sources for religious groups proves not altogether random but actually significant in directing our attention to the sphere of religion as the proper and effective pioneer in blunting the expectedly disastrous results of pluralist dissension. In this respect the positive consequences of the Reformation's most negative and horrific features cannot be disallowed. The priority of the neutralization of religious faction reinforces the notion of the upcoming so-called American

Revolution as the last war of religion in European history.[89] For if a stable multicellular condition could be realized in the religious sphere, such an arrangement could be applied more broadly and specifically in the secular sphere. Hume would certainly be instructive and influential, but the role of Adam Smith needs recognition. It has been argued that Madison is alluding to Smith in *Federalist* 10 in the following: "a religious sect may degenerate into a political faction in a part of the Confederacy, but the variety of sects dispersed over the entire face of it, must secure the national Councils against any danger from that source." And again in *Federalist* 51: "In a free government the security for civil rights must be the same as for religious rights. It consists in the one case in the multiplicity of interests, and in the other in the multiplicity of sects." For Smith's analysis of the relationship among religious sects, when left alone by government, follows this pattern. The fanatical zeal and rigid purposes of any one sect, when faced by the same thing among the rest, will dictate a more moderate and reasonable stance. Competition makes it less likely as to the success of a sect selling its frenzied or absurd product.[90] And of course the intervention of government into what has become a more private or local matter in a neutralized sphere could only lead to the capsizing of the entire constitution of this arrangement.

But the complexity of the arrangement did not end there. The refinement and the enlarging of public views are achieved by representation on both the federal and state levels by the passage of such public issues "through the medium of a chosen body of citizens whose wisdom may best discern the true interest of their country," making the sacrifice to narrower interests less likely.[91] By concluding with a number of not entirely rhetorical questions, Madison indicated a concern for sufficient security in opposing and preventing "the concert and accomplishment of the secret wishes of an unjust and interested majority"—security in the reduction of factional passions and removal of the evil to a state, on the more local level of the federal structure. In a later number of the *Federalist Papers*, Madison expressed confidence in this intricate combination of federalism, representation, and factional diversity for the unique affirmation of liberty and pluralism. Europe had discovered the principle of representation, but America could claim the merit of its application to extensive republics.[92] In noting the innovations deployed for the advancement of private rights and public happiness, Madison went on to laud this unprecedented step:

> Happily for America, happily, we trust for the whole human race [the leaders of the Revolution] pursued a new and more noble course. They accomplished a revolution which has no parallel in the annals of human society. They reared the fabrics of governments which have no model on the face of the globe.[93]

In his remarkable paean to the uniqueness of this innovation, Madison resolved the issue of the problem and potentiality of pluralism that Montaigne had foreseen two centuries earlier: the dangers of factionalism could be transcended by the affirmation of pluralism in an extended, rationalized structure. What was soon to elicit wonder and respect from De Tocqueville as well as Talleyrand in their viewing of this new republic proved somehow quite incomprehensible to its second president, John Adams.[94]

With his associates Madison contrived, offered, and persuaded a constitution without parties, apparently party proof. Securing even further the nonpartisan nature of government, the first six presidents, through John Quincy Adams, were readers of Bolingbroke's *The Idea of a Patriot King* and, along with so many of their contemporaries, particularly Washington and Jefferson, took as their model the king or president who stood above party.[95] Yet despite their model and its ideal of eschewing the taint of factionalism, they came to agree with the definition given by Burke: "party as a body of men united for promoting by their joint endeavors the national interest, upon some particular principle in which they all agreed." Such a party of principle sought to combat and dissolve all factional parties and thereupon itself dissolve.[96] Nevertheless, Madison and Jefferson found themselves the organizers of a Republican party that was in deliberate opposition to the early dominance of the Federalists. Later, as Lord Bryce effectively expressed it, the force of party was as necessary to the machinery of government and particularly the whole mass of the national and state governments as steam to the engine of a locomotive.[97]

It was not only party that was inevitable. In an atmosphere still intellectually dominated by Bolingbroke, a Federalist member of the House of Representatives observed in 1798 the notion of rival parties as being not only inevitable but desirable, for in their very contention "a middle course is produced generally conformable to the public good."[98] Apparently something of the American colonial experience was being called forward. Despite their ideal of standing above party, Madison and Jefferson nevertheless created their Republican party in effective opposition to the initial Federalist predominance. The ideal of unanimity was wearing thin for Presidents Monroe and John Quincy Adams, with parties pursuing "fusion policy" and with the obfuscations presented to the growth of parties in the Era of Good Feelings; it would require a total rethinking of party's place in government to break the hold of Bolingbroke and Burke, directed toward the ultimate goal of unanimity and the evaporation of party. That decisive break came with Martin Van Buren, not so much as the promoter of Andrew Jackson for president in 1828 and Van Buren's growing differences with the incumbent President Adams, but much more as the engineer and advocate of government by two distinct, well-organized parties. The new order of government associated with Van Buren and projected by his Albany Regency required the engagement of a broad, popular electorate; party discipline and loyalty; the control of patronage; and spoils to the victors—all coupled with a clear sense of the benefits of forsaking the traditional mystique of social harmony and frankly espousing the constructive nature of political competition and conflict.[99]

The long and often tortuous two centuries' journey from 1628 to 1828 in the Anglo-American world of a European civilization charted a shift from the ideal of coercive orthodoxies, enforced harmony, and unity to a sort of exalted game played between recognized, opposing contestants wherein both not only could but must survive. The triumphant achievement derived from the fact and recognition that a regime's political opponents were to be neither jailed, exiled, nor exterminated, but rather respected as a possible source of criticism, moderation, and systemic correction.

Given the immense complexity and sophistication of the system, the relative isolation of the experiment, and the need for moderation, was it exportable? While the British parliamentary monarchy would remain exemplary for succeeding constitutionalism, liberalism, and organized political parties, these currents, shaped by the experience and fruit of the French Revolution, would on the continent make their tenuous way during the course of the nineteenth century.

But what of the world beyond Europe?

Aftermath

Do you know what is happening in the Orient? An entire world is being transformed, from the banks of the Indus to the Black Sea, in all that immense space, societies are crumbling, religions are being weakened, nationalities are disappearing, all the [old] lights are going out, the old Asiatic world is vanishing, and in its place the European world is rising. Europe in our times does not attack Asia only through a corner, as did Europe in the time of the crusades: She attacks . . . from all sides, puncturing, enveloping, subduing.

—Alexis de Tocqueville, "Second discours, sur la question d'Orient," 1840

He alluded constantly to Europe. . . . Then I noticed a small sketch in oils, on a panel, representing a woman, draped and blindfolded, carrying a lighted torch. The background was somber—almost black. The movement of the woman was stately, and the effect of the torchlight on the face was sinister. . . . To my question he said Mr. Kurtz had painted this.

—Joseph Conrad, *Heart of Darkness*

[We must not] be content with mere political democracy. We must make our political democracy a social democracy as well. . . . What does social democracy mean? It means a way of life which recognises liberty, equality and fraternity as the principles of life. These principles of liberty, equality and fraternity are not to be treated as separate items in a trinity. They form a union of trinity in the sense that to divorce one from

> the other is to defeat the very purpose of democracy. . . . We must begin by acknowledging the fact that there is complete absence of two things in Indian society. One of these is equality. On the social plane, we have in India a society based on the principle of graded inequality which means elevation for some and degradation for others. On the economic plane, we have a society in which there are some who have immense wealth as against many who live in abject poverty. On the 26th January 1950, we are going to enter into a life of contradictions. In politics we will have equality, and in social and economic life we will have inequality. . . . We must remove this contradiction at the earliest possible moment, or else those who suffer from inequality will blow up the structure of political democracy which this Assembly has so laboriously built up.
>
> —B. R. Ambedkar, speech to the Constituent Assembly (India), 1949

By 1914, as it plunged into the First World War, Europe had managed during the course of the previous century to increase its control over the rest of the world from 30 percent to 85 percent.[1] More significantly, in the same period it had broken the long Asian dominance in trade and production: by 1900 it accounted for 65 percent of world trade, accompanied by America with another 15 percent. But, of even greater importance, the immense forces Europe had generated and marshaled during the nineteenth century had allowed for this astonishing mastery of the globe through the ever-greater consolidation of the territorial (now nation-) state, the expanding productivity of capitalism, the application of science to industry, and the rising level of self-confidence, driven in no small measure by notions of white supremacy. More than any other single factor, the institutionalization of high productivity through capitalism would transform the lives of a now-burgeoning population both European and extra-European and would make the nineteenth century not simply Europe's "take-off" period but the decisive break in human history.[2] Furthermore, the relative degree of internal peace among the great states of Europe allowed it to save itself from internal competition by means of ruthless expansion throughout the globe.

Most studies of the present issues emergent and to be deployed throughout the globe will properly and expectably begin their analysis in 1800 or even later, although with reference to the preceding Enlightenment. Our approach has taken a longer, backward gaze and has sought deliberately to avoid the better-trod period of the nineteenth and early twentieth centuries with the full emergence of colonialism, imperialism, and the European world dominance. Yet to support the consideration and understanding of our two themes and their development, the next two hundred years, especially the nineteenth century, must be briefly suggested.

Edward Gibbon and Karl Marx constitute an unlikely pair. Yet each in his own way presents an understanding of the European order's expansion throughout the globe—one in terms of civilization, without ever using that word, the other in terms of the new, enterprising middle class, bearers of the monstrous forces of industrialization, capitalism, and aggressive commerce that will devour the world. One late in the eighteenth century, the other at mid-nineteenth century, together they chart the necessary preliminaries for the progress of Europe's overwhelming of the world. Here we can only briefly allude to and suggest the presence, this mastery, this transformation of context before the issue of universal human rights and the practicality of political dissent on a world scale could become a problem.

This aftermath has the modest intention of leading the reader out beyond the less familiar shades of the past into the familiar, more traveled currents of inquiry and debate.

At the end of the eighteenth century, Immanuel Kant darkly observed that "a whole continent, if it feels itself in a superior position to another one, will not hesitate to plunder it or actually to extend its rule over it."[3] He then went on to chart a secular vision of a cosmopolitan rule of law and constitutional order made possible by increasing communication among the continents. Kant considered a federal union of all peoples—a *civitas gentium,* rather than the annexations and amalgamations productive of universal monarchy—difficult but inevitable. The global vision implicit in his "Toward Perpetual Peace"—and the preposition *toward* (*zur*) needs to be emphasized as conveying a process never completely to be realized—reminds us of the Enlightenment's ideals and their apparent fragility in the face of the momentum of great impersonal forces. Two contemporary understandings of what has here been called Europeanization provide us with a global perspective on this process.

In the "General Observations," which appeared at the end of the third volume of his *Decline and Fall of the Roman Empire* (1781), Edward Gibbon mused on the reasons Europe now felt relatively secure in avoiding a fate similar to imperial Rome's. The question permitted his elegant mind to focus on the Asian homeland of the Mongols, who had pushed inconveniently against both Rome and China and in the later Middle Ages almost overwhelmed Islam; indeed, Eurasia came to appear as a fragile periphery of sedentary civilizations imposingly

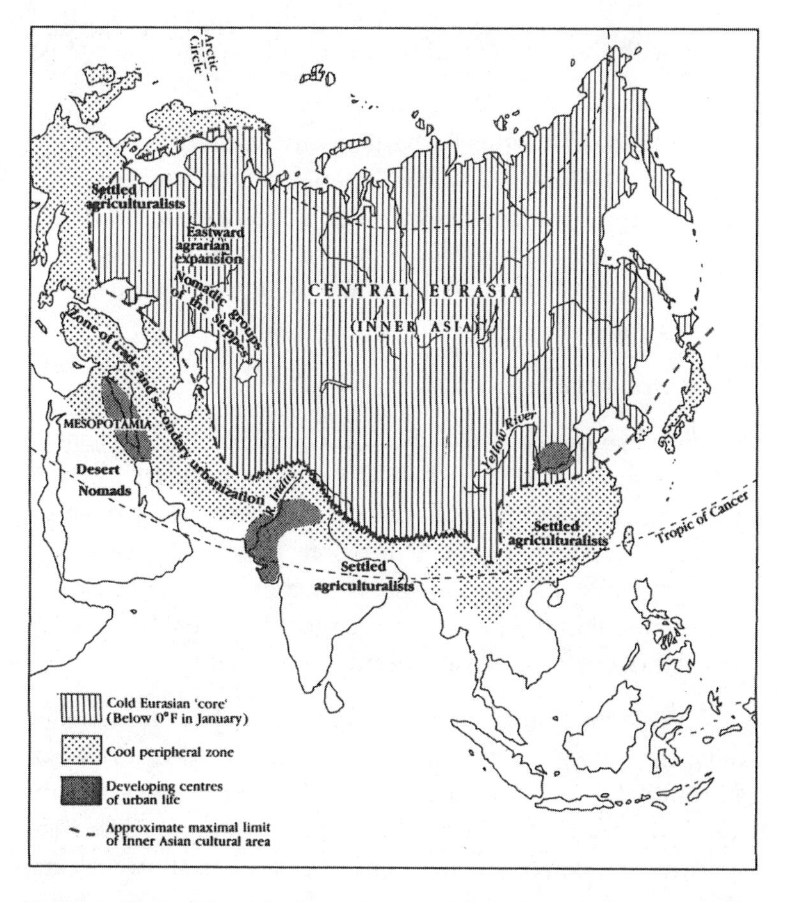

Figure 8. Central Eurasia. A modern rendering of the basic geopolitical conditions that persisted down to the end of the Middle Ages and began to disintegrate only in the early modern period: a nomadic heartland and the fragile fringe of civilizations—European, Moslem, Hindu, and Chinese. Courtesy of Cambridge University Press.

threatened by that great motor of history, the nomadic heartland (see fig. 8). But Gibbon saw the forces of European civilization as having virtually dissolved the Mongol threat. Even in the unlikely event that these "savage conquerors" could cut their way through the complex of well-organized, polite states, with their cultivated peoples, and penetrate to the Atlantic Ocean, then:

> Should the victorious Barbarians carry slavery and desolation as far as the Atlantic Ocean, ten thousand vessels would transport beyond their pursuit the remains of civilized society; and Europe would revive and flourish in the American world, which is already filled with her colonies and institutions.[4]

In a footnote, Gibbon adds:

> America now contains about six millions of European blood and descent; and their numbers, at least in the North, are continually increasing. Whatever may be the changes in their political situation, they must preserve the manners of Europe; and we may reflect with some pleasure, that the English language will probably be diffused over an immense and populous continent.[5]

Gibbon claims Europe to be "one great republic" in a moderately fluctuating balance among its most civilized states. Significantly, he sees Russia as having become a powerful and civilized empire, in effect Europeanized, limiting barbarism "to a narrow span." In his third reason against any reverse visited upon Europe such as ancient Rome suffered, Gibbon turns to the art of war, enhanced by gunpowder and other scientific advances: now, before the barbarians may conquer, "they must cease to be barbarians."[6] The Russia of Catherine II offered itself as a telling example: through a proportionate improvement in the arts of peace and civil policy, it had acquired a place among "the polished nations." It is unlikely, according to Gibbon's global vision, that any people might, in their presumed march toward possible perfection, "relapse into their original barbarism." His considerations conclude with the final step in civilization: the British penetration of the

Pacific Ocean under Cook, "inspired by the pure and generous love of science and mankind," that has introduced into the South Sea islands the plants and animals most useful to human life.[7]

Yet, in this undeniably satisfying global vision, the possibilities for triumphalism are muted by an undercurrent of anxiety and strain. The tensions among the various "polished" parts, then engaged in "temperate" competition, suggest the fragility of Gibbon's luminous balance. Europe, civilization, European civilization had apparently reached its self-conscious apogee. The very word *civilization* had gained currency, passing beyond the *civilité* of good manners to connote something more complex. Gibbon uses the term for the first and, apparently for him, only time in referring to "the progress of civilization" in the sense of "the refinements of life" as potentially corruptive of the sturdy ethic manifested by the German tribes.[8] Appearing in chapter 9 of his first installment of the *Decline and Fall*, published in 1776, the expression "the progress of civilization" abruptly recurs the following year, used in a more positive and potentially comprehensive sense by William Barron in the opening paragraph of his history of ancient colonization. The term was by no means a favorite of Gibbon's, but it had apparently caught on in English usage. In these same years Edmund Burke, who also adhered to the notion of Europe as a republic from which none of its citizens "could altogether be an exile," had arrived at the further notion of "the Western system" in a letter of November 1789 to his friend Lord Fitzwilliams.[9] In his *Reflections on the French Revolution*, he speaks similarly of the term *civilization*: of "our manners, our civilization, and of all good things which are connected with manners and with civilization."[10] Indeed manners seemed to provide something more fundamental than laws.[11] The multicellular character of Europe, Gibbon's republic of nations, had already entered the realm of international law a generation earlier in the work of Emeric de Vattel.[12] This complex system seemed to afford a mechanism of mutual stimulation and emulation, while admitting limit and control upon its members. Here again the British historian could contrast it to the stultifying, carceral uniformity of the earlier Roman Empire, which offered no check upon or redress from the almighty ruler:

> The division of Europe into a number of independent states, connected however, with each other, by the general resemblance of religion, language, and manners, is productive of the most beneficial consequences to the liberty of mankind. A modern tyrant, who should find no resistance either in his own breast or in his people, would soon experience a gentle restraint from the example of his equals, the dread of present censure, the advice of his allies, and the apprehension of his enemies.[13]

Such a fine balance, so dependent upon the moderation of its members, presented a frighteningly fragile order for accommodating the challenges of the oncoming century. Of aristocratic construction—an aristocracy of the mind, rather than of the social order—this tense balance lacked any sense of such new realities as nationalism and the more impersonal forces of economic growth and population increase, thus exposing its own vulnerability to such transformative currents. Europe itself, multicellular, polycentric, rich in its variety whatever the basic commonality, has well been defined as "composed of its differences, as a delicate unity of differences."[14] After 1790 its aristocratic character, of Enlightened minting, would suffer a pervasive transformation.

Sixty years later, at mid-century, Karl Marx presents us with a very different global vision. A new entity, long in gestation, had entered the lists to produce a class-ridden society and introduce the exponential increases of a capitalist economy to the globe:

> The bourgeoisie, wherever it has got the upper hand, has put an end to all feudal, patriarchal, idyllic relations. It has pitilessly torn asunder the motley feudal ties that bound man to his "natural superiors," and has left remaining no other nexus between man and man than naked self-interest, than callous "cash payment." . . . It has been the first to show what man's activity can bring about. It has accomplished wonders far surpassing Egyptian pyramids, Roman aqueducts, and Gothic cathedrals; it has conducted expeditions that put in the shade all former Exoduses of nations and crusades. . . . All fixed, fast-frozen relations, with their train of ancient and venerable prejudices and opinions, are swept away, all new-formed ones become antiquated before they can ossify. . . . The need of a constantly expanding market for its products chases the bourgeoisie over the whole surface of the globe. It must nestle everywhere, settle everywhere, establish connections everywhere. . . . The bourgeoisie, by the rapid improvement of all instruments of production, by the immensely facilitated means of communication, draws all, even the most barbarian, nations into civilization. The cheap prices of its commodities are the heavy artillery with which it batters down all Chinese walls, with which it forces the barbarians' intensely obstinate hatred of foreigners to capitulate. It compels all nations, on pain of extinction, to adopt the bourgeois mode of production; it compels them to introduce what it calls civilization into their midst, i.e., to become bourgeois themselves. In a word, it creates a world after its own image. . . . Just as it has made the country dependent on towns, so it has made

> barbarian and semi-barbarian countries dependent on the civilized ones, nations of peasants on nations of bourgeois, the East on the West.[15]

In this tsunami of revolutionary change that Marx analyzes so eloquently, what had only begun in 1848 accelerated and expanded in its intensity and effect up to the present—a total transformation not only of a world economy, but of human lives and the earth's surface. Among the new transforming currents affecting the globe at mid-century, a sinister change had developed regarding the notion of mankind—no longer a recent emerging consensus on the basic physical and moral homogeneity of humans apart from superficial differences, but now rather an emphasis upon the intrinsic heterogeneity of mankind, no matter the superficial similarities.[16] As Europe exploded upon the globe and its peoples, the tension within the concept of universality could be viewed from another angle provided by that most perceptive of analysts, Alexis de Tocqueville, in his appreciation of the British liberal colonial enterprise as reflecting two premises: the first, that all humans are equal, all cultures commensurable, and human progress can be calibrated upon a single scale; yet the second, that the English on account of their considerable accomplishments were somehow quite different, both individually and as a caste apart, and that this mentality proved more grating to indigenous peoples than the caste mentality of Brahminism. In the shrill light of de Tocqueville's insight, the evidence of a new European energy and self-confidence, all too often driven by racist attitudes, dispelled the former respect for China: Chinese and Indian cultures appeared to be enslaved to tradition and social convention, distrustful of innovation, and backward.[17]

In the latter part of the century the nation-state, the approved Western answer to the question of effective polity, drew unto itself the new forces of the age and consolidated itself. By the end of the nineteenth century, an ever-improved weaponry had reached alarming proportions. At Omdurman in 1898 the British effortlessly slaughtered more than ten thousand Sudanese with the modest loss of forty-eight of their own, a victory that was credited to the stupendous capacity of the new Maxim gun to administer death.[18] Major von Tiedemann, the German military attaché present, took due note of the matter.[19] Within two decades Europe turned this firepower upon itself in a first bout at suicide, 1914–18, that killed a thousand times the number slaughtered at Omdurman. And then, thirty years later, as if Europeans had not yet gotten the message—another sixty million, but on a grander, more global scale.

The nightmare of the *philosophes* had become reality: the civilizers had become the savages—but worse. In fact, it took the death camps of the Nazis and the general horror of World War II to awaken Europe, now the West, and even the global conscience of all peoples out of the sleepwalk that had allowed the issue of human rights largely to absent itself from the nineteenth and the first part of the twentieth centuries; indeed, the League of Nations had seen no need to attempt some statement regarding rights. It was in a brief moment of shared horror, 1945–48, that representatives of all the earth's peoples convened to compose what became the Universal Declaration of Human Rights—an act that probably would have been impossible any later, given the rising tide of national and cold war concerns after 1950. Guiding the difficult negotiations and making possible their success was Eleanor Roosevelt—a woman, no less—who, insofar as the ideal of a common humanity has long-range magnitude and resonance, can truly be considered the greatest person of the twentieth century. Although the declaration was nonbinding and reflected more an aspiration than an established reality, it served as an ideal and international measuring stick for the firm and full inclusion of women within the concept of humanity. At the same time, following two spasms of civilizational suicide, the mid-twentieth century managed to nurture out of the ashes of war no fewer than three modern democracies—the two defeated powers, Germany and Japan, and India, as a consequence of Britain's imperial withdrawal. Nevertheless, little room seemed to exist for self-congratulation on this score: the same mid-century that marked the declaration of human rights saw the minting of a new term, *genocide*.[20] Three occasions of it in the subsequent half century made the twentieth, in the opinion of one authoritative historian, the most murderous as well as the most revolutionary.[21]

Epilogue

There is a deeper objection to policies of multiculturalism that issue in the creation of group rights. This is that a stable liberal civil society cannot be radically multicultural but depends for its successful renewal across the generations on an undergirding culture that is held in common. This common culture need not encompass a shared religion and it certainly need not presuppose ethnic homogeneity, but it does demand widespread acceptance of certain norms and conventions of behavior and in our times, it typically expresses a shared sense of nationality. . . . In so far as policy has been animated by [adherence to abstract rules rather than to a common culture], the result has been further social division, including what amounts to low-level civil war between the races. As things stand, the likelihood in the United States is of a slow slide into ungovernability, as the remaining patrimony of a common cultural inheritance is frittered away by the fragmenting forces of multiculturalism.

—John Gray, *Enlightenment's Wake*, 1995

Do not let us make any mistake about this. The natural government of man is servitude. Tyranny is the normal pattern of government. It is only by intense thought, by great effort, by burning idealism and unlimited sacrifice that freedom has prevailed as a system of government. And the efforts which were first necessary to create it are fully necessary to sustain it in our own day. He who offers this thing we call freedom as the soft option is a deceiver of himself

> deceived. He who sells it cheap or offers it as the by-product of this or that economic system is a knave or fool. For freedom demands infinitely more care and devotion than any other political system. It puts consent and personal initiative in the place of command and obedience. By relying upon the devotion and initiative of ordinary citizens, it gives up the harsh but effective disciplines that underpin all the tyrannies which over the millennia have stunted the full stature of men.
>
> —Adlai Stevenson, speech delivered in Constitution Hall, January 1, 1959

> Provincializing Europe cannot ever be a project of shunning European thought. For at the end of European imperialism, European thought is a gift to us all.
>
> —Dipesh Chakrabarty, *Provincializing Europe,* 2000

Although it is not normally the office of a historian to enter upon the tricky currents of present politics and affairs, it becomes appropriate for us to consider the prospects of our two political principles under existing conditions by returning to the initial question at the beginning of this inquiry: If potentially universal, how currently exportable? For this study has sought to affirm the uniqueness of the West's sustained adherence to a principle of universal equality present in the idea of a common humanity and the implicit principle of freedom, also unique, present in the willingness to contend with dissent and its alternatives. Although the resulting judgments can only be speculative and subject to the limitations and prejudices of a particular historian, yet the weight of the previous analysis and the momentum of the two political principles themselves pose the question: To what extent is each effective in today's context?

With its inhering commitments to universality and equality, the idea of a common humanity operates as a formidable ideal that can be judged in terms of its own intrinsic integrity and momentum, despite the grave lapses among even its most eminent proponents. Thomas Jefferson, among other slaveholders, asserted that all men are created equal, thus posing the patent absurdity and glaring contradiction that perhaps can best be understood by resorting to the famous dictum that all are equal, but some are more equal than others. In many ways, quite apart from the immediate intention of the statement, when applied to the larger context of the present argument it provides us with an indictment of the terrible injustice in the blatant gap between ideal and practice that Europe allowed during its heyday of global imperialism. Nevertheless, the fact remains that given the human consciousness's quest for justice, and with the ideal serving as an immortal spur according to its own inexorable, implacable logic, there will in time appear, far down the track, one who actually believes and takes seriously the ideal and has the power to render it effective, an Abraham Lincoln. And a century after Lincoln the civil rights movement of the 1960s reminded us of the continuing need for reassertion and restatement of this ideal. No matter how apparently inexorable the presence of this ideal, it must always wait upon the historical circumstances for its advancement.

Since no idea operates in a vacuum, the practicalities of exporting programs of human rights demands consideration. An assessment rendered in 1993 regarding the prospects for the human rights program saw four threats to its progress: "unchecked population growth; ethnic religious and nationalist xenophobia; the world's fragile ecology; and the baleful results of unrestricted trade in armaments."[1] Unfortunately, in the succeeding years little has been done to correct these threats and the situation has in fact worsened; only with respect to Europe itself has population increase significantly abated—and there rather ominously. At the same time, the new, unexpected factor of global terrorism has further darkened and certainly complicated the prospects. An enduring tribalism, moreover, with its practice of honor killing, still rife in Islam, magnifies the plight of many Muslim women and thereby offers a frontier for human rights. But beyond any program of human rights, all too often burdened with exaggerated expectations and claims, even beyond any principle of equality, itself fraught with inner tensions and difficulties, there remains the quest for justice; an aspiration persists, burning in the conscience.

Freedom in the form of constitutional democracy represents a more precarious, complex, and ultimately intangible commodity, something much more immediately of human construction. Because we as Americans are currently in the mission of "spreading democracy," a realistic assessment of its exportability seems justified. For if the trumpet gives an uncertain sound, who will rally to the summons?

Ever since early 2001—9/11 simply accelerated the development—the United States has seriously compromised its moral leadership within the world community, howsoever fragile and tentative that role, and has become in effect a leading rogue state. Though the present administration cannot be solely blamed for an erosion of civil rights by previous administrations both Republican and Democratic, nevertheless it has proceeded to paint the world in black-and-white moralistic terms and has been able to impose a reduction of civil rights upon a willing, fearful populace. As in the Germany of 1933, so in the United States in 2001, and again in 2004, the effects of fear and confusion have caused citizens to value leadership and commitment, no matter to what, in place of any considered weighing of alternatives in the interest of justice. Democracy is so much more than holding elections; it requires respect for law, for the rules. The ability to set and maintain the example of lawfulness and moderation is crucial. Yet the enormity of Abu Ghraib, its continuance at Guantánamo and elsewhere—our very own gulag archipelago with its searing violation of legal procedures—all too long unaddressed and thereby enjoying the apparent compliance of the nation, have dispelled the image of America as generous, law abiding, and somehow removed from the ordinary evils of the world. Now we are very unspecial, like all the rest—but worse—a seeming difference lost, probably never to be recovered. The abandonment of law and all lawfulness leads us into untold embarrassments and difficulties. As Grotius had warned in his Prolegomena: "All things are uncertain the moment men depart from the law." Most recently, in the violation of what signifies for many the ark of international law and practice and the most recent abandonment of due process, a benighted executive together with a lamentably short-sighted Congress has provided the tools for the undoing of America throughout the world and in the later historical record. The secular vault of heaven has received a fatal crack.

Equally alarming are the tactics of the majority party: violating the boundaries between politics and religion, working for the obliteration rather than the reasoned contestation of its opposite. Rules, accountability, even laws are trashed or ignored by the congressional leadership itself, and the executive office now cherry-picks parts of the law it wishes to recognize and pursues their selective enforcement. A craven, demoralized opposition party, having fed at the same trough, proves itself incapable of operating effectively. With the supporting institutions of a presently threatened free press and a dangerously politicized judiciary, are the traditional checks and balances checking and balancing? Given the ugly face that America has abruptly acquired, the prospects for spreading freedom are dim indeed. An excessive reliance upon brute force has instead come to predominate—all in support of a way of life, a standard of living impossible to sustain here, much less extend to the rest of the planet.

In the present climate many an academic has come to see the university as the only remaining bulwark against the current monopolization of government by a highly conservative, ideologically driven party. For is not the current unfortunate condition to be understood in terms of a straightforward polarization between neoconservatism and the liberalism that abounds in the academic world? Each sees the worst in the other, its own intensity feeding upon the nutty fringe of its opponent, and represents the extreme of its own camp, while disallowing any space for compromise, negotiation, moderation. If there is a certain truth in such viewing of the political scene, then from the perspective of any effort to understand our own civilization and transmit pedagogically its unique features and aspirations to succeeding generations, the developments in American academe since the 1960s have proved counterproductive; they have worked in their own way to disassemble and traduce the valuable import of liberties and human experience that should work toward the reconstruction of liberalism as a coherent political philosophy rather than allow it to parade itself in its present ragged, often garish garb. Indeed, we seem to have here the supreme case of the baby having been thrown out with the bathwater. For without the principled reference, study, and appreciation of the Western development as the continuing agent and source of global initiatives, the pursuit of cultural diversity becomes baseless. Both American academe and the present administration, howsoever clearly opposed, together work to scuttle what should be positive and enduring in this unique civilization: the former undermining its inspiring past, its persisting import; the latter disassembling its constituted face.

Regarding any effort to recenter an Enlightenment that has been hollowed out, its perspectives fractured, we owe much of the difficulty to ourselves, the intellectual community. Most evidently in the literatures the delights of relativism, subjectivism, and nihilism have been indulged, with rampant energies expended in often ludicrous frivolities and trivial pursuits, making a mockery of the academy's humanities programs. Little wonder that such programs falter, fail to attract the serious student, lack funding and support. Better that such energies be revised and refocused in conveying a more modest, moderate view of Christianity, Europe, the West, and its legacy so that we may reapproach "the Rest" with understanding, with aid, stemming from a better self-knowledge.

It is difficult to end on a positive note. With so many fundamentals in disarray and threatened, one can well appreciate the resort of Greek drama to a *deus ex machina* as a way out of a dilemma. Such a way, if it exists for us, is not likely to be found in any one leader, especially one dangerously populist or charismatic, but more fundamentally in a redefinition and implementation of the public interest that may nurture a reordered opposition and dissent, a regeneration of public attitudes more generously oriented, and ideals recentered, made worthy of meaningful sacrifice.

More questions remain. Two unique and most valuable historical developments credited to European civilization have here been traced. How, if at all, are they related to each other? To what extent can the European/Western capacity for admitting and constructively using dissent moderate the excesses of universalism? And how are the sources of these two principles in Christianity and the classical tradition related to each other through time? Any reconsideration of the components that made possible the initial statement of natural rights pertaining to all men, beginning in the twelfth century and subsequently evolving, must recognize its foundations both in classical Stoicism and Christianity. Our story has revealed an increasing removal from the expressly religious to the secularity characteristic of European universalism. For no matter how universal Christianity's aspirations, as a specific religion it inevitably introduces an explicitly exclusive particularism in its theology and morals, which the secularity of the classical component transcends or loosens to achieve a fair degree of neutrality. In this process successive updates of Stoicism have played their part in the advancement of a relative neutrality on otherwise explosive, divisive issues harbored by religion. The impact of the Reformation's successive dissents shattered the front of a formal Christian unity and introduced the experience of fratricidal religious warfare, which Europe ultimately and uniquely managed to transcend to its own advantage. With a longer perspective Europe's dreadful experience, derived from the horrors of religious fundamentalism and the futility of theological definition, has here been judged positive in that it ended by inducing a mood of tolerance, compromise, and moderation in matters religious, as well as by the heightening of a secular neutrality. The new mood allowed multiple cultural engagements and the decisive transfer of religion from a public issue to a private matter of individual conscience. The Virginia Bill of Rights of 1776 consolidated this achievement: its sixteenth article, which pertains to religion, resulted from the direct intervention of James Madison.[2] The prevailing late eighteenth-century attitudes of benevolence, compromise, and, above all, moderation further secured this achievement.

In any analysis of their relationship, the universalizing force first engages our attention as the more pervasive, comprehensive, and enduring of our two principles. For with its complex composition it can either promote or suffocate self-criticism, review, and reasoned dissent. From the beginning, as constructed out of Christian and classical components, the fit was never perfect. Tension existed and persisted. There lurked within the unsteady, ever-readjusted composition, which, following the Reformation, gave way to a secularizing preeminence, the latent passion for destroying not only universality itself, but that moderation and spirit of compromise that made dissent and constituted opposition possible. Only the most cultivated, moderated, deft handling of Christian universality such as that evinced by the Jesuits in China, civilized and civilizing, could turn the powerful religious component away from evangelical extremes. Yet in the Chinese experiment this effort led to a neutering of Christianity for the Jesuits involved.

The ending of the slave trade in Great Britain and of slavery in general, 1807 and 1833 respectively, though somewhat outside the purview of our study, presents us with an extraordinary instance of the continuing presence and importance of the religious component to our equation. Therein a refreshed, explicitly Christian impulse, a case of evangelical Christianity applied to the gravest public social ill, demonstrates a decisive and resounding contribution to that universality implicit in the idea of a common humanity. The initiative of the Clapham Sect in mobilizing public opinion by means of a multidenominational Christian fervor produced perhaps the first pressure group in history to bring its influence to bear upon the existing political framework.[3] Such a public—rather than governmental—political initiative suggests at their best the continuing resources of Christian churches for the furthering of that universal equality, unity, and community announced at our beginning. Only silently and indirectly did the Enlightenment here play a part.[4]

Failing to obtain anything like the widespread public pressure and persistent government support evident in Great Britain, a comparable abolitionist effort in the new United States proved abortive. Despite the appeals of both Presidents Jefferson and Madison to the principle of humanity and to the violation of human rights, the secular language of the Enlightenment failed, ironically, where Christian basics had succeeded elsewhere. Within a strained Anglo-American world, difference in context and circumstances helped to explain the discrepancy.[5]

In the new millennium a most grotesque development has become evident. With the express reintroduction of the religious into politics in an extreme ideological and most ignorant form, five hundred years or more of tenuous progress have been reversed and thrown into question. Once God in a particularistic, politicized guise has been reintroduced, an Absolute that defies compromise or moderation drives an ideological wedge into a matrix constructed to avoid such extremes. A dormant native fundamentalism is reassembled to counter a foreign one. The self-appointed people of faith, somehow marvelously endowed with God, now carry their banner through the entire apparently tainted system for its correction; the godly bring to their task a radical conservatism reinforced by a misplaced patriotism. This faith-based initiative of a violent, sometimes even murderous, extremism undercuts possibilities for compromise; presently unchecked by any effective dissent or opposition, it drags the uncertain into the experience of fundamentalist conflict. No matter the crippling effect on diplomacy—negotiation becomes impossible, for how can the Righteous have any dealings with Evil? The reintroduction of religious and moral specificities only heightens the displacement of all that salutary moderation made possible by the achievements of the late eighteenth century. The present abruption of the Christian component further underlines the fact that if the peculiar merits of our system are to be retained and function properly in any worldwide appeal, the specifically Christian element in its presumed universality must be curtailed in public affairs and limited to the private sphere. For the story recounted here demonstrates the merciful predominance of the secular element and the tempering of the Christian.

As America's moral, economic, and political leadership disintegrates throughout the world and China's hitherto traditional hegemony of the Middle Kingdom enjoys a renewal, the question of human rights held by both Western and Chinese civilizations presses to the fore. Without intruding upon the current politics of human rights and the grounds for a future accord between or meld of both traditions, one might hazard that the Western view of human rights could only benefit from some of the possible correctives that Chinese humanism might supply:[6] to Western individualism, now exaggerated to the point of promoting hedonism and permissiveness and all too forgetful apparently of its own inhering sense of duties and responsibilities, the Confucian tradition brings a sense of moral potential that shifts the emphasis from the individual's primary relation to the state, to power, to the ruler, to the individual's relationship to society and to fellow human beings—to moral reciprocity. For its own part, the Western program can supply a much-needed legal, political grounding to Chinese notions of human rights. It can extend the principle of equality to the traditional Confucian program of rites, rather than rights, wherein hierarchical and dictatorial features still lurk.[7]

Beyond such a possibly fruitful interchange, the uniqueness of the Western tradition in the creation of a common humanity needs to be reaffirmed. From the beginning, the process of its universalization establishes a focus on all humans everywhere, a principle of equality, transcending any one particular political entity, not just in the most graced part of the earth, a principle continuously sustained by increasing intellectual rigor rather than occasional fine statements or exemplars. For only within a condition of basic equality can there be justice in the simplest understanding of the term—the persistent will to render unto each one's own, one's due, one's right. Second, this sense of an almost sacred individuality as a property of the self radiates from a legal, political, constitutional framework—an achievement that finds something of its explanation in our second political uniqueness here sketched, namely, the legality and recognition of political dissent. There persists the clumsy yet ultimately effective extending of human equality, dignity, and reciprocal recognition not just to people of color, but to women, where it would seem the basic and most decisive battles are still to be fought and won throughout the world.

Joseph Conrad tells us that all of Europe went into the making of Kurtz. Certainly the serpent of exclusion still lurked amidst the West's universalizing currents and its uniquely attained practice of political dissent. Yet Europe and its most significant transatlantic extension possessed other resources and the capacity to reassert them. Since 1800 and the clear, public enunciation of principles promotive of human rights, each generation would need to reclaim the idea and ideal of equality in its own way, circumstances, and space. For like freedom itself, the idea of equality, the bearer of natural human rights, howsoever fragile and debatable, would simply not go away. The spur forged in earlier centuries by elements of European thought and experience must await the direction of a better-endowed rider and a more coherent public.

Notes

Introduction

1. D'Avity, sigs. eij–eiij^{v} in the dedicatory letter to the chancellor, Pierre Seguier.

2. Gellner, 1992: 71, 77–79.

3. Gress, 1998: 558. Gerard Delanty's *Inventing Europe*, which came to my attention only belatedly during the process of publication, dates the emergence and comprehensive application of the term West from the moment of the western frontier's opening after 1492. Thence the lingering notion of Christendom as well as that of Europe itself becomes increasingly identified with a western crusading movement (14, 45–46). Such a view does not disallow the full emergence and recognition of the term West much later, about 1900.

4. Pocock, 2005: 238.

5. Sen, 1997: 22–30; 2005: 234–88. Such a position by no means discounts or minimizes the value and importance of such scattered moments or implicit traditions wherein Hinduism, Buddhism, Confucianism, or Islam suggests comparable or supporting notions toward a broader view of humanity, tolerance, and diversity. In fact, this very presence and reality make possible the reception of the Western stimulus and challenge, which has already attained some broader evidence of acceptance since the Universal Declaration of Human Rights in 1948 and subsequent covenants. At the same time, however, the fundamentally Western origins of human rights, coming in the wake of European imperialism and colonialism, hardly recommend their immediate support by Asian and African peoples and make all the more necessary the particular role of their "provincial" embodiment (Sen, 2005: 284–88 passim; Freeman, 52).

6. Chakrabarty, 124–29. With rare sensitivity this author seems to respond to just such an invitation for grafting or possible stimulus in his analysis of the Bengali notion of *hriday* (heart), which appears to be a local, yet intense, version of human sympathy or compassion, somehow darkened or blocked by custom. Here the contrast emerges between the Enlightenment understanding of compassion as natural, hence universal, and the Bengali understanding of it as special—so special and excep-

tional as to place its agents above the ordinary human. There would seem to be thus an invitation or room for some sort of adjustment between the universal and the mysteriously exceptional that could go beyond simply a "mutual supplementation." To the extent that any agreement between rival views of human rights requires acceptance of the whole package of one party to the neglect of anything of the others, Charles Taylor (1999) warns that such consensus would be unlikely or merely imposed. On the matter of the Hindu experience of compassion itself, Kwok (86) interestingly attributes to Buddhism "the dimension of kindness and compassion" in Chinese sensibilities. On this same matter see the remarks of Irene Bloom (102) on Mencius and compassion. Nor is the possibility of grafting or some sort of loose consensus entirely absent in Islamic thought, although the attitude here seems to be more one of already possessing all the essentials within itself than any willing openness. Norani Othman (173) affirms the Quranic notion of a "common human ontology" (*fitna,* nature) expressed in the Islamic idiom of a moral universalism. Othman's own inquiry is directed more to the issue of greater equality for women within *shari'a* than to any need for an initiative imparted or an accord with Western programs of human rights.

Chapter 1. The Renaissance Defining and Engagement of the Global Arena of Humanity

The epigraphs in this chapter are taken from Perry Anderson, *Lineages of the Absolute State* (London, 1974), 422; and Cicero, *De re publica,* trans. Clinton Walker Reyes, Loeb ed. (London, 1928), VI.19, 273–75.

1. Richards, 106–7; Harley, 1988a.
2. Cormack, 1997.
3. Elliott, 1986: 177–78; 361–62.
4. Buisseret, 2003: 24.
5. Ptolemaeus, I.i (sig. a): Geographia imitatio est picturae totius partis terrae cognitae, cum ijs, quae sibi quasi universaliter sunt annexa.
6. Cormack, 1991: 641–42.
7. Ibid., 644.
8. Ptolemaeus, vii.6 (sig. M4).
9. On the decisive nature of this controversy for the early definition of geography and more generally for the map as a commercial and political product, see the valuable study by Brotton, 138–53 passim. Cf. also Buisseret, 1992.
10. On the political reading and import of maps see Harley, 1988a in general and 1988b: 282, 301, and more recently Blair, 174–75.
11. Gadol, 198.

12. Cormack, 1997: 59–86; Pocock, 2005: 312.

13. Buisseret, 2003: 112.

14. On the idea of a politicization of oceanic space in the early modern period, see the interesting article by Elizabeth Mancke.

15. Scholars, guided by the faulty analysis of Pierre Chaunu, who did not take into account rampant smuggling, have allowed themselves to overlook the tremendous commercial precocity of Manila, made evident only recently by the work of Professors Flynn and Giráldez (1995a and 1995b). Here I must myself admit guilt in my paper (1995) presented serendipitously at the same session of the World History Association in Honolulu where the two scholars first revealed their program. In the construction and understanding of how the world economy first comes into being through the Manila exchange, Flynn and Giráldez begin with the centrality of China, representing one-quarter of the population of the earth, now giving up a paper currency for silver and thus establishing a voracious appetite for that metal; on the supply side both Spain (Peru and later Mexico) and Japan providing ample quantities of silver. By the mid-seventeenth century the ratio of silver to gold achieved an equilibrium throughout Europe, Asia, and America, thereby announcing the reality of a global economy. Concurrently the introduction of the sweet potato into China, also through Manila, and the concomitant presence of other American crops, peanuts and maize, more through the initiatives of the Portuguese and Dutch, served to transform the economy and the ecology as well as the diet of China and further magnify the reality of a truly global economy whose vital belt of exchange comes to be buckled at Manila after 1571. On sugar, etc. see Mazumdar.

16. Lindberg, 29–35.

17. Vescovini, 969–74.

18. Lindberg, 32.

19. Panofsky, 27; 75–76.

20. Ibid., 15.

21. Ibid.

22. Goldstein, 1965: 14–25; Seed, 1995: 118–26.

23. Phelan, 88.

24. On the recovery of the manuscript of Ptolemy's *Geographia* see Hankins, 119–27; on its content and import see Gadol, 69–71, 198–200.

25. The import of the cognitive resonances created by mapping and terrestrial globes warrants further consideration for the late Renaissance. On Mercator here see Akerman, 21, 24; on geography and possession see Blair, 174–75.

26. Buisseret, 2003: 14–28, on this new way of seeing and its reception, as well as the subsequent chapter, "The Painterly Origins of Some European Mapping," 29–48.

27. Edgerton, 1975: 98–99; Broc, 205–21, especially 205–7 and 217–21, for the intimate association and collaboration of painters and geographers in the ordering of space.

28. Rico, 2: 600; cf. Thrower, 51–53.

29. Goldstein, 1980: 30–34.

30. Näf, 1: 267, 270.

31. Lindgren, 155.

32. For the text of Santa Cruz's *Islario general* see Naudé, 127–70 at 140, 145.

33. Butzer, 353–57, 361; cf. also Mundy, 18. On the development of Spanish nautical science, its institutions, practices, and personnel, in the sixteenth century and its fateful curtailment, see the excellent article by Ursula Lamb, especially pp. 680–81 on Ovando and Velasco.

34. Favaro, 51–53.

35. Schmitt, 56–60.

36. Gusdorf, 3:1, 383.

37. Heylyn, I, fol. [A_3^v].

38. For Ptolemy's *Geographia* as an icon of mastery see Binding, 189, and for Ortelius in general. See also Skelton's introduction, titled "Bibliographical Note," to the Cleveland, Ohio reprint of the *Theatrum* (1964).

39. For an extended description and analysis of the title page, see Binding, 207–18, especially 211.

40. Pendergrass, 36.

41. Scammell, 412. For Charles V's motto *Plus oultre*, see Rosenthal. On Francis I's use of Juvenal's *unus non sufficit orbis* see Jardine and Brotton, 48.

42. Montaigne, 1965: 693, 695.

43. Ibid., 611, 857; cf. *Les essais de Montaigne*, ed. Pierre Villey and V. L. Saulnier (Paris, 1988), 3:13, 1116.

44. Godinho, 41; Bödeker, 1074–76.

45. Dupront, 53. Even in the hell that ostensible European universalism had created for the African and Indian peoples, the fragile, flickering survival of notions of humanity and natural rights can be found not only in the writings and actions of Las Casas but also with Tomás de Mercado, Bartolomé de Albornoz, and Alonso de Sandoval. On this see Blackburn, 150–56.

46. Giovanni Botero, *Le relationi universali* (Venice: Alessandro Vecchi, 1612), III.i.3–4. The pagination is in accordance with each individual part. On the basis of the numerous editions that I have examined at the John Carter Brown Library, a pagination consecutive throughout first occurs in the Bertani edition (Venice, 1671), a copy of which Professor Paul Grendler lent me. I have chosen to use here the 1612 Venice edition, the

last over which Botero could have exercised any control before his death in 1617. The large Roman numeral represents the *Parte*, the small Roman numeral, the *libro*, and the third figure, the page number. Regarding Europe as a cultural reality, Carlo Ginzburg credits Lorenzo Valla with one of the earliest uses of the word *Europe* in a cultural rather than a geographical sense: Europe as a distinct civilization based on competition and commerce but defined and unified by the Latin language. Valla's inaugural lecture, read at the university of Rome on October 18, 1455, is seen by Ginzburg as a prophecy of later European expansion (66).

47. Headley, 2005: 157–58.

48. Ibid., 160–65.

49. Buisseret, 2003: 55–57.

50. On the general condition of map production in the early sixteenth century, see Bagrow, 53–62, especially 60–61; Tooley, 12–47, especially 12–13.

51. On the importance of Gastaldi and the scope of his work, see Karrow, 216–49, especially 216, 226–27, 229.

52. For Ramusio in general, but with particular reference to his social context and network of leading associates, see Donattini, 55–100. For a useful biographical sketch of Ramusio, see Parks, 127–48. For a later work on Ramusio, see the introductions and annotations of Marica Milanesi in her definitive edition of the *Navigazioni e viaggi*, 6 vols. (Turin, 1978–88); see also Milanesi, 1984. Most recently Ramusio has been treated in another perspective by Liz Horodowich, "Armchair Travelers and the Venetian Discovery of the New World," *Sixteenth Century Journal* 36/4 (2005): 1039–62, which emphasizes the contextual constraints upon Ramusio at this time to the detriment of any appreciation of his formidable achievement.

53. Donattini, 81–83, 98; Parks, 129–38.

54. Donattini, 58, 99.

55. Ramusio, 1:8: "onde si può chiaramente comprendere che d'ogni intorno questo globo della terra è maravigliosamente abitato, né vi è parte alcuna vacua, né per caldo o gielo priva d'abitatori."

56. For some interesting elaborations upon the theme of the Copernican *propter nos*, quite apart from the study of Ramusio itself, see Sylvia Wynter, 251–86.

57. Penrose, given to loving description of the details of discovery, seems innocent of it. The one possible exception is the comprehensive study of Giuliano Gliozzi, *Adamo e il nuovo mondo*, which, though it exhaustively analyzes the manifestations of habitability and their implications, does not address the issue itself.

58. Romm, 1992: 37–38.

59. Arentzen, 320–21. On the iconic, nonrepresentational nature of the T-O map and how its misreading by the nineteenth century helped to contribute to the belief that the Middle Ages held to a flat-earth notion of the world, see the interesting analysis by Lesley B. Cormack, 1995: 363–85. It is unfortunate that this spook is still pervasive in our schools and annually joins in the celebration of Columbus Day through the media.

60. Romm, 1992: 128–31.

61. Ibid., 164–71; Randles, 5–76, especially 10–11 (hereafter cited as *CTA*).

62. Cicero, *De re publica*, VI.xix (Loeb edition, 272–74); cf. Macrobius, 284–86.

63. Flint, 65–80, especially 70–80. On the polygenetic view of human origins and racialist theories emerging in the course of the seventeenth century, see Gliozzi, 331–56, 514–621.

64. D'Ailly, 1: 206–15.

65. Ibid., 1: 206–8.

66. Goldstein, 1972: 19–51, especially 36–40.

67. Goldstein, 1965: 9–32, especially 18–25; Moretti, in *CTA*, 1: 241–84, especially 271–75.

68. Ravenstein, 71.

69. Ibid., 113, where the English translation of this letter, dated July 14, 1493, figures as document 9 of the appendix. Regarding Muslim thoughts on the problem of the earth's habitability, Ibn Khaldūn in his *Prolegomena* betrays some uncertainty. He estimates that the dry part of the earth covers half its total surface and the inhabited part about one-quarter of this amount, the southern part having the greatest wastes. While not excluding the possibility of occasional habitation in the torrid zone, he considers that the excessive heat makes the existence of a human population there highly unlikely. Interestingly enough, however, he observes that Ibn Rushd (Averroes) believes this torrid zone to be temperate and the regions lying south of it similar to those in the north and thus likewise inhabited. See Issawi, 1950: 38–40.

70. See Kish, 249–50, which refers to C. R. Beazley's edition of the remarkable "Directorium ad faciendum passagium transmarinum," *American Historical Review* 12 (1907): 810–57, especially 821–22, and 13 (1907): 66–115 (my own translation).

71. For the passage in Guicciardini's *Storia d'Italia*, I am indebted to my colleague Kenneth R. Bartlett, whose outstanding paper, "Burckhardt's Myopia: The Renaissance, Humanism, and the World," delivered at the Fourth International Conference of the World History Association, quoted at length the passage found in S. Alexander's translation, *History*

of Italy (New York, 1965), 182. I wish to thank him for bringing this passage to my attention.

72. *America pontificia primi saeculi evangelizationis, 1493–1592*, ed. Josef Metzler, 2 vols. (Vatican City, 1991), 1: 365.

73. Hanke, 65–102, especially 85–91.

74. Milanesi, 1984: 13–21.

75. Ibid., 54.

76. Broc, 237–38.

77. Milanesi, 1984: 219.

78. Ramusio, 2: 980–81.

79. Ibid., 2: 404–5.

80. Milanesi, 1984: 58.

81. Ramusio, 5: 6–9.

82. On the idea of the plenitude in Platonism, see the classic study by Lovejoy, 52, 111–12, 116.

83. Cosgrove, 65–89, especially 67, 75–81.

84. Bembo, *Opere*, 1: 138.

85. Singer, 234 (Introductory Epistle), 255–60 (First Dialogue).

86. Lovejoy, 111, 116–21.

87. Rosaccio, 4^{v}. The double-orb map is on pp. 1^{v}–2^{r}.

88. Goldstein, 1965: 25.

89. *Paradiso* 22.151 (ed. J. M. Dent [London, 1946], 278).

90. Ramusio, 5: 8–9.

91. Donattini, 88.

92. Padoan, 219–77, especially 235, 239, 262, 272–77. See also Ramusio, 2: 984–85.

93. Ramusio, 4: 141.

94. Ibid., 2: 981–82, 984–86; cf. 5: 7.

95. Ibid., 3: 22–23.

96. Ibid., 2: 979.

97. De Acosta, 102–3, 30–33, 39–40, 86–90, 106, 110–11, wherein Acosta dwells on the newly discovered habitability of the torrid zone as *muy templada*.

98. Ramusio, 1: 8.

99. Ibid., 5: 12.

100. Bembo, 1: 142.

101. Richardson, 67–98, especially 72, 88.

102. Gillies, 158, 162.

103. Richardson, 98.

104. Joseph Hall, 12. As late as 1652, Peter Heylyn, in his *Cosmographie*, includes in his Appendix, 4, [189]–197, a consideration of the unknown parts of the world, wherein Magellanica looms large.

105. Richardson, 95.

106. Harley, 1988b: 57–66, especially 62; Richardson, 98.

107. For a brief biographical sketch, see Markham, 1: xvi–xxxi, especially xviii, xxix; 2: 486, 502–3. On the mythical and utopian in later Spanish exploration, see the last two volumes of Juan Gil's *Mitos*.

108. Cro, 1: 38–43, 47–49; cf. Lestringant, xi. See also the remarkable memorial of the Chilean lawyer Juan Luis Arias to Philip III shortly after 1614, where the Southern Hemisphere is not only astrally favored, loaded with precious metals, and possessing a most salutary climate, but also populous, though given over to Lucifer, unless the king of Spain accepts the great commission: "the crown of universal empire of the globe in His hand, ready to place it on your head, if you value, as it should be valued, this Divine commission, and execute it with that zeal and devotion which the charge enjoins . . . [to] withhold the said zeal from the undertaking, it would doubtless be the greatest disaster that could happen to this kingdom and the most certain sign that God is withdrawing His hand from us." Markham, 2: 517–36, especially 532.

109. Delgado, xiii.

110. Celsus Kelley, 1961: 277–91, especially 284.

111. Celsus Kelley, 1966: 110–33; Atkinson, 410.

112. Ibid.

113. Ibid., 358–59.

114. Ibid., 358–66, 383–86.

115. Romm, 1994: 1: 77–116, especially 92–93.

116. Ibid., 105: "fere dedecus videtur fuisse tantas terras tamdiu ignorasse; non minus atque patrifamilias turpe esset si domus suae conclave praecipuum non nosset." *Pindarou Periodos* ([Wittenberg], 1616), 262.

117. *Les essais de Montaigne*, ed. Pierre Villey and V.-L. Saulnier, 3 vols. (Paris, 1988), 3: 13, 1116.

118. Ramusio, 2: 990.

119. Franck, fols. ccxxxiv–ccxxxv. I wish to thank my friend Philip L. Kintner for kindly providing me with a photocopy of the "America" section of the *Weltbuch*.

120. Sardella, 16 (my translation); encountered first in Moreau-Reibel, 536, but with incomplete reference.

121. Moreau-Reibel, 514–20, 531–35, has some interesting evidence on the growing importance of this right of communication developing in the legal literature of the late Middle Ages, wherein at the Council of Constance in 1415, the rector of the University of Cracow makes participation and communication among humans all obligations not only moral but juridical.

Chapter 2: The Universalizing Principle and the Idea of a Common Humanity

The epigraphs in this chapter are taken from Cicero, *De re publica*, trans. Clinton Walker Reyes, Loeb ed. (London, 1928), III.22, p. 211; Marcus Aurelius, *The Communings with Himself*, trans. C. R. Haines, Loeb ed. (Cambridge, Mass., 1953), IV.4, X.15, pp. 71, 73, and 275; and Nicholas Cusanus, *Of Learned Ignorance*, trans. Germain Heron (London, 1954), III.8, 151.

1. Although the Western identity and orientation of our civilization has a long pedigree, beginning first at that moment when Zeus in the form of a magnificent bull decided to bear the delectable Europa westward, followed by Diocletian's administrative division of the Roman Mediterranean world into two parts, *occidentalis* and *orientalis*, then the westward trek of *translatio imperii* and *studii*, and finally the Columbian experience, it was not until the late nineteenth century that the term *the West*, according to David Gress (p. 558), came to displace *European* to represent the entire collectivity of our civilization. Cf. Delanty, 14, 30–31, 44–47.

2. I am here drawing upon the significant exposition of this idea by Anthony Pagden, 1995: 11–62, especially 21–24 but largely as interpreted by my own review article of the book in Headley, 1996: 875–77.

3. Gauchet, 129, 215.

4. Ibid., 101–6, 124, 129.

5. Pagden, 1995: 22, 24.

6. Colish, I, 126–27, 152.

7. Bödeker, 1067, 1087–90.

8. Nicolet, 191–97, draws an important number of distinctions between the uniformity of the *citoyen* and the numerous qualifications associated with the *civis*.

9. Kristeva, 59.

10. Ibid., 66–69; MacIntyre, 1988: 149–52.

11. Cadoux, 297.

12. Ibid., 487, 524.

13. Ibid., 487, n. 4; cf. 5.10.10 and 6.10.1–9.

14. The text for this important statement can be found in Carl Mirbt, *Quellen zur Geschichte des Papsttums und des römischen Katholizismus*, Bd. I (Tübingen, 1967), 222–23, and its English translation in Brian Tierney, *The Crisis of Church and State, 1050–1300* (Englewood Cliffs, N.J., 1964), 13–14. Regarding the uniqueness of this dualism, I remain unpersuaded by the interesting effort of Ira M. Lapidas, "State and Religion in Islamic

Societies," *Past and Present* 151 (May 1996): 3–27, to suggest some sort of Islamic comparability: that whatever the separation of "state" and religious institutions, principally the *ulama*, the theological jurisconsults, lacked the clarity, defining force, and self-conscious traditions of sustained controversy that shape the medieval, the European, and the modern political experience of the West. This further uniqueness of our civilization, so fundamental and currently so abused, raises too vast an issue to be pursued here.

15. MacIntyre, 1988: 146–54.

16. Augustine, IV.4.

17. Ibid., 19.23, 24.

18. Ibid., 19.17.

19. Cassirer, 1963: 38–39.

20. Cusanus, 3.6.

21. Berman, 1983: 199–254.

22. Tierney, 1991: 298–99, 304; 1996: 28–29; 1997: 36, 142–45. On Innocent IV's commentary on the decretal or judicial determination of Innocent III's *Quod super his*, see the analysis of Muldoon, 1994: 16–21, 26, 87, 128.

23. Moreau-Reibel, 495, 504–8.

24. Headley, 1997: 12.

25. This last point derives from an observation made by J. H. Elliott (1995: 398–99) in his summing up of the conference held at the John Carter Brown Library, June 5–9, 1991, where in different words he distinguished between otherness and commonality—brothers, not others. But he then went on to consider the current excessive preoccupation of the profession with the issue of "otherness" and the privileged status that has been accorded "the observed" to the detriment of "the observers." Only after I had composed this book and it was going to the printer did I recover this well-expressed thought, which in many ways sums up one of the implications behind the present endeavor.

26. Hanke, 77.

27. Tierney, 1997: 267, 273, 286–87.

28. Grotius, 1957: *Proleg.*, 6, 10.

29. Tierney, 1997: 310–11, 324–25.

30. Black, 1984: 18–23, 49–52; 2003: 1:46; 13:105.

31. Rashdall, I, 3.

32. Huppert, 768–69.

33. See the stimulating articles by Céard and by Margolin; cf. also Headley, 1999a and 2005: 154, 160, where Giovanni Botero will follow suit.

34. Cf. Scaglione, 64–67, 229–57.

35. Selwyn, 8.

36. Botero, 4.ii.14.
37. Hay, 77–78.
38. "Palam igitur est solam Christianam rempublicam ad extremum perfectum vivendi modum in orbem terrarum induxisse" (509). I am here preferring the text offered by Hay, which comes from the Basle 1553 edition and represents the text as Polydore left it for the last edition in his lifetime (Hay, 78; cf. 56, n. 1). Other versions of the same passage are less expansive in their connotation; the Estienne, 1528, 140^{v}, reads: "In confesso igitur est, solam sacrosanctam Christianam rempublicam ad postremum perfectum vivendi modum introduxisse"; and Rome, 1585, 477, reads: "Palam igitur est, solam Christianam rempublicam ad extremum perfectum vivendi modum introduxisse." Here and also with "mild-tempered virtues" rather than "quiet virtues" for *pudici mores* I have chosen to depart slightly from Hay's rendering.
39. Headley, 2000: 1144–49.
40. Rousseau, 92. Figuring as part of an extended endnote to the *Origin of Inequality,* this point leads to the very famous case of the Hottentot, carefully educated in European civilization, ceremoniously divesting himself of same and all its accoutrements and returning to the religion and customs of his ancestors (93). What the English has rendered here as "admirers of European Civilization" is, according to the original, "aux admirateurs de la Police Européenne" (*Oeuvres complètes,* 3:221, Gallimard, 1964).
41. Elliott (1972) makes this point throughout this article, but specifically at its beginning and end.
42. Elliott, 1995: 404.
43. Schwaller, 3–15, 80–81. I want to thank Professor Schwaller for bringing this reference to my attention.
44. See, for example, the assessment by Adas, 166–98.
45. For the following several cases of contact and perception see my express indebtedness to Joan-Pau Rubiés in note 48.
46. Bernard Lewis (5–47) has some interesting thoughts on the rival ecumenical ambitions of world religions, of which he identifies three—Buddhism, Christianity, and Islam. Of the first and earliest, Buddhism was eventually rejected in its Indian homeland and became stalled in Southeast Asia. Islam alone emerged to dispute with Christianity the idea that there is a single truth for all the peoples of the earth and it is the duty of the faithful to share that truth by various means of conversion. It can be further argued that no matter how much more effective and sensible in practice the Muslim means of conversion have proved historically, whatever its potential universalism it is skewed from the start by its vision of the present world as divided between Dar al-Islam, the House of Islam, constituting Muslims, and Dar al-Harb, the House of War, consti-

tuting everyone else. In contrast, Christianity, whatever its flawed practices, which are all too historically evident, begins not with an almost ontological division between Muslims and *harbi* but with the centralizing idea of a single, common humanity to be realized through the extension of Christ's Body.

47. Here of course see the almost classic study by Marshall Hodgson, *The Venture of Islam*. In arguing for the continuity of Islam's cultural superiority over Christianity/Europe in this period, yet endowing this period as being marked by a "conservative spirit," Hodgson tortuously struggles to expunge the possible resonances of stagnation and decadence that the word *conservative* might harbor (2: 371–85). For an effective rejection of Hodgson's vain efforts in this respect see Issawi (1981: 85, 111–32), who shifts Hodgson's eighteenth century as the date of Western cultural surpassing of Islam to the fourteenth or fifteenth century at least with respect to "technology, most branches of science, economic activity and economic policy . . . scholarship and political institutions" (125), faulting Hodgson for being too concerned with levels and not sufficiently with trends (113). In justice to Hodgson, whose forte was Iranian, Issawi is concerned with Arabs and the Ottoman empire which at least militarily more than held its own until the later seventeenth century. On the general state of modern Islam, or, better, Islamdom, and its prevailingly repressive and inflexible tendencies, see the stimulating article by Mehdi Mozaffari, "Can a Declined Civilization be Reconstructed? Islamic Civilization or Civilized Islam?" *International Relations* 14, no. 3 (1998): 31–50, which essentially argues that the *Umma* of humankind be effectively extended to include the *Umma* of Islam and that Islamic Civilization be forsaken for a Civilized Islam. Obviously the events of 9/11, three years after the article's publication, have made such an unlikely accommodation even more difficult to realize.

48. I welcome the opportunity to express my gratitude to Joan-Pau Rubiés for allowing me to use these passages culled from his formidable study, first made available to me in typescript by Cambridge University Press for the purpose of obtaining my professional opinion. In correspondence with the author I have since learned that the history of this proverb, which appears rather compressed in the present magisterial study *Travel and Ethnology in the Renaissance* (113–16), will appear more fully in a separate article.

49. Botero, 2.ii.

50. Lach/Leibniz, 74. On the continuity of this appeal to the comparison between Europe and China regarding the two eyes down to the middle of the seventeenth century, one finds the witness of Peter Heylyn in his *Cosmographie*, 3:209.

51. O'Malley, 2, 334.

52. Adshead, 242.
53. Cummins, 85.
54. Ibid., 44–45.
55. Miller, 2000: 110–27, esp. 115, 121. Indeed, Miller's treatment of Stoicism in its accommodationist and universalizing capacities, as developed by Guillaume du Vair, Nicolas Fabri de Peiresc, Matteo Ricci, and Hugo Grotius, illuminates a major strand in the intellectual life of Europe at the turn of the century. Among the late sixteenth-century disciples of Epictetus could also be added San Carlo Borromeo, the prince of Catholic reformers.
56. Cummins, 46–47.
57. Jensen, 7, 61, 90–94, 108–12, 283.
58. Ibid., 8, 112, 118, 121, 146.
59. Admittedly, the momentary experience of a European, presumably Enlightened civilization was to prove most fragile and subject to national pluralization both within and without Western Europe. Immediately prior to the French Revolution and the explosion of nationalism and nation-states, the multicellular nature of European culture and civilized life allowed a transcellular civilization to emerge that was expressive of general human civilization. The celebrated notion of a "commonwealth of Christian Europe"—suggestive of that new common cultural reality that had come to displace what had heretofore been an ecclesiastical empire—Edmund Burke lived to see shattered by the chaos of revolutionary upheaval. The concept of civilization would soon become pluralized both internally within Europe itself along the most strident nationalist line—French, German, *civilisation*, *Kultur*—and externally beyond Europe as Europeans had increasingly to contend with other peoples, societies, and cultures. The hegemonic had to give way in time to a taxonomic, pluralistic view of civilizations—of peoples and of their respective cultures and societies, each organized into its appropriate civilization. The ambiguity—or, better, the internal tension—between the transnational or universal implication of civilization as a superior ideal and its exclusive, national manifestations, "between process and achieved fact," had to wait for the later nineteenth and twentieth centuries to be worked out. I want to thank Jerry Bentley for providing me with proofs of Prasenjit Duara's article, which later appeared in the *Journal of World History* 12, no. 1 (2001): 99–130, especially 105–7 and 123–25, as well as for reminding me of Febvre's article, especially 241–47, and for bringing to my attention Garth Fowden's arresting study of universalism and monotheism in an earlier time and place. Fowden's concept of commonwealth would extend to the entirety of the Western development and thus uniquely omit from it any prior stage of world empire,

even, apparently, in an ecclesiastical guise. On the distinctively multicellular character of European/Western civilization, see Jones (124).

60. Lach/Leibniz, 68–69.

61. Ibid., 68–75; Riley, 239.

62. Lach/Leibniz, 52.

63. This polarity of civilization—Europe/China—is further confirmed in Leibniz's thinking when in a letter of 1708 he speaks of China as an "oriental Europe," 94, n. 48 in Cook and Rosemont.

64. Riley, 228–35.

65. Marshall and Williams, 175–77; Kiernan, 152–55; cf. also Adas, supra n. 39 on the excessive confidence in machinery.

66. Cf. Le Roy, 95, 197, 418, 424–31; Gundersheimer, 104–5, 109, 114–16.

67. *Oxford English Dictionary*, 2nd ed., s.v. "civilization"; on Burke, see his *Reflections* 1989: 69.

68. *Le grand Robert de la langue française*, 2nd ed., s.v. "civilisation."

69. Victor Riqueti, marquis de Mirabeau, *L'ami des hommes ou Traité de la population* (Avignon, 1756), pte. 1, chap. 8 (p. 136): "La religion est sans contredit le premier & le plus utile frein de l'humanité: c'est le premier ressort de la civilisation; elle nous prêche & nous rappelle sans cesse la confraternité, adoucit notre coeur, éleve notre esprit." Although Pons (104) gives the date 1757 for first appearance and Fisch (717) gives 1756, Fisch goes on to explain that part 1 of Mirabeau's work actually appeared in 1757, yet it was backdated and already written in 1756. Curiously, Lucien Febvre, in his classic treatment of the term and idea along with its correlatives, overlooks Mirabeau entirely and settles ultimately on Baron d'Holbach in two different instances, 1766 and 1773 ("Civilisation: Evolution of a Word and a Group of Ideas," 222). For an extensive and searching analysis of the word *civilization*—its inner rift, its inhering obverse both at Mirabeau's time and in later development—see Jean Starobinski, chap. 1, which only came to my attention as the present study went to publication.

70. Cf. Starobinski, 2–7, 31–32.

71. *Grande dizionario della lingua italiana*, s.v. "civile," seq.

72. Ledyard and Watrows, 20, 32–38.

73. Ibid., 127; 144–46.

74. Gray, 2004: 356–57, 378–79.

75. Waley-Cohen, 1531.

76. Tierney, 1991: 322.

77. Vitoria, xiii, xxix–xxx, 231; Bireley, 79–80, 135, 177; Tuck, 1979: 46.

78. Tierney, 1997: 256–62; cf. Brett.

79. Tierney, 1997: 242–52.

80. Ibid., 251.

81. Ibid., 263.
82. Vitoria, 278–86.
83. Tierney, 1997: 310–11.
84. Skinner 2:176–77.
85. Bödeker, 3:1075–76; cf. Suárez, *De legibus*, 2.19.9 (my translation).
86. Oestreich, 1982: 14–15, 36–37, 58.
87. Ibid., 29, 33, 43.
88. Barbour, 1998: 170–73; 2003: 209.
89. Smith, 1976b: 5–10, 140–41; cf. 156, 237, 289–93. The tradition of Stoicism with its direct appeal to Epictetus and Marcus Aurelius continues down through Lord Shaftesbury and Adam Smith's own teacher, Francis Hutcheson, who in 1742 completed an annotated translation of the *Meditations*. Central to the current enthusiasm for Stoicism seems to be the idea of a pervasive universal benevolence coupled with the emerging, fateful notion of happiness: "The greatest possible quantity of happiness" to whose maintenance in the conduct of the great machine of the universe and in the promotion of a universal benevolence the all-wise Being is committed (Smith, 1976: 235–37).
90. Tierney, 324; Tuck, 1979: 53–60; 1999: 89–94.
91. Grotius, *Proleg*. 1, 28.
92. Zuckert, 1994: 136.
93. Grotius, *Proleg*. 6; Tuck, 1999: 97–99.
94. Grotius, *Proleg*. 16; nam naturalis iuris mater est ipsa humana natura . . .; also see Tuck, 1999: 98.
95. Grotius, *Proleg*. 12: quo sensu Chrysippus et Stoici dicebant iuris originem non aliunde petendam quam ab ipso Iove.
96. Ibid., 11.
97. Tierney, 1997: 325–26; cf. Brett in general on the multiple strands and their languages within late scholasticism and in Vázquez, passim and 204.
98. Zagorin, 2000: 34.
99. Zuckert, 1994: 141–45.
100. But see Tuck (1999: 13, 198–202 passim) for a significant presentation of an opposing interpretation persuasively rejected by Zagorin 2000. I must thank Paul Rahe for this reference.
101. The term *state of nature* seems to be curiously lacking here, yet its coining did not have to await John Locke. Earlier, in the "Praefatio ad lectores" to his *De cive* (1642), Hobbes had written: "Ostendo primo conditionem hominum extra societatem civilem (quam conditionem appellare liceat statum naturae) aliam non esse quam bellum omnium contra omnes" (Oxford, 1983, 81/14). This would be carried over into the 1652 English translation made by Hobbes himself (New York, 1949, 13).

102. Cooke 8, 67.
103. Hobbes, 1.14.5.
104. Ibid., 1.15.
105. Spinoza, 164; cf. 108.
106. Trevor-Roper, 235–38.
107. Hobbes, 1.13.
108. Also see Stanlis, 77, 107, 123–24.
109. Grotius, *Proleg.*, 19.
110. Hunter, 2001: 161–62, 194–95; cf. 157, 173–74.
111. Pufendorf, 190.
112. Seidler, 241, 249; cf. Döring, 178–96.
113. Krieger, 259–60.
114. Muller, xxxv, 30, and 37. In his incorporation of a Protestant scholasticism as well as a modernized Swedish-Lutheran collegiate system into his legislative reforms for Russia, Peter and his chief intellectual guide, Prokopovich, bishop of Pskov, leaned predominantly on the writings of Pufendorf: to engage a historical self-understanding for Russia in the emerging state system of an international law; to recommend especially Pufendorf's *De officio hominis et civis* for the education of a new bureaucracy and the preparation of government servants; and to include specifically Pufendorf for the education of the clergy and his proposed academy. In the immense *Ecclesiastical Regulation*, composed by Prokopovich, the only work other than patristic writings mentioned and indeed specified for the curriculum is Pufendorf's *Abbreviated Politics* (Cracraft, 212–16, 240; Muller, 36–37). For the second reference I am indebted to my colleague David Griffiths.
115. Laslett, nos. 2401–7.
116. Hunter, 2001: 148.
117. Hochstrasser, 41–42, 55, 62–67.
118. Pufendorf, 55/10.
119. Dufour, 573–77, 585–88.
120. Pufendorf, 222/61.
121. Krieger, 94–100; Pufendorf, 101.
122. Krieger, 92–94.
123. Pufendorf, 187/20.
124. Ibid., ix–x, xvi–xvii.
125. Ibid., 129/43.
126. Postema, 6, 22, 33, 89–93.
127. Sharp, 55.
128. MacIntyre, 1966: 150–54.
129. Locke, 1:40–41.
130. Ibid., 1:141–42.
131. Ibid., 2:26.

132. Ibid., 54.
133. Davis, 234.
134. Waldron, 207.
135. Locke, 2:34.
136. Aarsleff, 135.
137. Ibid., 130–31.
138. Gliozzi, 619–20; cf. Locke's *Essay*, 3:vi.12.
139. Gliozzi, 597; cf. 341–49. For racism in general, beginning with the Spanish Inquisition and African slavery but focusing on the more recent eighteenth to twentieth centuries, see Frederickson. For our purposes here, apart from its historical evidence, significant is the author's educing a profound issue at the outset of the study: namely, that unique to the West, unlike other societies such as Hindu, which are hierarchical and not committed to any notion of natural equality, there exists a dialectical interaction between the promise and norm of equality and an intense prejudice toward those who are believed to be somehow deficient (11–12).
140. Hodgen, 422, 452–53, 490.
141. Gliozzi, 601–3.
142. Mehta, 48–50.
143. Sharp, xix.
144. Waddicor, 52, 135–42.
145. Quoted in Crowe, 244. For text, *The Speeches of Abraham Lincoln* (Carlsbad, CA, 2005), 40. For an extended contrast on this point between Jefferson and Lincoln, see Diggins, 2000.
146. Locke, 2:30.
147. Ibid., 2.6, 7, 128, 182, 229; cf. 13.
148. Faucci, 67.
149. Marshall and Williams, 93.
150. Ibid., 181, 212.
151. Ibid., 239.
152. Ibid., 242–43; cf. Braude, 135–41.
153. Marshall and Williams, 246.
154. Rousseau, 84–86; cf. 102.
155. Rommen, 89–90.
156. Zuckert, 2000: 67.
157. Hunt, 2000a: 9.
158. Hunt, 1996: 36–37. Cf. Terence, *Heauton Timormenos* (The Self-Tormentor), 1:77: homo sum: humani nil a me alienum puto; Loeb, ed.
159. Hunt, 1996: 5.
160. Jellinek, 18–19; Hunt, 1996: 13–14.
161. Hunt, 1996: 14–15.
162. Oestreich, 1978: 76 (my translation).

163. Kant, "On the Common Saying," 1996: 291–96.
164. Cf. Taylor, 1996: 248–65; Hunt, 1996: 10–12, 119–31.
165. Kant, *Groundwork*, 1996: 73.
166. Ibid., 86.
167. Kant, *Toward Perpetual Peace*, 1996: 329.
168. Ibid., 332–33.
169. Nussbaum, 40–41.
170. Kant, *Toward Perpetual Peace*, 1996: 335.
171. Kant, *Perpetual Peace*, 1991: 108–9.
172. Kant, "Idea for a Universal History," 1991: 44–45.
173. Kant, *Perpetual Peace*, 1991: 106; cf. 117.
174. Nussbaum, 31.
175. Dante, I.3: Nunc autem videndum est quid sit finis totius humane civilitatis . . .
176. Kant, *Toward Perpetual Peace*, 1996: 336.
177. Ibid., 339–40.
178. Ibid., 344–45.
179. Ibid., 346.
180. Kant, *Perpetual Peace*, 1991: 102–3, 117.
181. Kant, *Toward Perpetual Peace*, 1996: 347.
182. Kant, 1996: 307.
183. Kant, *Metaphysics of Morals*, 1996: 487.
184. Kant, *Strife of the Faculties*, 1963: 146.
185. Ibid., 147–48.
186. Ibid., 154.
187. Herder, 1968: xxiv.
188. Herder, *Ideas*, 1968: 7; 1989: 255–56.
189. Muthu, 211.
190. Ibid., 226; 233–34.
191. Herder, 1968: 96, 100; 1989: 647, 651.
192. Muthu, 238.
193. Kant, 1996: 339.
194. Herder, 1968: 78.
195. Ibid., 107–8.
196. Palmer, 2:474.
197. Ibid., 358.
198. Paine, 37.
199. Ibid.
200. Ibid., 42.
201. Ibid., 90–91, 98.
202. Cf. Postema, 89.
203. Paine, 109–10.
204. Ibid., 82.

205. Ibid., 55.
206. Dreisbach, 138.
207. Paine, 128–29.
208. Ibid., 171–72.
209. Ibid., 172.

Chapter 3: The Emergence of Politically Constituted Dissent in the European World

The epigraphs in this chapter are taken from Frederick William Maitland, *A Historical Sketch of Liberty and Equality* (Indianapolis, 2000), 114; and Richard Price, *Observations on the Importance of the American Revolution and the Means of Making It a Benefit to the World: to which is added A Letter from M. Turgot . . .* (Dublin, 1785), 113–14 and 123–24. As a correction to the text: Rather than the "Jerseys" it was Delaware that required the Divinity test.

1. Foord, 1–2.
2. Headley, 1999b; on the theme of *monarchia universalis* see the work of Franz Bosbach.
3. Rahe, 46–48, 64–67.
4. Hume, *Moral Essays*, 14: 119.
5. Tillich, 162–63, 208–9.
6. Burke, 1981, 8: 341–44.
7. On the matter of conscience and authority in Luther before 1521, see Michael G. Baylor, *Action and Person: Conscience in Late Scholasticism and the Young Luther* (Leiden, 1977), 254–71, especially 267–70.
8. Roper, 126.
9. Luria, 30.
10. For the definitive exposition of the distinction being made here, see Maria Turchetti, 11–14, 290–99, 406–11.
11. Grotius, 1988: 1, 10–13, 134, 162. Cf. Salvian, *De gubernatione Dei*, ed. Franciscus Pauly, CSEL (Vienna, 1883), V-ii, 9–11 (104).
12. Lecler and Valkhoff, 2: 130–42.
13. Heckel, passim.
14. Ibid., 44–45, 52–55, 67, 82, 97.
15. Ibid., 146. On the rival confessions' cooperation with the emperor against the Calvinists at this point see Bodo Nischan, "Confessionalism and Absolutism: The Case of Brandenburg," in Andrew Pettegree et al., *Calvinism in Europe, 1540–1620* (Cambridge, 1994), 194, which seems to suggest here ultimately otherwise.
16. Heckel, 116–20, 166–67, 200, 205–6. On the workings of the majority principle see Winfried Schulze, "Majority Decision in the Imperial

Diets of the 16th and 17th Centuries," *Journal of Modern History* 58, suppl. (December 1986): 46–63, especially 50–51, 58–61. On the operation of the curias and their committees in the Reichstag, see Rosemarie Aulinger, *Das Bild des Reichstages im 16. Jahrhundert* (Göttingen, 1980), 210–27.

17. Schulze, 1978: 67–191, 297–301. On the Protestant exploitation of the Turkish threat see the work of Fischer-Galati.

18. Zagorin, 2003: 13.

19. On the practical difficulties and limitations of toleration within the individual territories of the empire, see the sobering account by Joachim Whaley, "A Tolerant Society? Religious Toleration in the Holy Roman Empire, 1648–1806," in *Toleration in Enlightenment Europe*, ed. Ole Peter Grell and Roy Porter (Cambridge, 2000), 175–95.

20. Cf. here Horst Dreitzel, "Toleranz und Gewissenfreiheit im konfessionellen Zeitalter: Zur Diskussion im Reich zwischen Augsburger Religionsfrieden und Aufklärung," in *Religion und Religiosität im Zeitalter des Barock*, ed. Dieter Bruer (Wiesbaden, 1995), 1: 115–28.

21. Niccolò Machiavelli, *The Prince and the Discourses* (New York, 1950), 110–21, 124–34.

22. Quoted by Holmes, 1988: 37; cf. *Rep.* IV.7.536.

23. Montaigne, 1965: 2:19, 504.

24. Haskins, 1–20.

25. Russell, 1990: 1–57, especially 28–29; Kishlansky, 618–20.

26. Robbins, 1982: 108–9.

27. Foord, 8.

28. Gunn, 226–27.

29. Ibid., 228.

30. Ibid., 229.

31. Rapin-Thoyras, 8: 268–69.

32. On the general background see Armitage's introduction and Foord, 113–21.

33. Bolingbroke, 111, n. 9.

34. Foord, 9; cf. 49–50, 232.

35. Shackleton, 7, 14.

36. Habermas, 60, 93–94.

37. Bolingbroke, 94, 132–39.

38. Ibid., 8–9.

39. Ibid., 88, 124; cf. Stourzh, 35–36, on Emeric de Vattel's later definition in 1758.

40. Bolingbroke, 70.

41. Ibid., 186–87.

42. Foord, 146–47.

43. Bolingbroke, 257–58.

44. Foord, 150.

45. Bailyn, 1968: 39–46, 54, 56.

46. Ibid., 126–27.
47. Robbins, 1958: 524–29.
48. Bailyn, 1968: 55, 128–29.
49. Mansfield, 1965: 15.
50. Ibid., 113.
51. Ibid., 121–22.
52. Foord, 105.
53. Ibid., 107.
54. Ibid., 157.
55. Ibid., 200.
56. Percival, 3; Foord, 231–32.
57. Foord, 16, 40.
58. Ibid., see 45, 61, 70, 71, 73, 92, 120, 130, 135, 156, 158 for examples.
59. Percival, 161.
60. Robbins, 1982: 250.
61. Pownall, 8–9.
62. Ibid., 15.
63. Ibid., 14.
64. Ibid., 31.
65. Foord, 318; cf. O'Gorman, 108; Dickinson, 208–9.
66. Mansfield, 1965: 173–200, esp. 180–84.
67. Burke, 1981, 2: 276.
68. Ibid., 278–79.
69. Ibid., 282–85.
70. Ibid., 287, 294.
71. Ibid., 312.
72. Ibid., 314–15.
73. Ibid., 321.
74. Ibid., 317.
75. Brewer, 70–73.
76. O'Brien, 99.
77. Foord, 364; Brewer, 94–95.
78. O'Brien, 213–14.
79. Foord, 412.
80. Ibid.
81. Ibid., 467.
82. Cf. Huizinga, 206–7.
83. Pocock, 1993a: 266–67; Bailyn, 1967: 22–54.
84. Bailyn, 2003: 133.
85. Hofstadter, 61–63.
86. Hume, 6:42.
87. Hume, 2.xvi.528; Marshall, 255–56; Adair, 350–55.
88. *Federalist*, no. 10: 61.

89. For the original minting of this notion and its different exposition see Armitage, 1994: 1–10.

90. Fleischacker, 324–27. The passage identified by Fleischacker in *The Wealth of Nations*, 2: 792–93, warrants more extensive quotation: "The interested and active zeal of religious teachers can be dangerous and troublesome only where there is, either but one sect tolerated in the society, or where the whole of a large society is divided into two or three great sects; the teachers of each acting in concert, and under a regular discipline and subordination. But that zeal must be altogether innocent where the society is divided into two or three hundred, or perhaps into as many thousand small sects, of which no one could be considerable enough to disturb the publick tranquility. The teachers of those great sects, whose tenets being supported by the civil magistrate, are held in veneration by almost all the inhabitants of extensive kingdoms and empires, and who therefore see nothing around them but followers, disciples, and humble admirers. The teachers of each little sect, finding themselves almost alone, would be obliged to respect those of almost every other sect, and the concessions which they would mutually find it both convenient and agreeable to make to one another, might in time probably reduce the doctrine of the greater part of them to that pure and rational religion, free from every mixture of absurdity, imposture, or fanaticism, such as wise men have in all ages of the world wished to see established."

91. *Federalist*, no. 10: 59.

92. Ibid., no. 14: 81.

93. Ibid., no. 14: 85.

94. Wood, 1969: 588–92; cf. 596–604.

95. Ketcham, 73, 105–8, 118–19 passim. I want to thank my colleague Don Higginbotham for bringing this work to my attention.

96. Ibid., 203.

97. Hofstadter, 71.

98. Ibid., 37; cf. Main.

99. Hofstadter, 225–31, 248–53.

Aftermath

The epigraphs in this chapter are taken from Alexis de Tocqueville, *Oeuvres complètes* (Paris, 1985), III/2, 290, quoted and translated in Jennifer Pitts, *A Turn to Empire: The Rise of Imperial Liberalism in Britain and France* (Princeton, 2005), 221; Joseph Conrad, *Heart of Darkness* (London, 1995), 29; and B. R. Ambedkar, *Three Historical Addresses of Dr. Babasaheb Ambedkar in the Constituent Assembly* (New Delhi, 1999), 53–54.

1. Lindquist, no. 50.

2. Coclanis, "The Expansion of Capitalism and the Western Imperial Project," a lecture given for the Humanities Program at UNC-Chapel Hill, February 19, 2005.

3. Kant, 1991: 117.

4. Gibbon, 2: 512–14. In the Womersley edition this remarkable intermezzo, "General Observations on the Fall of the Roman Empire in the West," appears at the end of chapter 38 in volume 2, 508–16.

5. Ibid., 514, n. 8.

6. Ibid., 514.

7. Ibid., 516, n. 15.

8. Ibid., 1: 243. I must thank Keith Windschuttle for calling this reference to my attention.

9. McShea, 9; I want to thank my colleague Ian Crowe for bringing this valuable article to my attention. Cf. also Burke, 1967, 6: 37.

10. Burke, 1987: 69.

11. Ibid., 68.

12. Whelan, 89.

13. Gibbon, 1: 106–7. Quoted from Hall, 1986: 14.

14. Delanty, 77.

15. Marx and Engels, *Communist Manifesto*, 417–19.

16. Pitts, 19. See also Porter, 244–45.

17. Pitts, 223–24, 40; Mehta, 2.

18. Lindquist, no. 53.

19. Ferguson, 270.

20. Lemkin, 79.

21. Hobsbawm, 7.

Epilogue

The epigraphs in this chapter are taken from John Gray, *Enlightenment's Wake: Politics and Culture at the Close of the Modern Age* (London and New York, 1995), 23–24; *The Papers of Adlai E. Stevenson, 1957–61*, ed. Walter Johnson et al. (Boston, 1959), 7: 326; and Dipesh Chakrabarty, *Provincializing Europe: Postcolonial Thought and Historical Difference* (Princeton and Oxford, 2000), 255.

1. Menand, 200.

2. Swanson, 128.

3. Ferguson, 118–22. I want to thank Terence McIntosh for reminding me of slavery's ending in the British Empire.

4. Hochschild, 366: the author speaks of "a newer kind of faith" and attributes the success to a matter of mobilizing "a just indignation" that suggest implicitly the decisive features of an aroused public and the real-

ity of an ideal of a common humanity. The penultimate sentence of the book reads: "The abolitionists placed their hopes not in sacred texts but in human empathy." What seems to be in play here is the Enlightenment's creation of a public sphere resonating a new sensitivity. Yet according to Thomas Haskell in his analysis of the economic, capitalistic origins of nineteenth-century humanitarian sensibility, most is owed to a "shift in the conventional boundaries of moral responsibility" (360), effected by an adroit recognition of the shape of the market.

5. Coughtry, 203–37; Du Bois, 51–133, especially 95, 110.

6. Apart from the present enterprise, as a layman one can decry not only the apparent hedonism and the loss of a sense of comparable duties that have come to be associated with the indiscriminate understanding of human rights but also the application of the concept, designed for individuals, to groups and its frivolous extension. In a remote footnote, the learned Brian Tierney (1988: 8, n. 32) gives examples of such inappropriate applications: "a right to sunshine," "to a tobacco free job," and most arresting of all, the right "to a sex break"—whatever that might entail.

7. Kwok, 87–91; cf. also Huang, 227–48, as well as the interesting remarks of Svensson, 211–13, on the flawed relativism and exceptionalism of China regarding human rights.

Bibliography

Aarsleff, Hans. 1969. "The State of Nature and the Nature of Man." In *John Locke: Problems and Perspectives: A Collection of New Essays*, edited by John W. Yolton, 99–136. London.

Acosta, José de. 1977. *Historia natural y moral de las Indias*. Seville, 1590; reprinted Valencia.

Adair, Douglas. 1957. "That Politics May Be Reduced to a Science: David Hume, James Madison, and the Tenth Federalist." *Huntington Library Quarterly* 20: 342–60.

Adas, Michael. 1989. *Machines as the Measure of Men: Science, Technology, and Ideologies of Western Dominance*. Ithaca.

Adshead, Samuel Adrian M. 1995. *China in World History*. 2nd ed. New York.

Akerman, James R. 1998. "Atlas, Birth of a Title." In *The Mercator Atlas of Europe*, edited by Marcel Watelet, 15–29. Pleasant Hill, Ore.

Ambedkar, B. R. 1999. *Three Historical Addresses of Dr. Babasaheb Ambedkar in the Constituent Assembly*. New Delhi.

———. 2002. *The Essential Writings of B. R. Ambedkar*. Edited by Valerian Rodriguez. Oxford.

Arentzen, Jörg-Geerd. 1984. *Imago Mundi Cartographica: Studien zur Bildlichkeit mittelalterlicher Welt- und Ökumenekarten unter besonderer Berücksichtigung des Zusammenwirkens von Text und Bild*. Munich.

Armitage, David. 1992. "The Cromwellian Protectorate and the Languages of Empire." *Historical Journal* 35, no. 3: 531–55.

———. 1994. "The American Revolution: The Last War of Religion?" *London Review of Books* 16. Reprinted in *Greater Britain, 1516–1776: Essays in Atlantic History* XIII, 1–10. 2004. Aldershot.

———, ed. 1997. *Bolingbroke: Political Writings*. Cambridge.

———. 1999. "The British Conception of Empire in the Eighteenth Century." In *Imperium/Empire/Reich: Ein Koncept politischer Herrschaft im deutsch-britischen Vergleich*, edited by Franz Bosbach and Herman Hiery, 91–109. Munich.

Arneil, Barbara. 1996. *John Locke and America: The Defense of English Colonialism*. Oxford.

Aron, Raymond. 1976. "The Crisis of the European Idea." *Government and Opposition* 11: 5–19.

Atkinson, Geoffrey. 1935. *Les nouveaux horizons de la Renaissance*. Paris.

Augustine, Aurelius. 1948. *The City of God*. Translated by Marcus Dods. New York.

Bagrow, L. 1948. "A Page from the History of the Distribution of Maps." *Imago Mundi* 5: 53–62.

Bailyn, Bernard. 1967. *The Ideological Origins of the American Revolution*. Cambridge, Mass.

———. 1968. *The Origins of American Politics*. New York.

———. 2003. *To Begin the World Anew: The Genius and Ambiguities of the American Founders*. New York.

Baker, Keith. 1990. *Inventing the French Revolution*. Cambridge.

Banning, Lance. 1988. "Second Thoughts on Virtue and Revolutionary Thinking." In *Conceptual Change and the Constitution*, edited by Terence Ball and J.G.A. Pocock, 194–212. Lawrence, Kans.

Barbour, Reid. 1998. *English Epicures and Stoics: Ancient Legacies in Early Stuart Culture*. Amherst, Mass.

———. 2003. *John Selden: Measures of the Holy Commonwealth in Seventeenth-Century England*. Toronto.

Barendse, R. J. 2002. *The Arabian Seas: The Indian Ocean World of the Seventeenth Century*. Armonk, N.Y.

Barron, William. 1777. *History of the Colonization of the Free States of Antiquity, Applied to the Present Contest between Great Britain and Her American Colonies*. London.

Bartlett, Kenneth R. 1999. "Burckhardt's Humanist Myopia: Machiavelli, Guicciardini and the Wider World." *Scripta Mediterranea* 16–17: 17–29.

Battaglia, Salvatore, ed. 1961. *Grande dizionario della lingua italiana*. Torino.

Beazley, C. R. 1907. "Directorium ad faciendum passagium transmarinum." *American Historical Review* 12: 810–57; 13: 66–115.

Bell, Terence, and J.G.A. Pocock, eds. 1988. *Conceptual Change and the Constitution*. Lawrence, Kans.

Bembo, Pietro. 1729. *Opere del Cardinale Pietro Bembo*. 4 vols. Venice.

Berman, Harold Joseph. 1983. *Law and Revolution: The Formation of the Western Legal Tradition*. Cambridge, Mass.

Binding, Paul. 2003. *Imagined Corners: Exploring the World's First Atlas*. London.

Bireley, Robert. 1999. *The Refashioning of Catholicism, 1450–1700: A Reassessment of the Counter Reformation*. Washington, D.C.

Black, Antony. 1984. *Guilds and Civil Society in European Political Thought from the Twelfth Century to the Present*. Ithaca.

———. 2003. *Church, State and Community: Historical and Comparative Perspectives*. Aldershot, U.K.

Blackburn, Robin. 1997. *The Making of New World Slavery: From the Baroque to the Modern, 1492–1800*. London and New York.

Blair, Ann. 1997. *The Theater of Nature: Jean Bodin and Renaissance Science*. Princeton.

Bloom, Irene. 1998. "Mencian Confucianism and Human Rights." In *Confucianism and Human Rights*, edited by Theodore De Bary and Tu Weiming, 94–116. New York.

Bödeker, Hans Erich. 1982. "Menschheit." In *Geschichtliche Grundbegriffe*, edited by Otto Brunner et al., 3: 1063–1128. Stuttgart.

Bolingbroke, Henry St. John, Viscount. 1997. *Political Writings*. Cambridge.

Bosbach, Franz. 1988. *Monarchia Universalis: Ein politischer Leitbegniff der frühen Neuzeit*. Göttingen.

Botero, Giovanni. 1612. *Le Relationi Universali*. Venice.

Braude, Benjamin. 1997. "The Sons of Noah and the Construction of Ethnic and Geographical Identities in the Medieval and Early Modern Periods." *William and Mary Quarterly*, 3rd ser., 54, no. 1: 103–42.

Brett, Annabel. 1997. *Liberty, Right and Nature: Individual Rights in Later Scholastic Thought*. Cambridge.

Brewer, John. 1976. *Party Ideology and Popular Politics at the Ascension of George III*. Cambridge and New York.

Broc, Numa. 1980. *La géographie de la Renaissance (1420–1620)*. Paris.

Brotton, Jerry. 1998. *Trading Territories: Mapping the Early Modern World*. Ithaca.

Browning, Andrew, ed. 1953. *English Historical Documents, Volume VIII, 1660–1714*. New York.

Buisseret, David, ed. 1992. *Monarchs, Ministers, and Maps: The Emergence of Cartography as a Tool of Government in Early Modern Europe*. Chicago.

———. 1998. "Locational Imagery in Early Modern Europe." Paper presented at the Folger Shakespeare Library Conference "Mapping the Early Modern World," March 13–14, Washington, D.C.

———. 2003. *The Mapmaker's Quest: Depicting New Worlds in Renaissance Europe*. Oxford.

Burke, Edmund. 1967. *The Correspondence of Edmund Burke, Vol. VI: July 1789–December 1791*, edited by Alfred Cobban and Robert A. Smith. Cambridge.

———. 1981. *The Writings and Speeches of Edmund Burke*, vol. 2, edited by Paul Langford. Oxford.

———. 1987. *Reflections on the Revolution in France*. Indianapolis and Cambridge.

———. 1989. *The Writings and Speeches of Edmund Burke*, vol. 8, edited by L. G. Mitchell. Oxford.

Burns, J. H. 2003. "Majorities: An Exploration." *History of Political Thought* 24, no. 1: 66–85.

Butzer, Karl W. 1992. "From Columbus to Acosta: Science, Geography and the New World." *Annals of the Association of American Geographers* 82: 345–68.

Cadoux, Cecil John. 1955. *The Early Church and the World*. Edinburgh.

Canny, Nicholas. 1998. "England's New World and the Old, 1480s–1630s." In *The Origins of Empire: The British Overseas Empire to the Close of the Seventeenth Century*, edited by Nicholas Canny, 148–69. Oxford.

Caracciolo, Angela Aricò, ed. 1990. *L'Impatto della scoperta dell'America nella cultura veneziana*. Rome.

Cassirer, Ernest. 1951. *The Philosophy of the Enlightenment*. Boston.

———. 1963. *The Individual and the Cosmos in Renaissance Philosophy*. Oxford.

Céard, Jean. 1982. "L'image de l'Europe dans la Littérature cosmographique de la Renaissance." In *La conscience européenne au XVe et au XVIe Siècle*, Actes du Colloque International; Collection de l'Ecole Normale Superieure de Jeunes Filles; no. 22, edited by Centre National de la Recherche Scientifique (France), 49–63. Paris.

Chakrabarty, Dipesh. 2000. *Provincializing Europe: Postcolonial Thought and Historical Difference*. Princeton and Oxford.

Chakravarti, Uma. 1987. *The Social Dimensions of Early Buddhism*. Delhi.

Colish, Marcia. 1985. *The Stoic Tradition from Antiquity to the Early Middle Ages*. Leiden.

Conrad, Joseph. 1995. *Heart of Darkness*. London.

Constable, Giles. 1985. "Religious Life in the Twelfth Century and Acceptance of Social Pluralism." In *History, Society, and the Churches: Essays in Honor of Owen Chadwick*, edited by Derek Edward Dawson Beales and Geoffrey Francis Andrew Best, 29–47. New York.

Cook, D. J., and H. Rosemont, Jr. 1992. "Leibniz and Chinese Thought." In *Discovering China: European Interpretations in the Enlightenment*, edited by Julia Ching and Willard G. Oxtoby, 82–92. Rochester, N.Y.

Cooke, Paul D. 1996. *Hobbes and Christianity: Reassessing the Bible in Leviathan*. Lanham, Md.

Cormack, Lesley B. 1991. "'Good Fences Make Good Neighbors': Geography as Self-Definition in Early Modern England." *Isis* 82: 639–61.

———. 1995. "Flat Earth or Round Sphere: Misconceptions of the Earth and the Fifteenth-Century Transformation of the World." *Ecumene* 1: 363–85.

———. 1997. *Charting an Empire: Geography at the English Universities, 1580–1620*. Chicago.

Cosgrove, Denis. 1992. "Mapping New Worlds: Culture and Cartography in Sixteenth-Century Venice." *Imago Mundi* 44: 65–89.

Coughtry, Jay. 1981. *The Notorious Triangle: Rhode Island and the African Slave Trade, 1700–1807*. Philadelphia.

Covell, Charles. 2004. *Hobbes, Realism and the Tradition of International Law.* London.

Cox, Jeffrey. 2003. "Master Narratives of Long-Term Religious Change." In *The Decline of Christendom in Western Europe, 1750–2000*, edited by Hugh McLeod and Werner Ustorf, 201–17. Cambridge.

Cracraft, James. 2004. *The Petrine Revolution in Russian Culture.* Cambridge, Mass., and London.

Cro, Stelio. 1994. *The American Foundations of the Hispanic Utopia: The Literary Utopia*, 2 vols. Tallahassee.

Crowe, Michael Bertram. 1977. *The Changing Profile of Natural Law.* The Hague.

Cummins, J. S. 1978. "Two Missionary Methods in China: Mendicants and Jesuits." *Archivo Ibero-Americano* 38: 33–108.

Cusanus, Nicholas. 1954. *Of Learned Ignorance.* Translated by Germain Heron. New Haven.

D'Ailly, Pierre. 1930–31. *Imago mundi.* 3 vols. Edited by Edmond Buron. Paris.

Dante Alighieri. 1985. *Monarchia*. Edited by Federico Sanguineti. Milan.

Davis, J. C. 1998. "Equality in an Unequal Commonwealth: James Harrington's Republicanism and the Meaning of Equality." In *Soldiers, Writers and Statesmen of the English Revolution*, edited by Ian Gentles, John Morrill, and Blair Worden, 229–42. Cambridge.

D'Avity, Pierre. 1637. *Le monde ou la description generale de ses quatre parties*. Paris.

DeBary, William Theodore. 1998. Introduction. In *Confucianism and Human Rights*, edited by William Theodore De Bary and Tu Weiming, 1–26. New York.

Dee, John. 2004. *The Limits of the British Empire*. Edited by Ken MacMillan et al. Westport, Conn., and London.

Delanty, Gerard. 1995. *Inventing Europe: Idea, Identity, Reality.* New York.

Delgado, Paulino Castañeda. 1983. *Los memoriales del Padre Silva sobre la predicación pacifica y los repartimientos*. Madrid: Consejo Superior de Investigaciones Científicas, Instituto "Gonzalo Fernández de Oviedo."

De Smet, Antoine. 1970. "Les géographes de la Renaissance et la cosmographie." In *L'univers à la Renaissance: Microcosme et macrocosme; Colloque international, October 1968*, 13–29. Brussels and Paris.

Dickinson, H. T. 1977. *Liberty and Prosperity: Political Ideology in Eighteenth-Century Britain*. London.

Diggins, John Patrick. 1984. *The Lost Soul of American Politics: John Adams, the Federalist and the Refutation of Virtue*. New York.

———. 2000. *On Hallowed Ground: Abraham Lincoln and the Foundations of American Liberty.* New Haven.

Diggins, John Patrick. 2003. *John Adams*. New York.

Donattini, Massimo. 1980. "Giovanni Battista Ramusio e le sue *Navigationi*. Appunti per una biografia." *Critica storica* 17: 55–100.

Donnelley, Jack. 1989. *Universal Human Rights in Theory and Practice*. Ithaca.

Döring, Detlef. 1998. "Samuel von Pufendorf and Toleration." In *Beyond the Persecuting Society: Religious Toleration before the Enlightenment*, edited by John Christian Laursen and Cary J. Nederman, 178–96. Philadelphia.

Dreisbach, Daniel L. 2000. "Church-State Debate in the Virginia Legislature." In *Religion and Political Culture in Jefferson's Virginia*, edited by Garret Ward Sheldon and Daniel L. Dreisbach, 135–65. London and Boulder.

Du Bois, W.E.B. 1965. *The Suppression of the African Slave Trade in the United States of America, 1638–1870*. New York.

Dufour, Alfred. 1991. "Pufendorf." In *Cambridge History of Political Thought, 1450–1700*, edited by J. H. Burns and Mark Goldie, 561–88. Cambridge.

Dunn, John. 1969, "Politics of Locke in England and America in the Eighteenth Century." In *John Locke: Problems and Perspectives; A Collection of New Essays*, edited by John W. Yolton, 45–80. London.

Dupront, Alphonse. 1946. "Espace et Humanisme." *Bibliothèque d'humanisme et Renaissance* 8: 7–104.

Durara, Prasenjit. 2001. "The Discourse of Civilization and Pan-Asianism." *Journal of World History* 12, no. 1: 99–130.

Dutt, Sukumar. 1957. *The Buddha and Five After-Centuries*. London.

Edgerton, Samuel Y. 1975. *The Renaissance Rediscovery of Linear Perspective*. New York.

———. 1987. "From Mental Matrix to *Mappamundi* to Christian Empire: The Heritage of Ptolemaic Cartography in the Renaissance." In *Art and Cartography: Six Historical Essays*, edited by David Woodward, 10–50. Chicago and London.

Elias, Norbert. 1978. *The History of Manners: Volume I, The Civilizing Process*. New York.

Elliott, J. H. 1972. "The Discovery of America and the Discovery of Man." *Proceedings of the British Academy* 48: 101–25.

———. 1986. *The Count-Duke of Olivares: The Statesman in an Age of Decline*. New Haven and London.

———. 1995. "Final Reflections: The Old World and the New Revisited." In *America in European Consciousness, 1493–1750*, edited by Karen Ordahl Kupperman, 391–403. Chapel Hill and London.

———. 2006. *Empires of the Atlantic World: Britain and Spain in America, 1492–1830*. New Haven and London.

Faucci, Dario. 1969. "Vico and Grotius: Jurisconsults of Mankind." In *Giambattista Vico: An International Symposium*, edited by Giorgio Tagliacozzo and Hayden V. White, 61–76. Baltimore.

Favaro, A. 1993. *Amici e corrispondenti di Galileo*, vol. 3: *Libreria editrice salimbeni*. Florence.

Febvre, Lucien. 1973. "Civilization: Evolution of a Word and a Group of Ideas." In *A New Kind of History and Other Essays*, edited by Peter Burke, translated by K. Folca, 219–57. New York.

Ferguson, Niall. 2003. *Empire: The Rise and Demise of the British World Order and the Lessons for Global Power*. New York.

Fiering, Norman S. 1976. "Irresistible Compassion: An Aspect of Eighteenth-Century Sympathy and Humanitarianism." *Journal of the History of Ideas* 37, no. 2: 195–219.

Fisch, Jörg. 1992. "Zivilisation, Kultur." *Geschichtliche Grunderbegriffe* 7, edited by O. Brunner, W. Conze, and R. Koselleck, 679–774. Stuttgart.

Fischer-Galati, Stephen A. 1959. *Ottoman Imperialism and German Protestantism*. Cambridge, Mass.

Fleischaker, Samuel. 2003. "The Impact on America: Scottish Philosophy and the American Founding." In *The Cambridge Companion to the Scottish Enlightenment*, edited by Alexander Broadie, 316–37. Cambridge.

Flint, Valerie I. J. 1984. "Monsters and the Antipodes in the Early Middle Ages and Enlightenment." *Viator* 15: 65–80.

Flynn, Dennis O., and Arturo Giráldez. 1995a. "Born with a 'Silver Spoon': The Origin of World Trade." *Journal of World History* 6, no. 2: 201–21.

———. 1995b. "Arbitrage, China, and World Trade in the Early Modern Period." *Journal of the Economic and Social History of the Orient* 38, no. 4: 429–48. Reprinted in 2001, *The Pacific World*, 4, 261–80.

———. Forthcoming. "Born Again: Globalization's Sixteenth-Century Origins." *Pacific Economic Review*.

Flynn, Dennis O., Arturo Giráldez, and James Sobredo. 2001. Introduction. *The Pacific World*, vol. 4, *European Entry into the Pacific*, xiii–xliii. Aldershot.

Foord, Archibald S. 1964. *His Majesty's Opposition: 1714–1830*. Oxford.

Fowden, Garth. 1993. *Empire to Commonwealth: Consequences of Monotheism in Late Antiquity*. Princeton.

Franck, Sebastian. 1534. *Weltbuch: Spiegel und Bildtnisz des gantzen Erdbodens*. Tübingen.

Frederickson, George M. 2002. *Racism: A Short History*. Princeton and Oxford.

Freeman, Michael. 2000. "Since There Is No East and There Is No West, How Could Either Be the Best?" In *Human Rights and Asian Values:*

Contesting National Identities and Cultural Representations in Asia, edited by Michael Jacobson and Ole Bruun, 43–58. Richmond, Surrey.

Frohnen, Bruce. 2005. "Burke and the Conundrum of International Human Rights." In *An Imaginative Whig: Reassessing the Life and Thought of Edmund Burke*, edited by Ian Crowe, 175–202. Columbia.

Furet, François. 1976. "Civilization and Barbarism in Gibbon's History," *Daedalus*, 105, no. 3:209–16.

Gadol, Joan. 1969. *Leon Battista Alberti: Universal Man of the Early Renaissance*. Chicago.

Gauchet, Marcel. 1997. *The Disenchantment of the World: A Political History of Religion*. New French Thought. Princeton.

Gellner, Ernest. 1988. *Plough, Sword and Book: The Structure of Human History*. London.

———. 1992. *Postmodernism, Reason and Religion*. London and New York.

Gibbon, Edward. 1994. *The History of the Decline and Fall of the Roman Empire*. Edited by David Womersley. Harmondsworth, Middlesex.

Gierke, Otto. 1934. *Natural Law and the Theory of Society, 1500 to 1800*. Edited by Ernest Barker. Cambridge.

Gil, Juan. 1989. *Mitos y utopias del descubrimiento*. Madrid.

Gillies, John. 1994. *Shakespeare and the Geography of Difference*. Cambridge.

Ginzburg, Carlo. 1999. "Lorenzo Valla on the 'Donation of Constantine.' " In *History, Rhetoric, and Proof*, 54–70. Hanover, N.H. and London.

Glendon, Mary Ann. 2001. *A World Made New: Eleanor Roosevelt and the Universal Declaration of Human Rights*. New York.

Gliozzi, Giuliano. 1977. *Adamo e il nuovo mondo: La nascita dell'antropologia come ideologia coloniale dalle genealogie bibliche alle teorie razziali, 1500–1700*. Florence.

Godinho, Vitorino Magalhâes. 1991. "Entre mythe et utopie: les grandes découvertes. La construction de l'espace et l'invention de l'humanité aux XVe et XVIe siècles." *Archives européennes de sociologie* 32: 3–52.

Goldstein, Thomas. 1965. "Geography in Fifteenth-Century Florence." In *Merchants and Scholars: Essays in the History of Exploration and Trade*, edited by John Parker, 9–32. Minneapolis.

———. 1972. "The Renaissance Concept of the Earth in Its Influence upon Copernicus." *Terrae Incognitae* 4: 19–51.

———. 1980. *Dawn of Modern Science: From the Arabs to Leonardo da Vinci*. Boston.

Gordon, Daniel. 1994. *Citizens without Sovereignty: Equality and Sociability in French Thought, 1670–1789*. Princeton.

Gould, Eliga J. 2000. *The Persistence of Empire: British Political Culture in the Age of the American Revolution*. Chapel Hill and London.

———. 2003. "Legal Geography of the British Atlantic." *William and Mary Quarterly* 60, no. 3: 471–510.

Gray, Edward G. 2004. "Visions of Another Empire: John Ledyard, An American Traveler across the Russian Empire, 1787–1788." *Journal of the Early Republic* 24, no. 3: 347–80.

Gray, John. 1995. *Enlightenment's Wake: Politics and Culture at the Close of the Modern Age*. London and New York.

Gress, David. 1998. *From Plato to NATO: The Idea of the West and Its Opponents*. New York.

Grotius, Hugo. 1919. *De iure belli ac pacis*. Edited by P. C. Molhuysen. Leyden.

———. 1957. *Prolegomena to the Law of War and Peace*. Translated by Francis W. Kelsey. New York.

———. 1983. "Freedom of the Seas." In *Grotius Reader: A Reader for Students of International Law and Legal History*, edited by L. E. van Holk and C. G. Roelofsen, translated by J. B. Scott, 59–93. The Hague.

———. 1988. *Meletius sive de iis quae inter Christianos conveniunt epistola*. Edited by Guillaume H. M. Posthemus Meyjes. Leiden and New York.

Guicciardini, Francesco. 1968. *History of Italy*. Translated by Sidney Alexander. New York.

Gundersheimer, Werner L. 1966. *The Life and Works of Louis Le Roy*. Travaux d'Humanisme et Renaissance 82. Geneva.

Gunn, J.A.W. 1968. "Party before Burke: Shute Barrington." *Government and Opposition* 3, no. 2: 223–40.

Gusdorf, Georges. 1969. *Les sciences humaines et la pensée occidentale*, vol. 3, part 1. Paris.

Habermas, Jürgen. 1995. *The Structural Transformation of the Public Sphere*. Translated by Thomas Burger. Cambridge, Mass.

Haggenmacher, Peter. 1990. "Grotius and Gentili: A Reassessment of Th. E. Holland's Inaugural Lecture." In *Hugo Grotius and International Relations*, edited by Hedley Bull, Benedict Kingsbury, and Adam Roberts, 133–76. Clarendon and Oxford.

Hall, John A. 1986. *Powers and Liberties: Causes and Consequences of the Rise of the West*. Berkeley.

Hall, Joseph. 1981. *Another World and Yet the Same*. Edited and translated by John Millar Wands. New Haven.

Hamilton, Alexander. 1961. *The Federalist*. Cambridge.

Hanke, Lewis. 1937. "Pope Paul III and the American Indians." *Harvard Theological Review* 30: 65–102.

Hankins, James. 1992. "Ptolemy's *Geography* in the Renaissance." In *The Marks in the Fields: Essays on the Uses of Manuscripts*, edited by Rodney G. Dennis, 119–27. Cambridge.

Harley, J. B. 1988a. "Maps, Knowledge, and Power." In *The Iconography of Landscape: Essays on the Symbolic Representation, Design and Use of Past Environments*, edited by Denis Cosgrove and Stephen Daniels, 277–312. Cambridge.

———. 1988b. "Silences and Secrecy: The Hidden Agenda of Cartography in Early Modern Europe." *Imago Mundi* 40: 57–76.

Haskell, Thomas. 1985. "Capitalism and the Origins of the Humanitarian Sensibility." *American Historical Review* 90: 339–61; 547–66.

Haskins, George Lee. 1948. *The Growth of English Representative Government*. Philadelphia.

Hay, Denys. 1952. *Polydore Vergil; Renaissance Historian and Man of Letters*. Oxford.

Headley, John M. 1994. "J. H. Elliott's Impact: On Exploring and Exploiting an Historiographical Issue." *Quaderni*, Nuova serie n. 6–7: 225–38.

———. 1995. "Spain's Asian Presence, 1565–1590: Structures and Aspirations." *Hispanic American Historical Review* 75, no. 4: 623–46.

———. 1996. "The Burden of European Imperialisms, 1500–1800." *International History Review* 18: 875–87.

———. 1997. "The Sixteenth-Century Venetian Celebration of the Earth's Total Habitability: The Issue of the Fully Habitable World for Renaissance Europe." *Journal of World History* 8, no. 1: 1–27.

———. 1999a. "Europe, Idea Of." In *Encyclopedia of the Renaissance*, edited by Paul F. Grendler, 2: 304–6. New York.

———. 1999b. "The Demise of Universal Monarchy as a Meaningful Political Idea." In *Imperium/Empire/Reich: Ein konzept des politischer Herrschaft im deutsch-britischen Vergleich*, edited by Franz Bosbach and Hermann Hiery, 41–58. Munich.

———. 2000. "Geography and Empire in the Late Renaissance: Botero's Assignment, Western Universalism and the Civilizing Process." *Renaissance Quarterly* 53, no. 4: 1119–55.

———. 2002. "The Universalizing Principle and Process: On the West's Intrinsic Commitment to a Global Context." *Journal of World History* 13, no. 2: 291–321.

———. 2004. "Thomas More's Horrific Vision: The Advent of Constituted Dissent." In *Confessionalization in Europe, 1555–1700: Essays in Honor and Memory of Bodo Nischan*, edited by John M. Headley, Hans J. Hillerbrand, and Anthony Papalas, 347–58. Aldershot, U.K. and Burlington, Vt.

———. 2005. " 'The Extended Hand of Europe': Expansionist and Imperialist Motifs in the Political Geography of Giovanni Botero." *Zeit-*

schrift für historische Forschung. Beiheft 34, Expansionen in der Frühen Neuzeit, 153–71.

Heckel, Martin. 1983. *Deutschland im konfessionellen Zeitalter*. Göttingen.

———. 1987. *Die Menschenrechte im Spiegel der reformatorischen Theologie*. Heidelberg.

Herder, J. G. von. 1968. *Reflections on the Philosophy of History and of Mankind*. Chicago and London.

———. 1989. *Herder Werke*, vol. 6. Frankfurt am Main.

Heylyn, Peter. 1652/2003. *Cosmographie*. Edited and introduced by Robert Mayhew. London/Bristol.

Higgins, Rosalyn. 1990. "Grotius and the Development of International Law in the UN Period." In *Hugo Grotius and International Relations*, edited by Hedley Bull, Benedict Kingsbury, and Adam Roberts, 267–80. Clarendon and Oxford.

Hobbes, Thomas. 1960. *Leviathian*. Edited by Michael Oakeshott. Oxford.

Hobsbawm, Eric. 2002. *Interesting Times: A Twentieth-Century Life*. London.

Hochschild, Adam. 2005. *Bury the Chains: Prophets and Rebels in the Fight to Free an Empire's Slaves*. Boston.

Hochstrasser, T. J. 2000. *Natural Law Theories in the Early Enlightenment*. Cambridge.

Hodgen, Margaret. 1964. *Early Anthropology in the 16th and 17th Centuries*. Philadelphia.

Hodgson, Marshall G. S. 1974. *The Venture of Islam: Conscience and History in a World Civilization*, vol. 2. Chicago.

Hofstadter, Richard. 1969. *The Idea of a Party System: The Rise of Legitimate Opposition in the United States, 1780–1840*. Berkeley and Los Angeles.

Holmes, Stephen. 1988. "Jean Bodin: The Paradox of Sovereignty and the Privatization of Religion." In *Nomos XXX: Religion, Morality and the Law*, edited by J. Roland Pennock and John W. Chapman, 5–45. New York.

———. 1993. *The Anatomy of Antiliberalism*. Cambridge, Mass., and London.

Hont, Istvan. 1987. "The Language of Sociability and Commerce: Samuel Pufendorf and the Theoretical Foundations of the 'Four-Stages Theory.' " In *The Languages of Political Theory in Early-Modern Europe*, edited by Anthony Pagden, 253–76. Cambridge.

Huang, Mab. 2000. "Universal Human Rights and Chinese Liberalism." In *Human Rights and Asian Values: Contesting National Identities and Cultural Representations in Asia*, edited by Michael Jacobsen and Ole Bruun, 227–48. Richmond, Surrey.

Huizinga, Johan. 1955. *Homo Ludens: A Study of the Play-Element in Culture*. Boston.

Hume, David. 1987. *Hume Essays: Moral, Political, and Literary.* Edited by Eugene F. Miller. Indianapolis.

Hunt, Lynn Avery. 1996. "Introduction: The Revolutionary Origins of Human Rights." In *The French Revolution and Human Rights, A Brief Documentary History,* edited by Lynn Avery Hunt, 1–32. Boston.

———. 2000a. "Paradoxical Origins of Human Rights." In *Human Rights and Revolutions,* edited by Jeffery N. Wasserstrom, 3–18. Lanham.

———. 2000b. The Psycho-Cultural Origins of Human Rights." Paper presented at the National Humanities Center.

Hunter, Ian. 2001. *Rival Enlightenments: Civil and Metaphysical Philosophy in Early Modern Germany.* Cambridge.

———. 2005. "Kant's Religion and Prussian Religious Policy." *Modern Intellectual History* 2, no. 1: 1–27.

Huntington, Samuel P. 1996. "The West: Unique, Not Universal." *Foreign Affairs* 75, no. 6: 28–46.

———. 2004. *Who Are We? Challenges to America's National Identity.* New York and London.

Huppert, George. 1971. "The Idea of Civilization in the 16th Century." In *Renaissance: Studies in Honor of Hans Baron,* edited by Anthony Molho and John A. Tedeschi, 759–69. De Kalb, Ill.

Ignatieff, Michael. 2001. *Human Rights as Politics and Idolatry.* Princeton.

Imbruglia, Girolamo. 1997. " 'My Ecclesiastical History': Gibbon between Hume and Raynal." In *Edward Gibbon: Bicentenary Essays,* edited by David Womersley, J. W. Burrow, and J.G.A. Pocock, 73–102. Oxford.

Ishay, Micheline. 2004. *History of Human Rights: From Ancient Times to the Globalization Era.* Berkeley and London.

Issawi, Charles, trans. and ed. 1950. *An Arab Philosophy of History.* Princeton.

———. 1981. *The Arab World's Legacy.* Princeton.

Jardine, Lisa, and Jerry Brotton. 2000. *Global Interests: Renaissance Art between East and West.* Ithaca.

Jellinek, Georg. 1901. *The Declaration of the Rights of Man and of Citizens: A Contribution to Modern Constitutional History.* Westport.

Jensen, Lionel M. 1997. *Manufacturing Confucianism: Chinese Traditions and Universal Civilization.* Durham, N.C.

Jones, E. L. 1987. *The European Miracle: Environments, Economics, and Geopolitics in the History of Europe and Asia.* 2nd ed. Cambridge and New York.

Kant, Immanuel. 1963. *On History.* Indianapolis and New York.

———. 1991. *Political Writings.* Edited by Hans Reiss. Translated by H. B. Nisbet. Cambridge.

———.1996. *Practical Philosophy.* Edited by Mary J. Gregor. Cambridge.

Karrow, Jr., Robert W. 1993. *Mapmakers of the Sixteenth Century and Their Maps*. Chicago.

Kelley, Celsus. 1961. "The Franciscan Missionary Plan for the Conversion to Christianity of the Natives of the Austral Lands." *Americas* 17: 277–91.

———. 1966. *La Austrialia del Espíritu Santo*. Cambridge.

Kelley, Donald R. 1976. "Vico's Road: From Philosophy to Jurisprudence and Back." In *Giambattista Vico's Science of Humanity*, edited by Giorgio Tagliacozzo and Donald Phillip Verene, 15–29. Baltimore and London.

———. 2002. *The Descent of Ideas*. Burlington.

Kelsey, Harry. 1987. "The Planispheres of Sebastian Cabot and Sancho Gutiérrez." *Terrae Incognitae* 19: 41–58.

Ketcham, Ralph Louis. 1984. *Presidents above Party: The First American Presidency, 1789–1829*. Chapel Hill.

Kiernan, V. G. 1995. *The Lords of Human Kind: European Attitudes to Other Cultures in the Imperial Age*. London.

King, James E. 1979. *Science in the Government of Louis XIV, 1661–1683*. Baltimore.

Kish, George, ed. 1978. *A Source Book in Geography*. Cambridge, Mass.

Kishlansky, Mark. 1977. "The Emergence of Adversary Politics in the Long Parliament." *Journal of Modern History* 49, no. 4: 617–40.

Koebner, Richard. 1961. *Empire*. Cambridge.

Koebner, Richard, and Helmut Dan Schmidt. 1964. *Imperialism: The Story and Significance of a Political Word, 1840–1960*. Cambridge.

Krieger, Leonard. 1965. The *Politics of Discretion: Pufendorf and the Acceptance of Natural Law*. Chicago.

Kristeva, Julia. 1991. *Strangers to Ourselves*. New York.

Kwok, D.W.Y. 1996. "On the Rites and Rights of Being Human." In *Confucianism and Human Rights*, edited by William Theodore de Bary and Tu Weiming, 83–93. New York.

Lach, Donald F. 1957. *The Preface to Leibniz' Novissima Sinica: Commentary, Translation, Text*. Honolulu.

Lal, Deepak. 1998. *Unintended Consequences: The Impact of Factor Endowments, Culture and Politics on the Long-Run Economic Performance*. Cambridge, Mass., and London.

———. 2004. *In Praise of Empires: Globalization and Order*. New York.

Lamb, Ursula. 1976. "Cosmographers of Seville: Nautical Science and Social Experience." In *First Images of America*, edited by Freddi Chiapelli, 2: 675–86. Berkeley and Los Angeles.

Laslett, Peter. 1971. *The Library of John Locke*. Oxford.

Lawrance, Jeremy. 1992. "The Middle Indies: Damiao de Góis on Prestor John and the Ethiopians." *Renaissance Studies* 6, no. 4: 306–24.

Lecler, Joseph, and Valkhoff, Marius-François. 1969. *Les premiers défenseurs de la liberté religieuse*. Paris.

Ledyard, John, and Stephen D. Watrous. 1966. *Journey through Russia and Siberia, 1787–1788: The Journal and Selected Letters*. Madison.

Leeuwen, Arend Theodoor van. 1964. *Christianity in World History: The Meeting of the Faiths of East and West.* London.

Lemkin, Raphael. 1944. *Axis Rule in Occupied Europe: Laws of Occupation, Analysis of Government, Proposals for Redress*. New York.

Lerner, Ralph. 1987. *The Thinking Revolutionary: Principle and Practice in the New Republic*. Ithaca.

LeRoy, Louis. 1575. *De la vicissitude ou variété des choses en l'univers*. Corpus des Œuvres de Philosophie en Langue Française. Paris.

Lestringant, Frank. 1994. *Mapping the Renaissance World: The Geographical Imagination in the Age of Discovery.* Berkeley.

Lewis, Bernard. 1993. *Islam and the West*. New York.

Lindberg, David C. 1970. *John Pecham and the Science of Optics: Perspectiva communis*. Madison and London.

Lindgren, Uta. 1995. "Was verstand Peter Apian unter 'Geographie'." In *Peter Apian: Astronomie, Kosmographie und Mathematik am Beginn der Neuzeit*, edited by Karl Röttel, 154–55. Boxheim.

Lindquist, Sven. 2001. *A History of Bombing*. Translated by Linda Haverty Rugg. New York.

Locke, John. 1960. *Two Treatises of Government*. Edited by Peter Laskett. Cambridge.

Lovejoy, Arthur O. 1957. *The Great Chain of Being*. Cambridge, Mass.

Luria, Keith P. 1996. "The Politics of Protestant Conversion to Catholicism in Seventeenth-Century France." In *Conversion to Modernities: The Globalization of Christianity*, edited by Peter van der Verr, 23–46. New York and London.

MacCormack, Sabine G. 1997. "History and Law in Sixteenth-Century Peru: The Impact of European Scholarly Traditions." In *Cultures of Scholarship*, edited by S. C. Humphreys, 277–308. Ann Arbor.

MacIntyre, Alasdair. 1966. *A Short History of Ethics*. New York.

———. 1988. *Whose Justice? Which Rationality*? Notre Dame.

Macrobius. 1981. *Commentarium in Somnium Scipionis libri duo* II.5, edited by Luigi Scarpa. Padua.

Mah, Harold. 2003. *Enlightenment Phantasies: Cultural Identity in France and Germany, 1750–1914*. Ithaca.

Main, Jackson Turner. 1973. *Political Parties before the Constitution*. Chapel Hill.

Maitland, Frederic William. 2000. *A Historical Sketch of Liberty and Equality: As Ideals of English Political Philosophy from the Time of Hobbes to the Time of Coleridge*. Indianapolis.

Mancke, Elizabeth. 1999. "Early Modern Expansion and the Politicization of Oceanic Space." *The Geographical Review* 89: 225–36.

Mansfield, Harvey Jr. 1965. *Statesmanship and Party Government: A Study of Burke and Bolingbroke*. Chicago.

———. 1991. *America's Constitutional Soul*. Baltimore and London.

Margolin, Jean-Claude. 1981. "Conscience européenne et réaction à la menace turque d'après le 'De dissidiis Europae et bello turcico' de Vivès (1526)." In *Juan Luis Vives*, edited by August Buck, 3: 107–40. Wolfenbütteler Abhandlungen zur Renaissanceforschung. Hamburg.

Markham, Sir Clements, trans. and ed. 1904. *The Voyages of Pedro Fernandez de Quiros, 1595–1606*. 2 vols. London.

Marshall, Geoffrey. 1954. "David Hume and Political Skepticism." *Philosophical Quarterly* 4: 247–57.

Marshall, P. J., and Glyndwr Williams. 1982. *The Great Map of Mankind: British Perceptions of the World in the Age of Enlightenment*. Cambridge, Mass.

Marx, Karl, and Friedrich Engels. 1946. "Manifesto of the Communist Party." In *Introduction to Contemporary Civilization in the West*, II: 414–35. New York.

Mazumdar, Sucheta. 1998. *Sugar and Society in China: Peasants, Technology and the World Market*. Cambridge, Mass., and London.

Mazzeo, Joseph Anthony. 1962. *Reason and Imagination: Studies in the History of Ideas, 1600–1800*. New York.

McIlwain, Charles Howard. 1947. *Constitutionalism Ancient and Modern*. Ithaca.

McLeod, Hugh. 2003. Introduction. In *The Decline of Christendom in Western Europe, 1750–2000*, edited by Hugh McLeod and Werner Ustorf, 1–26. Cambridge, Mass.

McShea, Bronwen Catherine. 2002. "High and Worthy Notions." *Reflections: The Newsletter of the Edmund Burke Society* 3, no. 4: 1–3.

Mehta, Uday Singh. 1999. *Liberalism and Empire: A Study in Nineteenth-Century British Liberal Thought*. Chicago.

Menand, Louis IV. 1993. "Human Rights as Global Imperative." In *Conceptualizing Global History*, edited by Bruce Mazlish and Ralph Buultjens, 173–204. Boulder, San Francisco, and Oxford.

Metzler, Josef, ed. 1991. *America pontificia primi saeculi evangelizationis, 1493–1592*. 2 vols. Vatican City.

Milanesi, Marica. 1984. *Tolomeo sostituito: Studi di storia delle conoscenze geografiche nel XVI secolo*. Milan.

Miller, Peter N. 1994. *Defining the Common Good: Essays Religious and Political in Eighteenth-Century Britain*. Cambridge.

———. 2000. *Peiresc's Europe: Learning and Virtue in the Seventeenth Century*. New Haven.

Miller, Peter N. 2002. "Nazis and Neo-Stoics: Otto Bremmer and Gerhard Oestrech before and after the Second World War." *Past and Present* 176: 144–86.

Minogue, Kenneth. 1989. "The History of the Idea of Human Rights." In *The Human Rights Reader*, edited by Walter Laqueur and Barry Rubin, 3–16. New York.

Minuti, Rolando. 1997. "Gibbon and the Asiatic Barbarians: Notes on the French Sources of the Decline and Fall." In *Edward Gibbon: Bicentenary Essays*, edited by David Womersley, J. W. Burrow, and J.G.A. Pocock, 21–44. Oxford.

Mitchell, L. G., William B. Todd, and Paul Langford. *The Writings and Speeches of Edmund Burke, Volume III*. Oxford.

Monfasani, John. 2006. "The Renaissance as the Concluding Phase of the Middle Ages." *Bollettino dell'Istituto Storico per il Medioevo* 108: 165–85.

Montaigne, Michel de. 1965. *The Complete Essays*. Translated by Donald M. Frame. Stanford.

———. 1988. *Les essais de Montaigne*. Edited by Pierre Villey and V. L. Saulnier. Paris.

Montandon, Alain. 1995. *Dictionnaire raisonné de la politesse et du savoir-vivre du Moyen Age à nos jours*. Paris.

Moreau-Reibel, Jean. 1950. "Le droit de société interhumaine et le 'Jus gentium': Essai sur les origines et le développement des notions jusqu' à Grotius." In *Académie de droit international de la Haye. Recueil des Cours*. II, 485–594.

Moretti, Gabriella. 1994. "The Other World and the 'Antipodes': The Myth of the Unknown Countries between Antiquity and the Renaissance." In *The Classical Tradition in the Americas* 1: 241–84. Berlin.

Mosher, Michael A. 2001. "Monarchy's Paradox: Honor in the Face of Sovereign Power." In *Montesquieu's Science of Politics: Essays in the Spirit of Laws*, edited by David Wallace Carrithers, Michael A. Mosher, and Paul Anthony Rahe, 159–230. Lanham, Md.

Muldoon, James. 1979. *Popes, Lawyers and Infidels*. Philadelphia.

———. 1994. *The Americas in the Spanish World Order: The Justification for Conquest in the Seventeenth Century*. Philadelphia.

Muller, Alexander, trans. 1972. *The Spiritual Regulation of Peter the Great*. Seattle and London.

Mundy, Barbara E. 1993. *The Mapping of New Spain: Indigenous Cartography and the Maps of the* Relaciones Geográficas. Chicago and London.

Muthu, Sankar. 2003. *Enlightenment against Empire*. Princeton.

Näf, Werner. 1944. *Vadian und seine Stadt St. Gallen*. St. Gallen.

Naudé, Françoise. 1992. *Reconnaissance du nouveau monde et cosmographie à la Renaissance*. Kassel.

Nederman, Cary. 1985. "Quentin Skinner's State: Historical Method and Traditions of Discourse." *Canadian Journal of Political Science* 18: 339–52.

Neill, Stephen. 1964. *A History of Christian Missions*. Baltimore.

Nenner, Edward. 1993. "The Later Stuart Age." In *The Varieties of British Political Thought, 1500–1800,* edited by J.G.A. Pocock, 180–208. Cambridge.

Nicolet, Claude. 1986. "Civis and Citoyen." *Government and Opposition* 21: 177–97.

Nussbaum, Martha. 1997. *Cultivating Humanity: A Classical Defense of Reform in Liberal Education*. Cambridge, Mass.

O'Brien, Conor Cruise. 1992. *The Great Melody: A Thematic Biography and Commented Anthology of Edmund Burke*. Chicago.

Oestreich, Gerhard. 1978. *Geschichte der Menschenrechte und Grundfreiheiten im Umriss*. Darmstadt.

———. 1982. *Neostoicism and the Early Modern State*. Cambridge.

O'Gorman, Frank. 1967. *The Whig Party in the Age of the French Revolution*. New York.

O'Malley, John W. 1996. "Jesuits." In *The Oxford Encyclopedia of the Reformation* 2: 333–38. New York and Oxford.

Othman, Norani. 1999. "The Grounding of Human Rights Arguments in Non-Western Culture: Shari'a and the Citizenship of Women in a Modern Islamic state." In *East Asian Challenge for Human Rights,* edited by Joanne R. Bauer and Daniel A. Bell, 169–92. Cambridge.

Padoan, G. "Sulla Relazione cinquecentesca dei viaggi nord-atlantici di Nicolò e Antonio Zen (1383–1403)." In *L'impatto della scoperta,* 219–77. Rome.

Padrón, Ricardo. 2004. *The Spacious Word: Cartography, Literature, and Empire in Early Modern Spain*. Chicago.

Pagden, Anthony. 1982. *The Fall of Natural Man: The American Indian and the Origins of Comparative Ethnology.* Cambridge.

———. 1994. "The Defence of Civilization." In *The Uncertainties of Empire: Essays in Iberian and Ibero-American Intellectual History,* edited by Pagden, 33–45. Aldershot, U.K.

———. 1995. *Lords of All the World: Ideologies of Empire in Spain, Britain and France c. 1500–c.1800*. New Haven.

———. 1998. "The Struggle for Legitimacy and the Image of Empire in the Atlantic to circa 1700." In *The Origins of Empire: The British Overseas Empire to the Close of the Seventeenth Century,* vol. I, edited by Nicholas Canny, 34–54. Oxford.

Paine, Thomas. 1992. *Rights of Man*. Edited by Gregory Claeys. Indianapolis.

Palmer, R. R. 1959–64. *The Age of the Democratic Revolution: A Political History of Europe and America, 1760–1800*. Princeton.

Panofsky, Erwin. 1991. *Perspective as Symbolic Form*. Translated by Christopher Wood. New York.

Pappin, Joseph L., III. 2005. "Burke and the Thomistic Foundations of Natural Law." In *An Imaginative Whig: Reassessing the Life and Thought of Edmund Burke*, edited by Ian Crowe, 203–27. Columbia.

Parks, George B. 1955. "Ramusio's Literary History." *Studies in Philology* 52: 127–48.

Peach, Bernard. 1979. *Richard Price and the Ethical Foundations of the American Revolution: Selections from His Pamphlets*. Durham, N.C.

Peck, Linda Levy. 1993. "Kingship, Counsel and Law in Early Stuart Britain." In *The Varieties of British Political Thought, 1500–1800*, edited by J.G.A. Pocock, 80–115. Cambridge.

Pelikan, Jaroslav Jan. 1993. *Christianity and Classical Culture: the Metamorphosis of Natural Theology in the Christian Encounter with Hellenism*. New Haven and London.

Pendergrass, Jan N. 1992. "Simon Grynaeus and the Mariners of *Novus Orbis* (1532)." *Medievalia et Humanistica* n.s., 19: 27–45.

Penrose, Boies. 1962. *Travel and Discovery in the Renaissance, 1420–1620*. New York.

Percival, Earl of Egmont. 1743. *Faction Detected by the Evidence of Facts*. London.

Phelan, John Leddy. 1970. *The Millennial Kingdom of the Franciscans*. Berkeley.

Phillipson, Nicholas. 1993. "Politics and Politeness in the Reigns of Anne and the Early Hanoverians." In *The Varieties of British Political Thought, 1500–1800*, edited by J.G.A. Pocock, 211–45. Cambridge.

Pitts, Jennifer. 2005. *A Turn to Empire: The Rise of Imperial Liberalism in Britain and France*. Princeton.

Plamenatz, John Petrov. 1960. *On Alien Rule and Self-Government*. London.

Pocock, J.G.A., ed. 1980. "1776: The Revolution against Parliament." In *Three British Revolutions: 1641, 1688, 1776*, 265–88. Princeton.

———. 1985. *Virtue, Commerce, and History*. New York.

———. 1988. "States, Republics and Empires: The American Founding in Early Modern Perspective." In *Conceptual Change and the Constitution*, edited by J.G.A. Pocock et al., 55–77. Lawrence, Kans.

———. 1993a. "Political Thought in the English-Speaking Atlantic, 1760–1790: (I) The Imperial Crisis." In *The Varieties of British Political Thought, 1500–1800*, edited by J.G.A. Pocock et al., 246–82. Cambridge.

———. 1993b. "Political Thought in the English-Speaking Atlantic 1760–1790: (II): Empire, Religion, and an End of Early Modernity." In *The*

Varieties of British Political Thought, 1500–1800, edited by J.G.A. Pocock et al., 283–317. Cambridge.

———. 1999a. *Barbarism and Religion, Volume I: Enlightenments and Edward Gibbon*. Cambridge.

———. 1999b. *Barbarism and Religion, Volume III: The First Decline and Fall*. Cambridge.

———. 2005. *Barbarism and Religion, Volume IV: Barbarians, Savages and Empires*. Cambridge.

Pocock, J.G.A. and Gordon J. Schochet. 1993. "Interregnum and Restoration." In *The Varieties of British Political Thought, 1500–1800*, edited by J.G.A. Pocock et al., 146–79. Cambridge.

Pons, Alain. 1995. "Civilité-Urbanité." In *Dictionnaire raisonné de la politesse et du savoir-vivre: De Moyen Âge à nos jours*, edited by Alain Montandon, 91–109. Paris.

Porter, Andrew. 1999. "Introduction: Britain and the Empire in the Nineteenth Century." In *The Oxford History of the British Empire*, vol. III, *The Nineteenth Century*, edited by Andrew Porter, 1–28. Oxford and New York.

Postema, Gerald J. 1986. *Bentham and the Common Law Tradition*. New York.

Pownall, Thomas. 1752. *Principles of Policy, Being the Ground and Reason of Civil Empire*. London.

Price, Richard. 1785. *Observations on the Importance of the American Revolution and the Means of making it a Benefit to the World: to which is added A Letter from M. Turgot. . . .* Printed for L. White et al. Dublin.

Ptolemaeus, Claudius. 1966. *Geographia*. Edited by Sebastian Münster. Amsterdam. 1540. Reprinted Basle.

Pufendorf, Samuel. 2003. *The Whole Duty of Man, According to the Law of Nature*. Edited by Ian Hunter and David Saunders. Indianapolis.

Rahe, Paul A. 2005. "The Book That Never Was: Montesquieu's *Considerations on the Romans* in Historical Context." *History of Political Thought* 26, no. 1: 43–89.

Ramusio, Giovanni Battista. 1978–88. *Navigazioni e viaggi*. Edited by Marcia Milanesi. 6 vols. Turin.

Randles, W.G.L. 1994. "Classical Models of World Geography and Their Transformation Following the Discovery of America." In *The Classical Tradition and the Americas*, vol. 1, *European Images of the Americas and the Classical Tradition*, edited by Wolfgang Haase and Meyer Reinhold, 5–76. Berlin.

Rapin-Thoyras, Paul de. 1953. "Dissertation on the Whigs and the Tories under Anne (1717)." In *English Historical Documents, 1660–1714, VIII*, 268–69. New York.

Rashdall, Hastings. 1951. *The Universities of Europe in the Middle Ages*. Oxford.

Ravenstein, E. G. 1908. *Martin Behaim: His Life and His Globe*. London.

Reinhard, Wolfgang. 1992. "Missionaries, Humanists and Natives in the Sixteenth-Century Spanish Indies: A Failed Encounter of Two Worlds?" *Renaissance Studies* 6, no. 4: 360–76.

Reiss, Hans. 1991. Introduction to "[Kant's] Reviews of Herder's Ideas of the Philosophy of the History of Mankind and Conjectures on the Beginning of Human History." In *Kant: Political Writings*, edited by Hans Reiss, 192–200. Cambridge.

Richards, Thomas. 1992. "Archive and Utopia." *Representations* 37: 104–35.

Richardson, W.A.R. 1993. "Mercator's Southern Continent: Its Origins, Influence and Gradual Demise." *Terrae Incognitae* 25: 67–98.

Rico, Francisco. 1984. "Il nuovo Mondo di Nebrija e Colombo: Note sulla geografia umanistica in Spagna e sul contesto intellettuale della scoperta dell'America." In *Vestigia: Studi in onore di Giuseppe Billanovich*, edited by Rino Avesani et al., 2: 576–606. Rome.

Riley, Patrick. 1999. "Leibniz's Political and Moral Philosophy in the 'Novissima Sinica,' 1699–1999." *Journal of the History of Ideas* 60, no. 2: 217–39.

Robbins, Caroline. 1958. " 'Discordant Parties': A Study of the Acceptance of Party by Englishmen." *Political Science Quarterly* 73: 505–29. Reprinted in 1982. *Absolute Liberty.*

———. 1959. *The Eighteenth-Century Commonwealthman*. Cambridge.

———. 1982. *Absolute Liberty: A Selection from the Articles and Papers of Caroline Robbins*. Hamden.

Robert, Paul, and Alain Rey. 1985. *Dictionnaire alphabétique et analogique de la langue française: Le grand Robert de la langue française*. 2nd ed., rev. and enlarged. Paris.

Robertson, John. 1997. "Gibbon's Roman Empire as a Universal Monarchy: The Decline and Fall and the Imperial Idea in Early Modern Europe." In *Edward Gibbon and Empire*, edited by Rosamond McKitterick and Roland Quinault, 247–70. Cambridge.

———. 1998. "Universal Monarchy and the Liberties of Europe: David Hume's Critique of an English Whig Doctrine." In *Political Discourses in Early Modern Britain*, edited by N. T. Phillipson and Quentin Skinner, 349–73. Cambridge.

Robertson, William. 1827. "A View of the Progress of Society in Europe." In *The Works of William Robertson, D.D., Vol. III, The History of Charles V.*, 1–179. London.

Röling, B.V.A. 1990. "Are Grotius' Ideas Obsolete in an Expanding World?" In *Hugo Grotius and International Relations*, edited by Hedley

Bull, Benedict Kingsbury, and Adam Roberts, 281–300. Clarendon and Oxford.

Romm, James S. 1992. *The Edges of the Earth in Ancient Thought: Geography, Exploration and Fiction*. Princeton.

———. 1994. "New World and *Novos Orbos:* Seneca in the Renaissance Debate over Ancient Knowledge of the Americas." In *The Classical Tradition and the Americas*, edited by Wolfgang Haase and Meyer Reinhold. 1: 77–116. Berlin.

Rommen, Heinrich Albert. 1947. *The Natural Law: A Study in Legal and Social History and Philosophy.* St. Louis.

Roper, William. 1962. "Life of Sir Thomas More." In *Two Early Tudor Lives*, edited by R. S. Sylvester and D. P. Harding, 195–254. New Haven and London.

Rosaccio, Gioseppe. 1598. *Descrittione della geografia universale, libro primo,* which constitutes a supplement to *Geografia di Claudio Tolomeo Alessandrino, tradotta di greco nell'idioma volgare italiano da Girolamo Ruscelli, et hora nuovamente ampliata da Gioseffo Rosaccio*. Venice.

Rosenthal, Earl E. 1973. "The Invention of the Columnar Device of Emperor Charles V at the Court of Burgundy in Flanders in 1516." *Journal of the Warburg and Courtauld Institutes* 36: 198–230.

Rousseau, Jean-Jacques. 1992. *Discourse on the Origins of Inequality* (Second Discourse). *The Collected Writings of Rousseau*, vol. 3. Edited by Roger D. Masters and Christopher Kelly. Hanover, N.H., and London.

Rubiés, Joan-Pau. 1993. "New Worlds and Renaissance Ethnology." *History and Anthropology* 6: 157–97.

———. 2000. *Travel and Ethnology in the Renaissance: South India through European Eyes, 1250–1625*. Past and Present Publications. Cambridge and New York.

Rudolph, Lloyd, and Susanne Hoeber Rudolph. 1997. "Occidentalism and Orientalism: Perspectives on Legal Pluralism." In *Cultures of Scholarship*, edited by S. C. Humphreys, 219–51. Ann Arbor.

Russell, Conrad. 1979. *Parliaments and English Politics, 1621–1629*. Oxford.

———. 1990. *Unrevolutionary England, 1603–1642*. London and Ronceverte.

Ruston, Roger. 2002. "Theologians, Humanists and Natural Rights." In *Religious Liberty and Human Rights*, edited by Mark Hill, 14–44. Cardiff.

Sardella, Pierre. 1948. *Nouvelles et spéculations à Venise au début du xvie siècle*. Paris.

Scaglione, Aldo D. 1991. *Knights at Court: Courtliness, Chivalry and Courtesy from Ottonian Germany to the Italian Renaissance*. Berkeley.

Scammell, G. V. 1969. "The New Worlds and Europe in the Sixteenth Century." *Historical Journal* 12: 389–412.

Schmidt, H. D. 1966. "The Establishment of 'Europe' as a Political Expression." *Historical Journal* 9, no. 2: 172–78.

Schmitt, Charles B. 1978. "Filippo Fantoni, Galileo Galilei's Predecessor as Mathematics Lecturer at Pisa." In *Science and History: Studies in Honor of Edward Rosen*, edited by Erna Hilfstein, Pawel Czartoryski, and Frank D. Grand, 53–63. Wroclaw and Warsaw.

Schulze, Winfried. 1978. *Reich und Türkengefahr im späten 16 Jahrhundert*. Munich.

Schwaller, John F. 1999. "Don Bartolomé de Alva: Nahuatl Scholar of the Seventeenth Century." In *A Guide to Confession Large and Small in the Mexican Language, 1634* (Bartolomé de Alva), edited by Barry D. Sell, John Fredrick Schwaller, and Lu Ann Homza, 3–15. Norman, Okla.

Schwarzenberger, Georg. 1990. "The Grotius Factor in International Law and Relations: A Functional Approach." In *Hugo Grotius and International Relations*, edited by Hedley Bull, Benedict Kingsbury, and Adam Roberts, 301–12. Clarendon and Oxford.

Seed, Patricia. 1995. *Ceremonies of Possession in Europe's Conquest of the New World, 1492–1640*. Cambridge.

Seidler, Michael J. 2002. "Pufendorf and the Politics of Recognition." In *Natural Law and Civil Sovereignty: Moral Right and State Authority in Early Modern Political Thought*, edited by Ian Hunter and David Saunders, 235–51. Houndmills, U.K. and New York.

Selwyn, Jennifer D. 1997. "'Procur[ing] in the Common People These Better Behaviours': The Jesuits' Civilizing Mission in Early Modern Naples, 1550–1620." *Radical History Review* 67: 4–34.

Sen, Amartya. 1997. *Human Rights and Asian Values*. New York.

———. 2005. *The Argumentative Indian: Writings on Indian History, Culture and Identity*. London.

Shackleton, Robert. 1988. "Montesquieu, Bolingbroke and the Separation of Powers." In *Essays on Montesquieu and on the Enlightenment*, 3–15. Oxford.

Sharp, Andrew, ed. 1998. *The English Levellers*. Cambridge.

Shils, Edward. 1997. *The Virtue of Civility: Selected Essays on Liberalism, Tradition, and Civil Society*. Indianapolis.

Shirley, Rodney W. 1983. *The Mapping of the World: Early Printed World Maps, 1472–1700*. London.

Singer, Dorothea Waley. 1950. *Giordano Bruno: His Life and Thought*. With annotated translation of *On the Infinite Universe and Worlds*. New York.

Skinner, Quentin. 1978. *The Foundations of Modern Political Thought*. Vol. 2. Cambridge.

Smith, Adam. 1976a. *An Inquiry into the Nature and Causes of the Wealth of Nations*. Edited by R. H. Campbell and A. S. Skinner. New York.

———. 1976b. *The Theory of Moral Sentiments*. Edited by D. D. Raphael and A. L. Macke. Oxford.

Spinoza. 2000. *Ethics*. Edited by G.H.R. Parkinson. Oxford.

Stanlis, Peter J. 1958. *Edmund Burke and the Natural Law.* Ann Arbor.

Starobinski, Jean. 1993. *Blessings in Disguise, or, The Morality of Evil*. Translated by Arthur Goldhammer. Cambridge.

Stein, Peter. 1980. *Legal Evolution: The Story of an Idea*. Cambridge.

Stourzh, Gerard. 1988. "Constitution: Changing Meanings of the Term from the Early Seventeenth to the Late Eighteenth Century." In *Conceptual Change and the Constitution*, edited by Terence Bell and J.G.A. Pocock, 35–54. Lawrence, Kans.

Strauss, Leo. 1953. *Natural Rights and History.* Chicago.

Strugnell, Anthony. 1991. "Postmodernism versus Enlightenment and the Problem of the Other in Raynal's *Histoire des deux Indes*." In *Studies on Voltaire and the Enlightenment Century,* edited by Hans-Jürgen Lüsebrink and Manfred Tietz, 169–82. Oxford.

Svensson, Marina. 2000. "The Chinese Debate on Asian Values and Human Rights: Some Reflections on Relativism, Nationalism and Orientalism." In *Human Rights and Asian Values*, edited by Michael Jacobson and Ole Bruun, 199–206. Richmond, U.K.

Swanson, Mary-Elaine. 2000. "James Madison and the Presbyterian Idea of Man and Government." In *Religion and Political Culture in Jefferson's Virginia*, edited by Garrett Ward Sheldon and Daniel L. Dreisbach, 119–32. Lanham, Md.

Taylor, Charles. 1996. *Sources of the Self: The Making of Modern Identity.* Cambridge.

———. 1999. "Conditions of an Unforced Consensus on Human Rights." In *East Asian Challenge for Human Rights*, edited by Joanne R. Bauer and Daniel A. Bell, 124–44. Cambridge.

Thrower, Norman J. W. 1996. *Maps and Civilization: Cartography in Culture and Society.* Chicago and London.

Tierney, Brian. 1988. "Villey, Ockham and the Origin of Individual Rights." In *Weightier Matters of Law and Religion: A Tribute to Harold J. Bloom*, edited by John Witte Jr. and Frank S. Alexander, 1–31. Atlanta, Ga.

———. 1991. "Aristotle and the American Indian—Again: Two Critical Studies." *Cristianesimo nella Storia* 12: 295–322.

———. 1996. "Religious Rights: An Historical Perspective." In *Religious Human Rights in Global Perspective: Religious Perspectives*, edited by J. D. van der Vyver and John Witte, 17–45. The Hague and Boston.

———. 1997. *The Idea of Natural Rights: Studies on Natural Rights, Natural Law, and Church Law, 1150–1625*. Atlanta.

Tillich, Paul. 1948. *The Protestant Era*. Chicago.

Tooley, R.V. 1964. "Maps in Italian Atlases of the Sixteenth Century." *Imago Mundi* 3: 12–47.

Trevelyan, George Macaulay. 1926. *The Two-Party System in English Political History*. Oxford.

———. 1930. *Romanes Lectures Decennial Issue, 1921–1930*. Oxford.

Trevor-Roper, H. R. 1957. *Man and Events: Historical Essays*. New York.

Tuck, Richard. 1979. *Natural Rights Theories: Their Origin and Development*. Cambridge.

———. 1987. "The 'Modern' Theory of Natural Law." In *The Languages of Political Theory in Early Modern Europe*, 99–119. New York.

———. 1993. *Philosophy and Government, 1572–1651*. New York.

———. 1999. *The Rights of War and Peace: Political Thought and the International Order from Grotius to Kant*. Oxford.

Turchetti, Maria. 1984. *Concordia o tolleranza? François Bauduin e i "moyenneurs."* Geneva.

Ustorf, Werner. 2003. "A Missiological Postscript." In *The Decline of Christendom in Western Europe, 1700–2000*, edited by Hugh McLeod and Werner Ustorf, 215–25. Cambridge.

Vergilius, Polydorus. 1528. *De inventoribus rerum*. Paris.

———. 1585. *De rerum inventoribus libri octo*. Rome.

Vescovini, Graziella Frederici. 1969. "L'inserimento della 'perspectiva' tra le arti del quadrivio." In *Arts libéraux et philosophie au moyen âge: Actes du Quatrième Congrès international de philosophie médiévale, 27 August–2 September 1967, 969–74*. Montreal and Paris.

Vitoria, Francisco de. 1991. *Political Writings*. Edited by Anthony Pagden and Jeremy Lawrance. New York.

Vivanti, Corrado. 1962. "Alle origini dell'idea di civiltà: le scoperte geografiche e gli scritti di Henri de la Popelinière." *Rivista storica Italiana* 74: 225–49.

Waddicor, Mark H. 1970. *Montesquieu and the Philosophy of Natural Law*. The Hague.

Wade, Ira Owen. 1969. *The Intellectual Development of Voltaire*. Princeton.

Waldron, Jeremy. 2002. *God, Locke, and Equality: Christian Foundations of John Locke's Political Thought*. Cambridge.

Waley-Cohen, Joanna. 1993. "China and Western Technology in the Late Eighteenth Century." *American Historical Review* 98, no. 5: 1525–44.

Whelan, Frederick G. 1988. "Vattel's Doctrine of the State." *History of Political Thought* 9: 59–90.

Wills, Garry. 1978. *Inventing America: Jefferson's Declaration of Independence*. Garden City.

Wilson, Douglas L. 2000. "Jefferson and Bolingbroke: Some Notes on the Question of Influence." In *Religion and Political Culture in Jefferson's Virginia*, edited by G. W. Sheldon and D. L. Dreisbach, 107–18. Oxford.

Wood, Gordon S. 1966. "Rhetoric and Reality in the American Revolution." *William and Mary Quarterly* 23, no. 4: 1–32.

———. 1969. *The Creation of the American Republic, 1776–1787*. Chapel Hill.

Woodward, David. 1987. "The Manuscript, Engraved, and Typographic Traditions of Map Lettering." In *Art and Cartography: Six Historical Essays*, edited by David Woodward, 174–212. Chicago and London.

Wynter, Sylvia. 1991. "Columbus and the Poetics of the *Propter Nos*." *Annals of Scholarship* 8: 251–86.

Yolton, John W., ed. 1969. *John Locke: Problems and Perspectives; A Collection of New Essays*. Cambridge.

Zagorin, Perez. 2000. "Hobbes without Grotius." *History of Political Thought* 21: 16–40.

———. 2003. *How the Idea of Religious Toleration Came to the West*. Princeton and Oxford.

Zuckert, Michael. 1994. *Natural Rights and the New Republicanism*. Princeton.

———. 2000. "Natural Rights in the American Revolution: The American Amalgam." In *Human Rights and Revolutions*, edited by Jeffrey N. Wasserstrom, Lynn Hunt, and Marilyn B. Young, 59–78. Lanham, Md.

Index

Page references in italics refer to illustrations